S. (Sidney) Levett Yeats

The Honour of Savelli

A Romance

S. (Sidney) Levett Yeats

The Honour of Savelli
A Romance

ISBN/EAN: 9783744777063

Printed in Europe, USA, Canada, Australia, Japan

Cover: Foto ©ninafisch / pixelio.de

More available books at **www.hansebooks.com**

THE HONOUR OF SAVELLI

A Romance

BY
S. LEVETT YEATS

GROSSET & DUNLAP
PUBLISHERS - NEW YORK

PREFACE.

In writing this book the Author has made no effort to point a moral; all that has been done is an attempt to catch the "spirit of the true Romance," and to amuse. The book was partly written in the intervals of work in India, and was completed during the leisure allowed by furlough on medical certificate. In dealing with this period of Italian history, in which the story is set, the Author would say he has taken Dumas for his model, but hopes that he has worked out his scheme on original lines; and he has used, as far as possible, the language in which an Italian living in the beginning of the sixteenth century would express himself. At the time the book was written the Author had not read Mr. Stanley Weyman's brilliant novel, "A Gentleman of France." Had he done so the style of the present book would doubtless have been much improved from the lessons taught by a master-hand. The Author, in bringing this to the notice of the reader, would humbly add that he is making no challenge to break a lance with so redoubted a knight as the creator of Gaston de Marsac.

CONTENTS.

CHAPTER	PAGE
I. A Bolt from the Blue	1
II. Ruin	12
III. Madame D'Entrangues	24
IV. A Fool's Cap and a Sore Heart	33
V. D'Entrangues Scores a Point	48
VI. Bernabo Ceci	58
VII. The Garden of St. Michael	69
VIII. Temptation	83
IX The Marzocco Inn	92
X. Niccolo Machiavelli	102
XI. The Letter to D'Amboise	114
XII. The Ambuscade	128
XIII. Rome	144
XIV. George of Amboise	155
XV. The Gift of Bayard	171
XVI. Friend or Foe	183
XVII. The Vatican	195
XVIII. The Opal Ring	211
XIX. Exit the Ancient Brico	223
XX. "A Brown Paul—a Little Copper"	237
XXI. The Rescue of Angiola	249
XXII. The Ride to St. Jerome	262
XXIII. The Pavilion of Tremouille	271
XXIV. Too dearly Bought	280
XXV. The Vengeance of Corte	292
XXVI. Concerning many Things	301
XXVII. My Lord, the Count	313

PRELUDE.

I.

He rydes untoe ye Dragon's Gate,
And blowes a ryngynge calle:
A gallant Knyghte in armoure bryghte,
'Twere sadde toe see him falle.
Deare Sayntes of Mercy steele hys harte,
And nerve hys arme withalle!

II.

Noe glove bears he uponne hys creste,
And lettynge droppe hys visor's barres,
I sawe hys starke soule lookynge forthe,
Toe meete ye whysperes of ye starres.
True Knyghte of God, whose arme is stronge,
Whose harte is pure, whose lance is longe.

III.

Lette wyn, lette lose, belyke 'tis true,
Ye issue of ye daye will bee,
Notte toe ye dreamers; butte toe those
Who stayke their alle on victorie.
Notte to ye skiffes uponne ye streames,
Butte ye stronge shippes uponne ye sea.

Vanity Fair, 12th October, 1893.

THE HONOUR OF SAVELLI.

CHAPTER I.

A BOLT FROM THE BLUE.

"I do not drink with a thief!"

D'Entrangues spoke in clear, distinct tones, that rose above the hum of voices, and every one caught the words. In an instant the room was still. The laughter on all faces died away, leaving them grave; and twenty pairs of curious eyes, and twenty curious faces were turned towards us. It was so sudden, so unexpected, this jarring discord in our harmony, that it fell as if a bolt from a mangonel, or a shot from one of Messer Novarro's new guns, had dropped in amongst us. Even that, I take it, would have caused less surprise, although for the present there was a truce in the land. Prospero Colonna turned half round in his seat and looked at me. Our host and commander, old Ives d'Alegres, who was pouring himself out a glass of white vernaccia, held the decanter in mid-air, an expression of blank amazement in his blue eyes. Even the Englishman, Hawkwood, who sat next to me, was startled out of his habitual calm. Every eye was on us, on me where I sat dazed, and on D'Entrangues, who was leaning back slightly, a forced smile on his face, the fingers of one hand playing with the empty glass before him, whilst with the other he slowly twisted his long red moustache. I was completely taken aback. Only that afternoon I parted from D'Entrangues, apparently on the best of terms. We had played together, and he had won my crowns. It is true he was not paid in full at the time; but he knew the word of a Savelli. On leaving, Madame D'Entrangues asked me to join her hawking party for the morrow, and he urged the invitation. I accepted, and backed my new peregrine against D'Entrangues' old hawk Bibbo for ten crowns, the best of three flights, and the wager was taken. Never indeed had I known him so cordial. I did not like the man, but for his wife's sake was friendly to him. Of a truth, there were few of the youngsters in Tremouille's camp who were not in love with her, and some of us older fellows too, though we hid our feelings better. I was grateful to Madame. She had been kind to me after the affair of San Miniato, when a Florentine pike somehow found its way through my breastplate. Indeed, I may say I owed my recovery to her nursing. In return, I had been of some service to her in the retreat up the valley of the Taro, after Fornovo—she called it saving her life. In this manner a friendship sprang up between us, which was increased by the opportunities we had of meeting whilst the army lay inactive before Arezzo. Long years of camp life made me fully appreciate the society of a woman, remarkable alike for her beauty and her talent; and she, on the other hand, felt for me, I was sure, only that friendship which it is possible for a good woman to hold for a man who is not her husband.

I do not for one moment mean to imply that Doris D'Entrangues was perfection. I knew her to be wayward and rash, sometimes foolish if you will; but withal a pure woman. I soon found she was unhappy, and in time she got into a way of confiding her troubles to me, and they were not a few, for D'Entrangues was—what all men knew him to be. Finding that I could be of help to Madame, I avoided all difference with the husband, and for her sake was, as I have said, friendly to him. Perhaps my course of action was not prudent; but who is there amongst us who is always guided by the head? At any rate, I expiated my fault, and paid the price of my folly to the end of the measure.

As I sat in the now silent supper-room with the man's words buzzing in my ears, a curious recollection of a scene that occurred about a month ago came back to me. Madame and I had over-ridden ourselves hawking, and I had dismounted at her request and gathered for her a posy of yellow coronilla and scarlet amaryllis. This, in her quick impulsive way, she held to her husband's face when we met him, a half-league or so on our way back, saying, "See what lovely flowers Di Savelli has given me!" He snatched them from her hand, and flung them under his horse with an oath, adding something which I did not catch. Madame flushed crimson, and the incident ended there, for I did not care to press the matter.

It all came back to me now, in the oddest manner, as I sat staring at D'Entrangues. He had come in late to the supper, and, after greeting D'Alegres, slipped into the seat opposite me in silence. Across him two men were discussing a series of thefts that had recently disturbed us. They were not common thefts, such as are of daily occurrence in a military camp; but were the work of some one both daring and enterprising. Even then the matter would not have attracted the attention it did but for the loss of a ruby circlet by the Duchesse de la Tremouille, which, besides its intrinsic value, was the gift of a king. Madame de la Tremouille made an outcry, and the duke, as the matter touched him, was leaving no stone unturned to find the thief. It had come to be that every robbery in the camp was put down to this same light-fingered gentleman; and Visconti, one of the two men who were discussing the question, was loudly lamenting the loss of a rare medallion of which he had just been relieved. Throughout their conversation D'Entrangues, though once or twice addressed, spoke no word, but maintained a moody silence. When the wine was circling round I, being warmed, and wishing to stand well with the husband of Madame, made some rallying allusion to our match for the morrow, and offered to drink to him. His reply is known.

The silence which followed his speech was so utter that one may have heard a feather fall; and then some one, I know not who, laughed shortly. The sound brought me to myself, and in a fury, hardly knowing what I was doing, I jumped up and drew my dagger, but was instantly seized by Colonna and Hawkwood. The latter was a man of great size, and between him and Colonna I was helpless.

"Give him rope," whispered Hawkwood, and his voice was kind, "this is not an affair to be settled with a poniard thrust."

The whole room was in an uproar now, all crowding around us; D'Entrangues half-risen from his seat, his hand on his sword, and I quivering in the grasp of my kind enemies. Old Ives d'Alegres rushed forwards, "Silence, gentlemen!" he called out, "remember I command here. Savelli, give up that dagger; D'Entrangues, your sword. Now, gentlemen, words have been used which blood alone cannot wash out. M. d'Entrangues, I await your explanation!"

"Liar!" I shouted out, "you will give it to me at the sword's point," and big Hawkwood's restraining arms tightened over me.

"Thanks," replied D'Entrangues, "you remember the sword at last; a moment before I saw in your hands your natural weapon."

"A truce to this, sirs! I await you," interrupted D'Alegres.

"Your pardon," said D'Entrangues. "Gentlemen, you want an explanation. It is simple enough. We have a thief in our midst, and he is there."

"A thief—Di Savelli!" called out a dozen voices, and Ives d'Alegres said, "Impossible! you are mad, D'Entrangues."

"No more so, sir, than you, or any one of us here. I confess, though, I thought I was mad when I first knew of it, for this man has been my comrade, we have fought side by side, and he has borne himself as a gallant soldier. I thought I was mad, I say, when I first knew of this; but the proofs are too strong."

"What are they?" D'Alegres spoke very shortly.

"You shall have them. You all know there have been a series of unaccountable thefts amongst us lately. The duchess's rubies have gone. Hardly a lady but has lost some valuable, my wife, amongst other things, a bracelet. The thief did not confine his attentions to the fair sex; but visited us men as well. They were not common thefts. From the circumstances attending them, the robber must have known us intimately, and had easy access to our quarters. Up to now the matter has been a mystery. A lot of people have been wrongly suspected, and two poor wretches are now swinging on the gibbet, condemned for nothing that I know of."

"It was done by my orders, sir," said D'Alegres, "the matter is beside the point."

"I stand corrected, General. Some little time ago a fortunate chance revealed to me who the culprit was. I made no sign, but set to work until complete proofs were in my hands."

"You have said so before. Why beat about the bush? If you have proofs, produce them?"

"A moment, sir. May I ask any of you to state what your most recent losses have been?"

"My medallion by Cimabue," put in Visconti in his drawling voice.

"Fifty fat gold crowns in a leather bag," grumbled Hawkwood, "the residue of the Abbot Basilio's ransom. God send such another prize to me, for I know not how to pay my lances."

There was a little laugh at Hawkwood's moan, but it soon stilled, and, one by one, each man stated his latest loss.

"I will add to these Madame's bracelet," said D'Entrangues, "and shall not be surprised if the duchess thanks me for her rubies to-morrow."

"Tremouille has sworn to crucify the thief if he is found."

"The duke knows the value of his gems."

"He ought to be consoled, for he has a true wife left, and, his eminence of St. Sabines tells me, such a possession is more precious than rubies," drawled Visconti.

"Gentlemen, you interrupt M. D'Entrangues. Let us end this painful scene."

"There is but one thing more, sir. I ask you now to have this"—D'Entrangues indicated me with an insolent look—"this person's quarters searched."

Whilst he was speaking, D'Alegres gave a whispered order to a young officer, who left the room immediately, although with a somewhat discontented air at being sent away. As D'Entrangues finished, the door was opened, a couple of files of Swiss infantry entered, and with them Braccio Fortebraccio, our provost-marshal. At a sign from D'Alegres one of the files surrounded me, the other D'Entrangues, and Braccio called out in a loud voice, "Ugo di Savelli, and Crépin D'Entrangues, I arrest you in the king's name!"

"At your service, provost," said D'Entrangues with a bow, "my sword is already given up. May I ask, sir," he continued, turning to D'Alegres, "if you will put my proofs to the test?"

"At once. Provost, lead your prisoners to M. di Savelli's quarters."

"Thank God!" The expression burst from me, so great was my relief. I was sure of being acquitted, and madame or no madame, I should kill D'Entrangues the following day, even though I knew Tremouille had sworn to hang the next man caught duelling within the jurisdiction of his camp. We were, as I have stated, at Arezzo, and had passed the winter there, in the truce following the expulsion of the Duke of Bari from Lombardy. It had, however, become necessary to menace the Pope, who was hilt deep in intrigue as well as crime, and Tremouille leaving Monsignore d'Amboise in Milan, marched south, and with the aid of our Florentine allies, held the Borgia and Spain in check. Acting under the advice of Trevulzio, Ives d'Alegres, and others, the duke had not entered the town; but kept us in camp near Giove, outside the walls. The gates of the city and the citadel were, however, at the same time strongly garrisoned, and Trevulzio held command within. It was all the more urgent to keep the main body of the troops outside the walls, as they were composed, with the exception of a few French regiments, mainly of mercenaries, and by holding the town with picked men, upon whom he could rely, Tremouille would be able, in case of any change of front on the part of his mercenaries, to have them between two fires. Ives d'Alegres, who then acted as lieutenant-general to the duke, was immediately in command of the camp, and had fixed his headquarters in a large villa, the property of the Accolti, and it was here that the supper, which ended so disastrously for me, was given. My own quarters were but a bow-shot or two away, in the direction of the town. When we reached them, I was surprised to find at the door, my servant Tarbes in the hands of two of the marshal's men, a half troop of French lancers drawn up before my tent, and my own small *condotta* of ten lances, which I had raised for the war by pawning my last acre, all under guard. As if any attempt at rescue were possible! I saw in a moment that this accounted for D'Entrangues' late arrival at the supper: but entered the tent sure of the results. A dozen blazing torches threw a clear enough light, and D'Alegres briefly requested the provost to begin the search. The practised hands of the field police did this very effectually, but to no purpose, and I felt that the faces of all were looking friendly towards me. D'Entrangues seemed nervous, and his sallow cheek was pale.

"Send for Tarbes," he said, and at a word from the provost my knave was led in. This man was a Spaniard, whom I had taken into my service, some little while ago, on the recommendation of D'Entrangues. Except on one occasion when he lost, or maybe stole, a pair of silver spurs, for which I cuffed him roundly, he had served me well. At the present moment he seemed overcome with fear, trembled in every limb, and refused to look at me.

"Signor Tarbes," said the provost, "do you know what the wheel is?"

The man made no answer, and Braccio went on—

"Signor Tarbes, we want a little information which I am persuaded you possess. If you give it freely, we will be merciful; if you prevaricate, if you attempt to conceal anything, we will do to you what we did to the death hunters after San Miniato—you remember?"

"Speak freely, Tarbes. There is no fear," I added.

"Even your master, the excellent cavaliere, advises you, and I must say advises you well," continued Braccio. "Signor Tarbes, you will now show us," and he rubbed his hands together softly, "where the valiant knight, Ugo di Savelli, keeps his prizes of war, the spoils of his bow and spear—I was going to say fin——"

"Have a care, sir," said D'Alegres sternly, "you are here to do your duty, not to play the jester." Braccio shrank back at his look, and the general turned to Tarbes, "In brief, we want to know, if your master, M. di Savelli, has any concealed property here? Will you answer at once, or do you prefer to be put to the question?"

"I will speak—say anything, my lord—only have mercy. I swear what I say is true. His excellency, my master, has nothing beyond what you have seen—and what lies in the leather valise under this rug."

Now this rug in question lay flat on the turf, on which my tent stood, and at the time of the search D'Alegres and others were standing on it. Owing to this, and to the crowded state of the tent, it had hitherto escaped the attention, which it would doubtless have received sooner or later, for nothing ever passed Braccio's eyes. In a moment the rug was swept aside, and, as the torches were held to the turf, it was evident that it had been dug away and then replaced somewhat carelessly.

Braccio was in his element.

"*Pouf!*" he exclaimed, "a clumsy amateur after all! I thought better of his valour. Here! give me a pike! And hold the torches so!"

With a sharp point of the pike he quickly cleared away the turf, and, stooping down, lifted up from the hole he exposed, a small brown valise, which had been concealed in the earth. The interest was now intense. Every one crowded round Braccio. Even the vigilance of the guards over me completely relaxed. I felt a touch on my shoulder, and, looking back, saw Hawkwood.

"Would you like to go?" he whispered rapidly. "My horse is ready saddled—you know where to find him."

I thanked him with a look; but shook my head, and the giant fell back.

"Shall I break it open, excellency?" and Braccio held the bag out to D'Alegres.

"My master has the key," put in Tarbes; "I know no more."

"I—the key!" I exclaimed. "Villain, the bag is not mine!"

"It bears your arms, however;" Braccio pointed to a little metal plate on which they were distinctly engraved.

"You must, I am afraid, submit to the further indignity of being searched," said D'Alegres.

There was no hope in resistance and I endured this. Braccio himself searched me, and almost as soon as he began, pulled from an inner pocket of my vest a small key, attached to a fine gold chain.

"Here is the noble knight's key," he exclaimed, "and see; it fits exactly!" He turned it in the lock, opened the valise, and emptied the contents out on a rough camp table. A low murmur went up, for amongst the small heap of articles was Hawkwood's leather bag, and madame's bracelet, whilst something rolled a little on one side, and fell off softly to the turf. A soldier picked it up, and placed it face upwards on the table—the lost medallion.

One by one D'Alegres held up the articles sadly, and I looked round in my agony on the faces of those who but an hour ago were my friends. They had all shrunk back from me, and I was alone within the circle of the guards. D'Entrangues stood with folded arms, and a smile on his lips, and Tarbes glanced from side to side, like an ape seeking chance for escape. I looked towards Hawkwood, but even his face was hard and set.

"I do not see the duchess' rubies here," said D'Alegres.

"I am prepared to produce them to-morrow," replied

D'Entrangues; " in the meantime, I trust you have sufficient proof?"

"Give M. d'Entrangues his sword. You need not fight this man," D'Alegres added, pointing to me, " even if he challenges you. Were you a French subject," he said to me, " I would hang you in your boots; as it is I will submit the case to the duke. D'Entrangues, I hold you to your word about the rubies. Provost, see that your prisoner is carefully guarded. You will answer for him with your life."

"Prisoner, your excellency! There are two."

"I have restored M. d'Entrangues his sword."

"There is still another," and the provost pointed to Tarbes.

"Pah!" exclaimed D'Alegres, " hang him out of hand —come, gentlemen!"

One by one they went out. Not another look did they give me. I heard the tread of feet, and the sound of voices in eager conversation, dying out in the distance. I stood as in a dream. Tarbes had been dragged away speechless, and half fainting. When he was outside he found voice, and I heard him alternately cursing D'Alegres, and D'Entrangues and screaming for mercy. Braccio touched me on the arm.

"Come, signore," he said, "*you*, at any rate, have a few hours left."

CHAPTER II.

RUIN.

I STARTED at the man's words, and my rage and despair may be imagined, when I saw that he proposed to bind me, a noble, like any thief! From this I hoped to escape by bringing on death, and, on a sudden, hit the guard next to me on the face, with all my force. Down he went like an ox, and I made a rush to the tent door, little doubting that I should be cut down, and put out of my misery. But they were too quick. I was one, and they were many. In a hand turn I was tripped up, my wrists securely fastened behind my back, and any further resistance on my part impossible. The man whom I felled, scrambled up, and attempted to brain me with the butt of his pike as I went down; but Braccio struck him senseless with the hilt of his sword, and this time he lay in a huddled heap, quiet enough.

I besought Braccio to give me my parole, swearing on the faith of a gentleman, on the honour of a Savelli, that I would not attempt escape, and would go with him quietly, if I were but free from the ignominy of the cords that bound me.

"Shut the cage door, keep your bird," he laughed brutally, "I have to answer for you to-morrow, and I weigh the faith of a gentleman, and the honour—God save the mark —of a Savelli, as *that*," he snapped his fingers, " when it comes to a consideration of Braccio Fortebraccio's head. So your knighthood must even go as you are, with my love-knots on you. Here, two of you, take charge of this tent, and see after Arnulf there—I never thought his skull so thin—march!"

And in this manner was I led out, two men in front of me, two behind, one on either hand, all with their weapons ready, whilst the provost himself brought up the rear, with his drawn sword in one hand and a lighted torch in the other. Not that light was needed, for the moon had risen, and was in its full. I believe, however, that Braccio held the torch, so that the additional light might the more clearly show who his prisoner was, and I hung down my head as, with quick steps, we marched to the military prison.

"*Qui vive là,*" the challenge rang out crisply, and on the instant the provost replied, "France and Tremouille."

"Pass on," and the sentry, one of Bucicault's arquebusiers, looked at us curiously as we went by. And now, to add to my shame, we met, face to face, a group of late revellers returning to the camp.

"*Diable!*" called out a gay voice, "our respectable provost is at work I see. What have you got there, Braccio?"

I shuddered, for I recognised Bellegarde, a young noble of the Franche Compte, who had come to seek glory in the Italian war.

"Close up, men—another of my strayed lambs brought back to the fold, Viscompte—pardon me—it is late, and I must hurry on."

But Bellegarde was merry with wine. "Not till you have drunk our health," he laughed, barring the way with his drawn rapier, as he added, "Lowenthal here has a skin of wine from the Rhineland, have a pull at it, man, and let us see the prisoner."

"*Blitzen!* Der brisoner first, he will hang pefore der herr brovost," and the half-drunk Lanzknecht thrust his wine-skin towards me.

" Gentlemen—gentlemen! have you a care! See here, Viscompte," and Braccio whispered to Bellegarde.

" My God!" said the latter; and then hastily, " Come on, Lowenthal! Let them go."

" Let der brisoner drink. Would you debrife a boor man of his liquor?" replied Lowenthal, and to hide my face, I seized the skin, and raised it to my lips. Even Braccio held the torch away, and Von Lowenthal failed to recognise me in the half-light. My throat was red-hot with thirst, and sick as I was with shame, I drank greedily, and handed the wine-skin back to the German.

"*Blitzen!*" he said, giving it a shake, " you drink like an honest man. Now, herr brovost, a health to Germany, in honest German wine. What! No! Then drink to der halter, man, and Lowenthal will knight you," swaying to and fro, he attempted to draw his sword.

Matters were at a crisis, for Braccio was not to be trifled with any longer. At this juncture, Bellegarde and the others with him again intervened, and dragged Von Lowenthal away. The provost instantly pressed forwards with a hurried good-night. We did not go so fast, however, as not to perceive, from the noises behind us, that the Lanzknecht had subsided to earth, and was apparently abandoned there, with his wine-skin, by his companions. The sound of his voice, engaged in a drunken monologue, reached us.

" Der rascal Braccio, der knight of der noose und halter. I will gif him der accolade. I——" But we lost the rest as we hurried on, the guards smiling to themselves, and Braccio very ill-tempered.

In a few paces we passed D'Alegres' headquarters, and through an open window, I saw half-a-dozen of my late companions playing at dice, and heard Hawkwood's bass calling the mains. A few steps more brought us to our point, a fortified wing of the Villa Accolti itself, and Braccio, thrusting me into a strong room, turned the key of the door, and with a gruff order, which I did not catch, walked away. Now, indeed, was I in a distressful state, and the agony of my mind so great, that I heeded not the pain of the cords, but paced up and down like any caged animal. I fully recognised that I was the victim of a deeply laid plot on the part of D'Entraugues, and saw clearly that I was completely in his hands. It was a stroke of genius on his part, not to interfere in any way to save his creature, the wretched Tarbes. That hasty order of D'Alegres had removed the only danger of his scheme being laid bare. I tried to think out some plan of action; but to no purpose, for my mind was altogether confused and bewildered, and I was incapable of thought. The room in which I was confined was bare of all furniture, not even a camp-stool. There was only one window, and that, iron-grated, was set high up, near the ceiling. The moonlight straggled through the grating in long white ribbons, and dimly showed up the walls around me. Hour after hour passed away. I could hear the occasional barking of dogs, the distant cries of the sentinels as they called to one another, and the sound of the guard being relieved at my door. Then the moon sank and the morning came. From sheer weariness I threw myself on the floor, and fell into a troubled sleep, from which I was aroused by the cords biting into my flesh. This, and the constrained position in which my arms were held, gave me torture. I attempted by shouting to attract the attention of the sentinel over me; but though I heard the clod tramping up and down, I received no answer.

At length, about the sixth hour, I made another effort to get some one to hear me. I fortunately chose a moment when the guards were being visited. After a short discussion outside, an under-officer entered the cell. I begged him to free me from the cords, pointing out that escape was impossible, swearing that I would not attempt it, and ended by offering him five crowns for the good office. He hesitated at first, but either pity for my condition, or the bait of the crowns moved the man, for he freed me with a touch of his dagger, and for another five crowns I obtained from him the promise of procuring for me a change of attire from my tent. I had, hidden in a belt, worn under my shirt, thirty crowns, and this I reached with some difficulty, owing to the stiffness of my arms, and paid him the money. I specially begged he would get for me a pair of Spanish leather boots, that were lying in my quarters, for the sole of one of my *contigie* had come off during the struggle of last night. The honest fellow promised to do his best, and shortly returned with the articles I wanted, and in addition brought me some food and a cup of wine, for which he refused all payment, saying that I had treated him generously enough. To eat was out of the question, but the wine was grateful, and, after drinking it, I devoted myself to putting my attire in order. And here I may mention an odd circumstance, to wit, that my gold cross of St. Lazare, which I wore pinned to my breast at the supper, had by some chance remained intact, despite the struggle I had gone through, and was still hanging in its place by a shred of the ribbon. I carefully unfastened it, and placed it for security in my belt. To me it seemed an omen of fortune, this lost little tag of honour which clung to me. I succeeded indifferently well in arranging my dress, and so passed a full hour. Heavens! when I recall that night, although more was to befall me, I do not think I ever endured such misery; nor has the noiseless file of time ever been able to eradicate the memory of those hours.

At about noon Braccio entered the cell. He raged beyond measure at finding me loosed of my bonds, and insisted at first on securing me again. I shrewdly suspected, however, that Messer Braccio was a trifle afraid of the consequences of his violence the night before, and that his furious language was in this case but bluster. I showed a bold front therefore, and the under-officer putting in a word for me, the provost gave in with apparent reluctance. He informed me that my affair was to be dealt with by the duke in person, and that I should make ready to go with him. I replied that I was prepared to go at once, and without more ado was escorted to the main building of the villa. I could see that a considerable crowd was collected, and from the litters and riding-horses that were being led to and fro, perceived that some ladies had heard the news, and were come to gratify their curiosity at my expense, and see such trial as I was to undergo. I was led into the great hall, which was full of people, and in the gallery above the dais saw, amongst other ladies, the Duchesse de la Tremouille, and by her side Madame d'Entrangues. The latter kept her eyes down, and fanned herself with a fan of peacock feathers, which, even at that moment, I was able to recognise as my gift. On the dais was a table with seats set about it, which were as yet empty. At the steps of the dais stood D'Entrangues, and beside him a small man cloaked in a sad-coloured mantle, with a keen, cleanly-shaven face, and watchful eyes. He held in his hand a small packet, and surveyed me with no little interest. D'Entrangues did not meet my look, and his hang-dog face was turned towards the doorway immediately opposite to him. In a moment or so that door was opened, and the duke entered, talking earnestly with a cavalier of a most gracious and distinguished presence. Tremouille himself was a small, slightly-built man, of features in no way remarkable; but redeemed in some part by the alert intelligence of his glance. In early life he had met with an accident which left him lame ever after. Yet he was a good horseman and of a constitution that nothing could tire. As for his companion, his face was then strange to me; but in after times when I was admitted to his intimacy and honoured with his friendship, I came to know him as great beyond all men; and this I do not say in gratitude for the debt I owe him; but simply to add my humble testimony to that of others, his companions-in-arms, and equals in station, who with one consent allow him to be the glory of his age, and of knighthood. Immediately behind Tremouille came D'Alegres and Trevulzio, who had raised himself to his present high position, and was a most capable soldier. These four took their seats at the table, and the numerous and brilliant staff of officers who accompanied them ranged themselves behind. From the manner in which the stranger took his seat, I gathered, and I was not mistaken, that he was there as one of my judges, and for the moment I wondered who he was. That he was of the highest rank was clear from his aspect and bearing, and from the fact that he wore round his neck the collar of the Holy Ghost. The proceedings of this public court-martial began at once. It is needless to set them down in full detail. D'Entrangues stated his case, D'Alegres briefly set forth the action taken by him, and Visconti and Hawkwood testified to having found their property in my possession, under the circumstances already explained. I will do them the justice to say that they did so with evident and genuine reluctance. Tremouille, who had doubtless heard all this before, listened patiently to the end, and then asked me what I had to say. What could I say? I looked at the faces around me and saw no sympathy. I looked up at the gallery where the ladies sat, and caught a whisper:

"I do not care—I know it is false; he is not guilty."

The words gave me courage. The charge was false. As false as hell. Then I found tongue. I asked if it were possible that I, a noble, whose career had hitherto been blameless, could have suddenly become so vile as to sink to common theft? I pointed out my long years of service, and called D'Alegres and Trevulzio, under whose banners I had served, to witness if they had ever known me sully my honour.

"It is known, M. di Savelli, that you are hard put for money," said Tremouille.

I admitted the fact, and also admitted that at the time I stood there I owed money lost at play; but that the sum did not amount to more than fifty crowns, and there was twice that amount due to me from the military chest. I then went on to point out how unlikely it was that, even if I had stolen the jewels, I should have hoarded them up and not turned them into money, for which I allowed I was pressed, and wound up by saying I was the victim of a conspiracy, and that I was prepared to assert my honour, man to man, against D'Entrangues, or any other who would take up his cause.

"What say you, my lord of Bayard?" and Tremouille turned to the stranger who sat beside him. Even whilst waiting for his answer, and on the cross with anxiety as I was, I could not help looking with the greatest interest at the man. This then was the celebrated Pierre du Terrail, the noblest knight in Christendom. Vague rumours that he was about to join the army of Tremouille, with a high command, had reached us. But we had merely looked upon them as rumours. And now he had come, apparently suddenly, and without warning. I felt sure that he brought war with him, but had no more time to think, for he answered—" A fair offer—M. d'Entrangues can do no less than accept."

But Trevulzio then cut in, pointing out, that practically the case was proved. That to allow me the ordeal by combat would upset all the course of military discipline, under which he thought the matter should be decided. Even if the ordeal of battle was allowed, and I won, it would not prove my innocence in the face of the damning evidence against me.

"If there is any shadow of doubt, your excellency," and D'Entrangues advanced to the table, "this will clear it up. Messer Vieri, kindly hand that package to the duke."

The man whom he addressed, who was no other than he whom I had remarked, on entering the justice room as D'Entrangues' companion, stepped forward and placed the packet before Tremouille, who opened it amidst a dead silence.

"Messer Vieri, how did you obtain this?" asked Tremouille.

"The matter is simple, excellency," replied the banker, "but first may I ask if madame the duchess recognises the trinket?"

The circlet was handed to the duchess, who said in a low voice—

"It is mine: it was stolen from me a month ago—on the seventh of March."

"On the eighth of March a packet was delivered to me at my house of business by one Tarbes, calling himself servant to the Cavaliere di Savelli. He did not know the contents of the parcel; but it was sent to me for safe keeping by his master, so he said. I gave him a receipt for it. I myself did not know what the nature of the packet was until to-day; but hearing the charges preferred against the cavaliere, I opened the case and at once recognised madame's circlet, which I have the pleasure to restore."

"How did you come to hear these charges against the Cavaliere di Savelli?" asked Bayard.

"I was informed of them by the knight, Messer d'Entrangues."

"That is to say, M. d'Entrangues must have known that the jewels were pledged to you. Is this not odd?"

It was a straw of hope that floated to me, and I could scarcely breathe. D'Entrangues, however, replied boldly, "I was told of the matter by one Tarbes, a servant to M. di Savelli."

"You forget to add," I burst out, "that he was a creature of yours, whom I employed on your recommendation."

D'Entrangues made no reply, and Bayard said, "M. d'Entrangues appears to have usurped the functions of the provost and played catchpole. Could we not see this Tarbes?"

"Call Tarbes," said the duke.

Braccio came forward and explained that he had been dealt with summarily, under the orders of the lieutenant-general.

"Mine!" said D'Alegres in astonishment.

"Yes, excellency, he was the prisoner whom your excellency ordered me to hang last night."

"A pity," remarked the duke, and Trevulzio, between whom and D'Alegres there was little love, smiled.

"I suppose you have nothing to say to this?" said Tremouille to me.

"I was not in the camp on the seventh."

"Where were you?"

But this question I could not answer for I caught Madame d'Entrangues' eye imploring me to silence. I looked back at the duke, and as I did so felt that Bayard had followed my glance, and that his eyes were resting on madame's face. He glanced down almost as soon as I did and turned to me, and there was a grave encouragement in his look from which I took heart. To me it was a great thing to show I was not at or near the camp on the seventh; and yet if I did so I would ruin a woman's name. It had been a harmless frolic, I swear this, as I know I will come to judgment before a higher tribunal than that of man; and yet had I spoken there would have been but one construction. I hated D'Entrangues, too, and this would have struck at a vital part. For a second I hesitated, and looked up once more at madame. She was pale as death.

I looked at Bayard, and his glance seemed to penetrate my thoughts.

"I cannot say!"

There was a sound of a gasping sigh, and a heavy fall. The peacock fan fluttered slowly down from the gallery to my feet, and lay there with its hundred eyes staring at me.

"This ruins you," exclaimed D'Alegres.

"Think again before you reply," said the duke: "I will give you time."

"I thank your excellency; but I have no further answer."

Tremouille shrugged his shoulders with a disappointed air, and dropped his chin between his clasped hands, his elbows resting on the table, a favourite position of his. Whilst he was thus considering, Bayard was whispering earnestly to Trevulzio, and the old soldier seemed to assent, and his hard face almost softened as he looked at me. They then turned their gaze on D'Entrangues, and Trevulzio, with a shake of his head, noted something briefly on a slip of paper and passed it on to D'Alegres. The lieutenant-general looked surprised; but after a moment nodded assent, and in his turn passed the paper on to the duke, saying "I agree." Tremouille read the paper slowly, and then they consulted together in low tones.

And now, in a few brief words I heard my sentence, and it was carried out at once. Braccio himself hacked off my spurs, my sword was brought in and solemnly broken, and I was warned to leave the camp within an hour, on pain of being hanged as a thief. Such property as I had was declared confiscate, and the men of my *condotta* were to be enrolled, by force if necessary, under another banner. How I went through it all I do not know. I cannot say how I passed down that great hall with the eyes of all fixed on me, a dishonoured man, an outcast, and a leper. One thing, however, did happen. Whilst the sentence was being carried out, Tremouille sat apparently absorbed in thought. When the provost broke my sword he rose to leave the room, and as he passed D'Entrangues the duke stopped.

"Monsieur," he said, " you have mistaken your vocation. His majesty does not desire his officers to be thief-hunters. For such talents as yours you will doubtless find room elsewhere, and I have to tell you that the king—my master—regrets he has no further need of your services."

CHAPTER III.

MADAME D'ENTRANGUES.

WHEN I left the door of the justice room I had to pass through the main court-yard, and run the gauntlet of open scorn and contempt, bestowed upon me by all assembled there. It was a great thing for them, for those whom the French call *canaille*—we have no such appropriate word in our own tongue—to see a noble dragged in the dust and covered with infamy. And they did not spare me, taunt and jeer passed from mouth to mouth. Some even would have gone so far as to strike at me, had not their officers prevented them.

"Ah, *Croque-mort!*" exclaimed an arquebusier, "you should hang;" but the man stepped back a half-pace at my look, and, gaining the outer gate, I pressed on, hardly knowing whither my steps led me. I soon found out I was going in the direction of Arezzo itself, and as that was as good as any other place for me at present, I made no alteration in my course; but anxious to get on as fast as possible, quickened my pace almost to a run, until I was tired out, and perforce compelled to go slower.

This happened when I had covered about a mile, and was beginning the ascent leading to the town; and here I heard behind me the clatter of horses' hoofs, and looking back beheld a party riding in my direction. I turned aside, and, concealing myself behind the stem of a locust tree, waited until the riders should pass. This they did in a few moments, and I saw it was Tremouille and his staff returning to the town. By the side of the duchess, who was riding with her husband, was Bayard, mounted on a bay English horse, which he managed with infinite grace and dexterity.

Madame de la Tremouille was in the best of humours, most probably at the recovery of her circlet, for she was laughing gaily as she said something; but they went by too rapidly for me to catch the words. I waited until the troop was lost in the yellow dust which rose behind them, and then, stepping forth from my hiding-place, became aware that I was not alone; but that a body was hanging from a branch of the tree close to where I was standing, and this I had not noticed in my eagerness to escape observation. It needed but a glance to recognise Tarbes, my scoundrel, who had paid so long a price for his treachery; he was swinging there dead enough, overreached and destroyed by the master-villain.

The sight of my dead knave brought up an angry wave of hatred in my heart towards D'Entrangues, and I prayed that I might not die until I was even with him. So great was the uprising of my anger, that at the time I bitterly regretted not having seized the opportunity to wound him, by plainly answering Tremouille's last question. With my rage against D'Entrangues, there came an almost similar feeling towards Madame, and I began to accuse her in my heart of being the original cause of my misfortunes, and of conspiring, by her silence, to set the seal of my ruin. I did not stop to think that I was ruined already, and that it mattered little whether Madame allowed me to be silent or not. I only felt that she had made me pay too great a price for her reputation, and that she had sacrificed me mercilessly.

When I hastened from the scene of my condemnation, I had no other idea but of death, of self-destruction rather than life as it would be now to me; but I put aside all these thoughts for I had to live for revenge. That would be my first object, and until it was achieved I would not rest. With this in my mind I gained the St. Clement Gate of Arezzo, passing through without notice.

Walking down the Via San Dominico, I turned to the right by the Borgo di San Vito, and here I was recognised and hooted. Pressing hurriedly forwards, and aided opportunely by the passage of a body of men-at-arms, coming through the street in a direction opposite to that of my followers, I succeeded in shaking off my tormentors, and turning again to the right up a narrow street, entered a barber's shop to have my beard removed in order to disguise myself as far as possible. The barber, a fussy little fellow, placed me before a mirror of polished steel, and as he set to work stropping a razor on the palm of his hand, I removed my cap, and for the first time observed that the hair of my head was thickly streaked with grey.

"Your excellency has doubtless come to join the army," said the barber in a tone of inquiry as he drew his razor across my face.

"Ah, yes, yes; I have just come," I replied, and the little man went on—

"There have been great doings to-day. 'Tis said the duke has ordered the Count di Savelli to be executed for having in his possession a favour of Madame. They say the count stole it, but we know better, don't we, your excellency?" and the little fool chuckled to himself. He went on without waiting for an answer. "Ah, yes; the ladies can never resist us soldiers. I may tell you that I served with Don Carlo Baglioni, and can bear my pike—there now, I think that side is clean shaven—as I was saying before, it was hard on the Marquis di Savelli, a gallant noble whom I frequently saw—pardon, your excellency, it is but a scratch after all—had you not moved so suddenly, still only a scratch, nothing for a soldier. The Marquis di Savelli, as I said, was a regular customer of mine, and he had a lovely head of hair, your excellency. It was not so much before I took him in hand. *Ecco!* but in a month you should have seen! He came in here in his free easy way, and flung me ten crowns. 'Buy a ribbon for Madonna Giulia with that, Messer Pazzi,' says he; 'and harkee, send me over six more bottles of your elixir of St. Symmachus. *Maldetto!*' he exclaimed, twisting his curls between his fingers, 'but she adores me now.' Now who, I say, could *she* have been but —*tchick? Diavolo?* it is done; never a cleaner shave in Rome itself. If your excellency's fortune grows as well as your hair, I could wish you no better luck."

I rose in silence, and, flinging him a crown, bade him pay himself, and receiving my change, hurried out, declining all Messer Pazzi's entreaties to bear with me a bottle of his precious elixir of St. Symmachus or any other accursed balsam. I saw at a glance that the removal of my beard caused a considerable alteration in my appearance, and imagined if I could but change my attire, my most intimate friends would not know me unless they observed closely; and even then might perhaps fail to recognise me. This view, as it turned out, was not quite correct, and I had yet to learn how difficult a thing it is to arrange a complete disguise.

A few doors further on I laid out some of my money in the purchase of a stout leather buff coat, a long dark mantle, and a cap to match. The cap was ornamented with a single black feather; and when I had donned these garments I felt that, wrapped in the cloak, with the cap pulled well over my eyes, and the feather standing defiantly out to the side, that I wanted but a fathom of sword to make myself as ruffianly-looking a bravo as ever trod the purlieus of Naples or Rome. But the sword was some difficulty, for my crowns had dwindled to sixteen. Fortunately I had on my finger a sapphire ring, and this I pledged for twenty crowns, and made my way to the armourer's. I there selected a long straight weapon, with a plain cross handle and a cutting blade, such as would be useful for rough work, and, after some haggling, got it for ten pieces. The armourer assured me that it was a sound blade, and I may say it did me good service. It now hangs in my bed-chamber, a little chipped, it is true, but as bright and as fit for use as the day I paid for it, with a heavy heart, in Don Piero's shop, near the gate of St. Lawrence in Arezzo.

I began now to feel the want of food, for beyond the cup of Chianti brought to me by the under-officer I had tasted nothing since yesterday evening, and therefore stepping into an ordinary called for a flagon of wine and a pasty. Whilst engaged in assaulting these, half-a-dozen men, whom I recognised as belonging to the garrison, entered the hostel, but to my joy I saw I was not known to them, and after a casual glance at me they fell to eating their meal.

I was however perforce compelled to listen to their conversation, which was carried on in the loud tone men of their class affect, and found to my annoyance that they were discussing me, and the events of the day. In order to escape this I was about to rise, when I heard one of them mention D'Entrangues' name, and stopped to listen.

"He has left for Florence, and, it is said, intends to offer his sword to the Signory," said one.

"And the other?"

"Heaven knows! Perhaps Braccio's arm has reached him, poor devil!"

"Well, he was a good soldier and a stout lance."

"*Basta!*" said the first speaker. "What does a little lightness of finger matter? Play it in a small way, you're a thief, and food for Messer Braccio, curse him! Play it on a big scale and you're a prince. I for one don't think the less of Di Savelli because perhaps his hand at cards was always too good, and he made that little error in the matter of the rubies. A gentleman is sometimes driven to hard straits. I was a gentleman once and ought to know. I give you a toast—Here's to a long sword and a light hand!"

They drank with acclamation, and then set to a-dicing. I had however heard enough, and settling my account with the host, stepped forth into the street, intending to depart from the town by the Porta San Spirito or Roman Gate, leaving the camp over my shoulder, and to make my way to Florence as soon as possible. There I would meet D'Entrangues, and kill him like a mad dog. I ground my teeth with rage when I thought I had no horse, nor even the means to purchase one, and must trudge it like any *contadino*. But if I had to crawl on my hands and knees, I was determined to reach Florence and D'Entrangues.

It was however not yet sundown, and my idea was to leave the city when it was well dusk to avoid all possible chance of recognition. I meant to have passed the interval in the inn; but, as I felt this was impossible, it was necessary to find another spot where I could lay in quiet. With this end in view I crossed the Piazza di Popolo in an easterly direction, and went on until I came to the Franciscan church, into which I entered, not, I am sorry to say, with any desire for devotion, but merely because I was less likely to be disturbed there than anywhere else I could imagine. I was right, in so far that on entering the church I found it, as I thought, empty, but on looking round I saw beneath the newly-completed wheel-window, the work of Guillaume de Marseille, a kneeling figure, apparently absorbed in prayer. I had approached quite close before I became aware that I was not alone, and was about to turn away, when, perhaps startled by the sound of my footfalls on the marble pavement, the person rose hurriedly and looked towards me. It was Madame D'Entrangues. Her glance met mine for a second as that of a stranger, but as I was moving away some trick of gesture, or perhaps the hot anger in my eyes, told her who I was, for, calling my name, she came towards me with outstretched hands.

"Di Savelli," she said, for I made no advance, "do you not know me?"

"Madame," I bowed, "I am unfit to touch you."

"No, no—a thousand times no! It is I who am unworthy."

I still remained silent, and she asked with a passionate emphasis—

"Man, have you never sinned?"

The words struck me like a shot. I felt in a moment I had no right to stand in judgment.

"God knows," I replied, "I have, and I have been punished."

With that she took hold of my hand, and then suddenly burst into tears, weeping over me with words I cannot repeat. It was not for me to fling reproaches, and I softened and did what I could to appease her.

"I could not help it," she said, "I was not strong enough to speak or to let you speak. Oh, you do not know what such a thing is to a woman!"

"Let it pass, madame. What is dead is dead."

"I cannot. And yet, what can I do?" Her tears began afresh.

In a little time she grew better, and I seized the opportunity to point out the danger she ran of being seen speaking to me, and suggested that she should make her way home. It was impossible to escort her myself, but I would walk a little way behind, keep her in sight, and see she came to no harm. I urged this all the more as I saw it was growing late, and that she was without any attendants and far from the camp.

"You mistake," she said; "I have not far to go. In fact I am at present the guest of the convent here."

"And——" I did not finish the sentence, but she understood. I had forced myself to ask, to hear, if possible, confirmation of D'Entrangues' movements.

"He," she answered—"he has left the army and gone towards Florence."

"And you?"

"I stay here for the present."

Her tone more than her words convinced me that she had been abandoned by D'Entrangues, and it added another mark to my score against him.

"Why should I not tell you?" she continued. "After, when it was all over, the duke struck his name off the army, and he left in an hour. Before he went, he came and told me all, laughing at your ruin. I did not know man could be so vile. God help me—it is my husband I speak of! He offered to take me with him, but I refused; and he left, mocking like a devil, with words I cannot repeat. He was not done with you or with me, he said, as he went. I came here at once, and perhaps when Madame de la Tremouille returns to France, I shall be enabled to go with her in her train."

"Excuse my asking it," I said, "but have you——?"

"Oh, yes," she smiled sadly, "it is not that in any way."

At this moment I looked up and saw that it was sunset. Through the wheel-window the orange beams streamed in a long banner, and lit up the figure of the saint above us.

The rays fell on madame's pale face, and touched with fire the gold of her hair. We stood before each other in a dead silence.

"Good-bye," I said, extending my hand.

She placed her own in it and our eyes met.

It was a moment of danger to both. Leper as I was, I had but to lift my hand, but to say a word, and here was one who would have followed me like a dog. I felt her weakness in her look, in the touch of her hand, which shivered as it lay in mine like a captive bird. At once a fire leapt up within me. I had lost all—everything. Why not throw revenge after my losses, and with her by my side seek a new fortune with a new name? The grand Turk needed soldiers, and what mattered it whether it was cross or crescent that I served?

But the woman became strong as I grew weak.

"Go!" she said faintly.

I dropped her hand, and, turning without a word, strode down the aisle. As I reached the church door the bells of the Angelus rang out, and yielding to a sudden impulse I looked back.

Madame was on her knees before the saint.

CHAPTER IV.

A FOOL'S CAP AND A SORE HEART.

I WAS not so dense as to fail to grasp the extent of the peril I had escaped, or to fully realise the evil strength of the temptation, which came upon me as suddenly as a sneeze. It is rare in matters of this kind for wicked thoughts to be of slow growth; they spring at once to life, full-armed. I thanked God in my heart that I was able to sweep aside the base desire, which covered my soul like a black cloud, and refrained from taking advantage of madame's momentary weakness. I could not but see I was to blame myself.

I, the elder and the stronger, should have foreseen the probable consequences of a friendship such as ours, and my sorrow for her was mixed with the deepest regret for my part in the transaction. I banished all idea of attacking D'Entrangues through his wife, wondering at the littleness of spirit which had ever conceived such a thought. If it were possible, I would have kicked myself. Perhaps such victory as I gained over my heart was due to the secret springs of my vanity being touched, to the fear of the loss of my self-respect, and this mingling with my pity and regret, gave me the strength to win at the moment of temptation. It is difficult to tell; I have lived long enough in the world to know that the mysteries of the heart will remain veiled to the end. Occasionally we may lift the curtain a little, but more no man has done.

What had happened, however, explained clearly to me the motive for D'Entraigues' conduct. He, at any rate, must have seen, long before either of us, how affairs stood with the wife whose life he embittered; but he made no effort to save her, contenting himself with striking an assassin's blow, which had taken from him the last shred of respect madame may have felt for him, and which had in part recoiled on his own head. Be this as it may, his stroke was successful, in that to all intents and purposes it had utterly blasted me. I was worse than dead. It was no ordinary revenge. In those troublous times, a blow from a dagger could have easily rid him of a wife of whom he was sick, or a man whom he hated, and no one would have thrown the matter in his teeth. But with devilish cruelty, he inflicted wounds which could never heal, and left his victims to live. It was impossible to hit such a man back, in a way to make him feel to the utmost extent the agony he had administered; the only thing was to take from him his worthless life: this he doubtless valued most of all things, and I meant to deprive him of it, if he stood at the altar of Christ. Moved by such thoughts, and with my cloak drawn well over the lower part of my face, I hastened towards the Roman Gate, reaching it just as it was to be closed for the night. In fact, as I passed out, the huge doors came together behind me with a groaning, and at the same time I heard the dull boom of the evening gun from the camp, followed immediately by the distant peals of the trumpets of the cavalry brigade.

The sun had now set, and night came apace; a grey haze enveloped the town behind me; above, in the deep violet of the sky, a few stars were shining, soon to be dimmed by the rising moon; from the east a bank of clouds was rapidly approaching, the advance guard of a storm from the Adriatic. To the west, there was still light

enough to see the Chiana, lying like a silver thread, flung
carelessly to earth in long folds, and the rugged outlines of
the roadless Chianti hills stood up in fantastic shapes
against the horizon. South-east was the peak of Monte
Eavulto; due west, beyond Bucine, Mount Luco was yet
visible. I halted for a moment, hesitating what course to
take; whether to cross the swamps of the Chiana valley,
and make my way over the Ambra to Montevarchi, and on
to Florence; or to skirt the camp, cross the Arno at one of
the fords between Laterino and Giove, and go on through
the Prato Magno.

As the crow flies, Florence was but a few leagues distant; but I obviously would have to journey by side-paths,
over hill and across valley to avoid observation, and this
would occupy at least two days, unless my travels were
permanently stopped by my being cut off by a privateering
party from the camp, or by any other untoward accident.
Neither contingency was unlikely, for the writ of the king
ran barely a league from the army, and the country was full
of banditti. In fact, for a half-pistole one might have had
a priest's throat cut. I decided on the former route. So
muffling myself well in my cloak, for the wind blew chill,
with my sword resting in the loop of my arm, I set forward
at a round pace, and avoiding the camp, directed my steps
towards Bucine. As far as Chiani I knew the road. Beyond that there was nothing but quagmire and swamp;
still I had little doubt of finding my way by the moon,
which would soon show, and if, perchance, I fell in with
nighthawks, well then, there was little to be gained from
me but hard knocks; and it would be an opportunity to
test the temper of the blade I had purchased from Don
Piero, the armourer.

In this mind I pressed on, intending to lie at Bucine
for the night, or, if no better accommodation offered, to

sleep as a soldier should, wrapped in my cloak, with the sky for a roof. As I went on, I found I was relying a little too much on my knowledge of the road, and a blue mist, which rose from the ground, made it impossible to pick my way by landmarks. Stumbling along, I took a good two hours to do what should have been done in one, and, by the time I reached Chiani, began to think it would be well to reconsider my decision in regard to making Bucine that night. It was then that I suddenly remembered that Chiani was held by a piquet of Swiss infantry, and any attempt to enter would be impossible, as the gates were doubtless shut. I was a little put out, for had I only recollected the fact before, I might have been saved the extra mile or so of hard work I had to reach within a few yards of Chiani, merely for the pleasure of turning back. The moon, come out by this time, shone fitfully through the bank of clouds, which was shifting uneasily overhead, and the wind, rising steadily, marked rain. I stirred myself all the faster, for I was in no mind to add a wetting to my misfortunes, and a drop or two of rain that caught me, showed I had but little leisure to lose. I made out a narrow cattle track, and hurried along this; but before I covered a mile the moon was obscured, and the wind dropped. It now began to rain, and the darkness was so thick, that I could only just follow the road. Soon the track died away into nothing, and I found myself floundering, over my ankles in mud, and up to the waist in wet rushes. At any moment I might strike a quicksand, with which these marshes abound, so I used my sword as a search-pole, stepping only where I found foot-hold, a dozen inches or so below the surface of the bog. In this perplexity, imagine my relief to see the blaze of a fire shoot up beyond a small rising ground before me, and throw an arc of light into the darkness, against which the falling rain glittered like fine wires of silver. I shouted aloud and to my joy got an answer.

"Who is there? What is the matter?"

"A traveller," I replied, "who has lost his way in this cursed swamp. Whoever you are, you will make a friend and find a reward if you lead me out of this."

"Come straight on, there is no danger beyond getting your feet wet."

"They are that already," I answered, and pressed on, having absolutely to force my way through the wet rushes, which wound themselves round me impeding my progress terribly. Moreover, so sticky was the slime below, that I thought every moment it would pull the boots off my feet. Struggling on in this manner for a hundred yards or more, guided by the fire, and an occasional shout from my unknown friend, I at last touched hard ground, and with a "Thank heaven!" got out of the swamp, and found myself at the foot of the hillock, behind which the fire was blazing.

"Which way to Bucine?" I called out.

"Are you out of the swamp?"

"Yes!"

"Then come round the shoulder of the hill to your right, and follow your nose. You will find shelter here. Bucine you could never reach to-night, and a dog should not be out in this weather."

"True, friend," I muttered, and with a loud "thanks" to the apparently hospitable unknown, I followed his directions, and rounding the hillock, saw before me, spluttering in the rain, a huge fire of pine-logs, at the entrance to a hut of the rudest description. Inside, I perceived a sitting figure, over which the light from the fire alternately cast a glare, and then left it in darkness. I made my way to the open door, which hung back on hinges of rope, and entered without further ceremony.

"Humph!" snorted my host, without moving from his position. "I said it was no night for a dog to be out, I did not say anything of a wolf."

This change of tone was not so surprising, for dripping wet, covered with mud, and white with fatigue, my general appearance was but little calculated to re-assure any one. Yet, as I hung my cloak on a rough wooden peg which caught my eye, I could not help laughing in mockery as I answered:

"Wolves, friend, come to wolves' lairs."

He took no notice of my remark; but pointing to a heap of rushes opposite to him, said, "Sit down there." He then rose, and went towards the fire with an unlit torch in his hand. This gave me some opportunity of observing him. I saw he was of spare, but elastic figure. His head was bare, and his white hair hung in matted locks over a lean neck to his shoulders. His dress was fantastic, and entirely out of place with his surroundings. It consisted of a tight fitting jerkin of parti-coloured velvet, with puffed breeches to match, pulled over thick black hose. On his feet were the ordinary sandals of the peasantry, and, as he stooped to light the torch-wood, I saw his face was seamed with wrinkles, and that his lips moved rapidly, as if he was speaking, although no sound issued from them. He did not delay about his business; but hastened in, and sticking the torch in a hole in the floor between us, resumed his seat, and said abruptly—

"Let me look at you?"

Apparently his scrutiny was satisfactory, and I did nothing to interrupt him.

"Hungry?"

"No. All that I ask is to be allowed to rest here till to-morrow."

"That is well, for I have no food to offer you; but here is some wine in this skin."

He reached to a corner and pulled out a small wine-skin. This he placed before me with the single word "drink."

"No, thanks." The whole manner and aspect of the man were so peculiar, that, although I was much fatigued, I judged it prudent to decline. His quick eye seemed to read my thoughts, for he laughed a little bitterly as he said—

"Tush, man! There is no fear. You bear too long a sword to have a purse worth the picking, and you are not supping," a look of hate passed over his features as he dropped out slowly, "with the Borgia. See, I will give you a toast—Revenge." He took a pull at the skin and flung it to me.

"I drink to that," I said, tasting the wine in my turn. Here then was another who, like me, sought for consolation in vengeance. We sat in silence for some minutes, each absorbed in his own thoughts. The heat from the fire had warmed the hut so, that the blue steam began to rise from my damp clothes. My companion reclined on his elbow tracing some diagram on the floor with a poniard, which from its shape was evidently of Eastern make. The rain, which now increased in violence, had almost quenched the log-fire, and was invading our shelter, for the roof began to leak. There being no wind the torch burned steadily, throwing sufficient light for us to distinguish each other. I began to wonder what manner of man this was before me, dressed in a motley of court-fool and peasant, and my curiosity was aroused to such an extent, that for the time I forgot my own troubles. Nevertheless I made no sign of inquiry, knowing there is no means so sure of obtaining information as to seem not to desire it. My new friend kept his eyes fixed on the point of his dagger, the muscles of his queer-webbed face twitching nervously. At length he became conscious of my scrutiny, for lifting his eyes, he looked me in the face, and then made a motion of his hand towards the wine-skin.

"No more, thanks."

"There will be that left for to-morrow before we start."

"Then you also are a traveller?"

"If you so put it; but I have been here for a week."

"An odd retreat to choose."

"Any hole will do for a rat."

"True; but we were wolves a moment ago," I smiled.

"I did not say I was," he replied drily, "but you looked wolf all over when you came in. Give me your hand."

I stretched out my hand, and he held my open palm near the torch, bent over it, and examined the lines keenly.

"Yes," he muttered half to himself, "strong fingers that can close over a sword-hilt, a soldier too, and one who has seen wars. Too much conscience ever to be great. You will never die a prince as Sforza did. Stay—what do I see? A man changed to a wolf—no—wolf you will never be. A bitter enemy, a woman who loves you, and a free heart for yourself. Sorrow and danger, bale and ruth, then calm waters and peace. There! Are you satisfied? If the devil does not upset this, it is the map of your life. Can you read mine?"

"No," I replied, withdrawing my hand, and somewhat surprised at the general accuracy of this man's knowledge of my past. Yet, I could not help crossing myself as I thought of his allusion to the foul fiend.

"Ay!" he sneered, "cross yourself. Peter and Paul are old and blind. They do not see. Pray if you like. God is too far above the stars to hear you. Go on your knees and beat at the skies with your lamentations. You will surely see the light of a seraph's wings. Do I not know—have I not seen the deep? Some day you will know, too."

He stopped as suddenly as he burst out, and betook himself to his old trick of moving his lips rapidly, forming words without any sound. I began to think I was with a madman, and rapidly cast up the chances of a struggle. I was physically the stronger, but armed as he was, with an unsheathed dagger, the odds were against me. Perhaps it would be prudent to begin the assault myself, and taking him by surprise, overpower him. When, however, I came to consider that I was in a manner his guest, that he had shown me kindness, and given no signs of personal violence, I was ashamed of my fears.

"You say you are going to Bucine?" He asked the question in his usual abrupt manner; but his tone was composed.

"It lies on my road."

"And on mine, too. Shall we travel together? I could point out the way."

"Certainly. It is very good of you."

"Well, it is time to sleep, and the torch has burnt to an end."

As he spoke he stretched himself out at full length, and, turning his back to me, appeared to sink at once into slumber. I watched him for some time by the embers of the torch, wondering if I was wise in accepting his companionship, and then, overpowered by fatigue, lost myself in sleep, heedless of the rain, which dripped in twenty places through the roof.

I slept profoundly, until aroused by my shoulder being gently shaken, and looking up, beheld my host, as I must call him, bending over me. I thought I had slept for a few minutes only, and saw to my surprise that it was well in the morning, and the sun shone brightly. All traces of cloud were gone, though soft billows of mist rolled over the olive gardens, and vineyards of Chianti grape, that stretched towards Montevarchi.

"Heavens, man! How you sleep! I was right when I hinted you had a good conscience."

I scrambled up with a hasty Good-morning; and a few minutes afterwards, having finished the remains of the wine in the skin, we started off in the direction of Bucine. My companion had politely never inquired my name, and I had been equally reticent. He placed on his head a silken fools'-cap, and the bells on it jingled incessantly as he walked along with a jaunty air, at a pace that was remarkable for a man of his age. He seemed to have lost the melancholy that possessed him during the night, and conversed in so cheerful and entertaining a manner, that in spite of myself, I was interested and withdrawn from my unhappy thoughts. He kept up his mood to Bucine where, notwithstanding our strange appearance, we attracted, to my relief, less attention than I imagined we should draw.

With appetites sharpened by our walk, we did full justice to the meal I ordered at the only hostel in the place. Here I played host, as a return for my entertainment, and in conversation my acquaintance said that he was bound for Florence. I told him that also was my point, and invited him to bear me company on the road, to which he willingly agreed. I made an attempt here to hire a horse; but not even a donkey was procurable, all available carriage having been seized upon for the army. So once more descending the hill on which Bucine is situated, we forded the river and continued our journey.

At the albergo we heard that a body of troops were foraging along the banks of the Arno, and resolved to make a detour, and, crossing Monte Luco, to keep on the sides of the Chianti hills, if necessary avoiding Montevarchi altogether. My companion maintained his high spirits until we reached the top of the spur of Monte Luco, known to the peasantry as the Virgin's Cradle. Here we stopped to breathe and observe the view. I looked back across the Chiana valley, and let my eye run over the landscape which stretched as far as the Marches. In the blue splash, to the south of the rugged and conical hill of Cortona, I recognised Trasimene, and beyond it lay Perugia. I turned to call my friend's attention to the scene, and at first did not perceive where he was. Another glance showed him standing on the edge of the cliff, a little to my left, shaking his clenched hand in the direction of Perugia, whilst on his face was marked every sign of sorrow and hate.

Curious to see what this would result in, I made no attempt to attract his attention, but in a moment he shook off the influence which possessed him, and rejoined me with a calm brow. We thereupon continued our journey with this difference, that my companion was now as silent as hitherto he had been cheerful. My own dark thoughts too came back to roost, and in a gloom we descended the Cradle, pushing our way through the myrtle with which it was covered, and walked on, holding Montevarchi to our right.

We kept a sharp look-out for the foragers, and seeing no signs of them, made up our minds, after some consultation, to risk going to Montevarchi, which we reached without mishap a little after noon. It was not my intention to halt there more than an hour or so, which I, hoping I would have better luck than at Bueine, intended to spend in trying to hire an animal of some kind to ride.

We stopped at the Bell Inn, near the gate, and after a deal of bargaining, which consumed a good hour, the landlord agreed to hire me his mule for two crowns. The rascal wanted ten at first. Just as the matter was settled a dozen or so of troopers rode in, and, spying the mule, in the twinkling of an eye claimed it for carriage purposes.

It was in vain the landlord protested that it was his last beast, that it had been hired to the noble cavaliere, meaning me, and many other things beside. The soldiers were deaf to his entreaties, and although I had more than a mind to draw on the villains, I had the good sense to restrain myself, for the odds were too many against me. I therefore hid my chagrin under a smile, and the mule was led away amidst the lamentations of mine host, who was further put out of pocket by a gallon or so of wine, which the troopers consumed, doubtless in honour of the prize they had taken, neglecting in the true fashion of the *compagnes grandes* to pay for it. It was a fit lesson to the landlord, for had he not, in his cupidity, haggled for an hour over the hire of the animal, he might have been the richer by two crowns and still owned his mule. Thus it is that avarice finds its own punishment.

On going off, the leader of the troop, a man whom I knew by sight and by reputation as a swashbuckler, if ever there was one, made me a mock salute, saying, in allusion to my quietness in surrendering my claim to the mule, " Adieu, Messer Feather-Cap—may your courage grow as long as your sword." This taunt I swallowed ruefully, and immediately set about my departure. My companion, who was not mixed up in the altercation, joined me silently, and we followed in the direction taken by the troopers, pursued by the maledictions of the innkeeper, who vented his spleen on us as the indirect cause of his misfortune.

The foragers, who owing to the warmth of the weather had all removed their breast-plates, which were slung to their saddles, were going at a walking pace ; and it was amusing to see how the mere sight of their presence cleared the streets. Noting, however, that they did not appear to be bent on personal injury, we did not think it necessary to go out of our course, or delay our departure until they left the town, and as we walked fast and they went slowly, by the time they reached the main square, we were not more than a dozen yards behind them.

At this moment we noticed the figure of a woman, apparently blind, for she was guided by a little dog attached to a string. The poor creature was crossing the pavement almost in front of the leader of the troop, and as she was right in the path of the troopers, we attempted to warn her by shouting, and she stooped irresolutely, hardly knowing which way to turn. The troop leader, without making any effort to avoid her, rode on in a pitiless manner, and she was flung senseless to the ground. In this her hood fell back, uncovering her face, and my companion, suddenly uttering a loud cry, ran forward, and seizing her in his arms, began to address her with every term of endearment, in the manner of a father to his child.

The troopers halted—discipline it will be observed was not great—and one of them with rough sympathy called to my friend to bear the girl, for so she looked, to the fountain, at the same time that their commander gave a loud order to go on, and to leave off looking at a fool and a beggar. I had, however, made up my mind there was a little work for me, and, drawing my sword, stepped up to the swashbuckler's bridle, and asked for a five minutes' interview there and then.

He burst into a loud laugh, "*Corpo di Bacco!* Here is Messer Feather-Cap with his courage grown. Here! two of you bind him to the mule."

But the men with him were in no mood to obey, and one of them openly said—

"It is always thus with the ancient Brico."

"Do you intend to give me the pleasure I seek," I asked,

"or has the ancient Brico taken off his heart with his corselet?"

For a moment it looked as if he were about to ride at me: but my sword was ready, and I was standing too close to him for any such treachery to be carried off. Flinging the reins, therefore, to the neck of his horse, he dismounted slowly and drew his sword. A number of the townsfolk, attracted by the scene, so far forgot their fear of the foragers as to collect around us, and in a few moments a ring was formed, one portion of which was occupied by the troopers.

Brico took his stand so as to place the sun in my eyes, a manifest unfairness, for we should have fought north and south; yet I made no objection, and unclasping my cloak let it fall to the ground behind me.

"*À vous!*" he called out, and the next moment we engaged in the lower circle, my opponent, for all his French cry, adopting the Italian method, and using a dagger to parry. For a few seconds we tried to feel each other, and I was delighted with the balance of my sword. It did not take me a half minute to see that he was a child in my hands, and I began to rapidly consider whether it would be worth the candle to kill him or not. Brico, who had commenced the assault with a stamp of his foot, and a succession of rapid thrusts in the lower lines, became aware of his weakness as soon as I did, and began to back slowly. I twice pricked him over the heart, and his hand began to shake, so that he could hardly hold his weapon.

"Make way there," I called out mockingly, "the ancient would like to run a little."

Maddened by this taunt, he pulled himself together and lunged recklessly at me in tierce; it was an easy parry, and with a strong beat I disarmed him. He did not wait, but with the rapidity of a hare turned and fled, not so fast, however, but that I was able to accelerate his departure with a stroke from the flat of my sword.

"Adieu, ancient Brico!" I called out after him as he ran on, followed by a howl of derision from the crowd, in which his own men joined.

It was lucky that I adopted the course of disarming him, for had the affair ended otherwise, I doubt not but that the men-at-arms would have felt called upon to avenge their leader, poltroon as he was. As it happened they enjoyed his discomfiture, and an old trooper called out to me—

"Well fought, signore—you should join us—there is room for your sword under the banner of Tremouille. What—no—I am sorry; but go in peace, for you have rid us of a cur."

Saying this, they rode off, one of their number leading the ancient's horse by the bridle.

I turned now to look for my companion. He was nowhere to be seen, and on inquiry I found that he had lifted the girl up, and supporting her on his arm, the two, followed by the dog, had turned down by the church, and were now not in view. It would, no doubt, have been easy to follow, and as easy to trace them; but I reasoned that the man must have purposely done this to avoid me; and after all it was no business of mine. I therefore returned my sword to its sheath and walked on.

CHAPTER V.

D'ENTRANGUES SCORES A POINT.

BEFORE I had gone fifty paces, however, I became aware that there was some law left in Montevarchi, for a warning cry made me look over my shoulder, and I saw a party of the city-guards, who had discreetly kept out of the way when Brico and I crossed swords, hurrying towards me. The same glance showed me that the ancient was already in their hands, and was being dragged along with but little regard to his comfort; and I felt sure that now, as the troop was gone, the citizens would wreak their vengeance on this hen-roost robber, and he would be lucky if he escaped with life. As for me, the catchpolls being out, they no doubt reasoned that they might as well net me. To stop and resist, would only result in my being ultimately overpowered, and perhaps imprisoned; to yield without a blow meant very much the same thing, and, in the shake of a drake's tail, I resolved to run, and to trust for escape to my turn for speed. So I set off at my roundest pace, followed by the posse, and the rabble who but a moment before were cheering me.

More than once I felt inclined to turn, and end the matter for myself; but the fact that this might mean laying aside all chance of settling D'Entrangues, urged me to my best efforts. Some fool made an attempt to stop me, and I was compelled to slash him across the face with my sword, as a warning not to interfere with matters with

which he had no concern. I hardly knew where I was
going; but dashed down a little bye-street, and was, after a
hundred yards, brought to a halt by a dead wall. I could
barely reach the top of it with my hands, luckily this was
enough to allow me to draw myself up, and drop over to
the other side, just as the police reached within ten feet of
me. I did not stop to take notes of their action, but was
off as soon as my feet touched ground, and found to my
joy that I was close to one of the unrepaired breaches in
the city wall, made six months ago by Tremouille's cannon.
Through this I rushed, and scrambling down a slope of
broken stone and mortar, found I would be compelled to
climb down very nearly a hundred feet of what looked like
the sheer face of a rock, before I could reach level ground.
There was not even a goat track. My agility was, however, spurred on by hearing shouts behind me, and prefer-
ring to risk death in attempting the descent, rather than
fall into the hands of messer the podesta, I chanced the
venture, and partly by holding on to the tough broom roots,
partly slipping, and aided by Providence and Our Lady of
San Spirito, to whom I hurriedly cast up a prayer, I managed to reach the bottom, and fell, exhausted and breathless, into a cistus hedge.

I was too beaten to go another yard, and had my pursuers only followed up, must have become an easy prey. As
it was I heard them reach the breach, where they came to
a stop, all shouting and babbling at the same time. One
or two, bolder than the others, attempted to descend the
ledge of rock, down which I escaped, but its steepness
damped their courage. They, however, succeeded in loosening some of the débris so that it fell over the cliff, and a
few of the stones dropped very close to me; but by good
hap I escaped, or else this would never have been written.
One great block indeed, just passed over my head, and I

vowed an altar-piece to Our Lady of San Spirito, who alone could have diverted that which was coming straight to my destruction; and I may add I duly kept my word. After a time the voices above began to grow fainter, and to my delight I found that the citizens, thinking it impossible I should have escaped like a lizard amongst the rocks, were harking back, and ranging to the right and left. I waited until all sound died away, and cautiously peeped out. The coast was clear. I had recovered my wind, and without more waste of time, I rose and pressed on in the direction of the hills, determined to chance no further adventures near the towns. Indeed, I had crowded more incident into the past few hours, than into the previous five-and-thirty years of my life, and my sole object, at present, was to reach Florence without further let or hindrance.

Keeping the vineyards between me and the town, I avoided all observation, and at a small wayside inn, filled a wallet which I purchased, with food and a bottle of the rough country wine, so that there might be no necessity for my visiting a human habitation during the remainder of my journey. With the wallet swung over my shoulder, an hour or so later I was ascending the slopes of Mount St. Michele, cursing the fallen pine-needles, which made my foothold so slippery, that I slid rather than walked.

Turning the corner of a bluff, I suddenly came upon half-a-dozen men, reclining under the pines in various attitudes of ease. They sprang up at once on seeing me, and one of them, presenting his arquebus, called on me to halt.

"You must pay our toll before you pass, Signore," said the man, who appeared to be the leader of the party.

"As you please," I replied, "but my only metal is cold steel."

"*Corpo di Bacco!*" he exclaimed. "I thought I knew

you, and your voice makes me certain. Surely I address the Cavaliere di Savelli?"

I bowed, a little confused at the thought of my disguise being so easily penetrated, and the bandit went on, turning to his comrades—

"Put down your gun, Spalle, this gentleman is one of us, and—hawks do not peck out hawks' eyes. Signore," he added, "you pass free. I had the honour to serve in your *condotta* during the Siena war, and doubtless you remember Piero Luigi?"

"I do," I said, and the memory of a bag of florins which accompanied this same Luigi on his disappearance one fine day came to my mind. I had not however seen the man for three years, but he was apparently of those who do not forget faces. As it turned out, however, he had seen me very recently without my knowing it.

"It is a pleasure to think I am not forgotten, and in a way, Excellency, you have paid your footing." The rascal was alluding to my stolen florins. "To think," he continued, "that you should have joined us! But I suppose it was the dice, and, to be sure, the rubies were worth ten thousand. You should have realised at once and vanished; but experience will come, and mayhap another chance. I saw the trial, Excellency, and we do not war with the profession, least of all with a new recruit. You are free to pass, or, if you prefer it, to accept our hospitality for a while."

I declined the proffered invitation with a brief thanks and went on, my blood boiling at the impertinence of the scoundrel who so familiarly claimed me as one of his own kind. Innocent myself, I was tasting to the dregs all the humiliation of the guilty, and it was only perhaps a lucky chance that saved me from the rope, or the still worse fate of the galleys at Pisa. Turn which way I would, my own country would never be a country for me again. I was cut out from my order, my infamy would be known wherever my name was heard, and my associates would henceforth have to be the vilest of mankind. Had I committed a murder, or even an act of treachery in war, that could have been wiped out; but to have sunk to the condition of a common thief, this was ignominy beyond repair. I therefore resolved, as soon as I pushed matters to a conclusion with D'Entrangues, that I should leave Italy and seek a new life in the strange countries beyond the seas which Messer Columbus, the navigator, had discovered, and there, my past being unknown, perhaps find a future of peace or the rest which fears no disturbing from this world.

My original idea had been to seek the dominions of the Turk, but they were too close to my shame; even the New World was hardly far enough. So I planned, and so doubtless would I have acted had not circumstances worked to give me back what I lost, as I thought hopelessly, and to bring home to my mind the certainty of that tender mercy of God, of which we on earth take too little account.

It was late in the evening before I halted and ate my dinner under an overhanging rock, sheltered from the north wind by a clump of pines. When I finished I rolled myself up in my cloak, and fatigue, together with a good conscience, combined to send me to a sleep as sound as it was refreshing. I was up before the sun and continued my way, determined to reach Florence by evening. I took no particular notice of the view, where I could see to my right the Prato Magno, and to my left all the valley of the Greve; but kept my eyes before me, intent on my thoughts.

At length, when passing Impruneta, where the black virgin is, Florence came in sight. There was a slight haze which prevented me from seeing as clearly as I could wish;

but I plainly made out the houses on the banks of the Arno, Arnolfo's Tower, the Palace of the Signory, the Cathedral, the Bargello, and the unfinished Pitti Palace, whilst beyond rose the convent-topped hill of Senario, where the Servites have their monastery.

As I looked, there was little of admiration in my heart, although the scene was fair enough; but I could give no mind to anything beyond the fact that I was at last within measurable distance of D'Entrangues, and that in a few hours my hand was like to be at his throat.

With these thoughts there somehow mingled up the face of Madame, and the scene of our last meeting. I put this aside, however, with a strong hand, and determined to think no more of her, although no such recollection could be anything but pleasant and sweet. Until I met her I had managed well enough without womankind, and for the future I would leave bright eyes alone. Yet I knew I was the better man for holding the privilege of her friendship. However, she had passed out of my life, and across the seas I would have other things to think of than the memory of my platonic friendship with Doris D'Entrangues.

It was close upon sunset when I entered the San Piero Gate, and found myself in Florence, and in a difficulty at the same time, in consequence of my wearing a sword. I luckily, however, remembered that La Palisse, the French leader, was then in the city, and explaining that I was from the army at Arezzo with a message to him, inquired particularly his abode, which I was told was in the palace of the exiled Medici in the Via Larga. It so happened that La Palisse was in constant communication with Tremouille, and this and my confident bearing imposed upon the guards. I supplemented my argument with a couple of crowns, and they let me pass without further parley. It will thus be seen that whatever the regulations may have been, they were easily broken. Indeed I found later on that they were, even at that time, a dead letter, and that the zeal of the guards was merely inspired by the prospect of making something out of me, which they did on this occasion. I knew Florence fairly well, having been there under circumstances very different to the present; but as I hurried along the crowded streets, I began to feel I was somewhat uncertain as to whither the roads led. I judged it prudent, however, not to make inquiries, but kept my eyes on the sharp look-out for an hostel suitable to my purse, which was diminishing at a fearful rate. I stopped for a while at a street stall to satisfy my hunger with a cake of wheat and a glass of milk, a wholesome but unpalatable beverage, and entered into conversation with the stall-keeper. It came out that I was in a difficulty about a lodging, and the man very civilly told me where one could be procured, and added to his kindness, seeing I was apparently a stranger to the place, by directing his son, a small bare-legged urchin, to guide me to the house, which he said was an old palace of the Albizzi, that had passed into the hands of the banker Nobili, and was rented out in tenements.

Heaven only knows through what bye-lanes and alleys the imp led me, chattering like an ape the whilst; but at last we reached the house which lay in the street di Pucci. An arrangement was soon entered into with the person in charge, and I paid in advance for two weeks the small rent asked for the room I took. I selected the room, because there was in it some furniture, such as a bed, a table and a couple of chairs, which, I was informed with some emphasis, had been seized from the last tenant in default of rent. I sent the boy away rejoicing, and was surprised to find that the housekeeper did not depart as well; but this worthy soon made it clear to me that a further payment was requisite on account of the furniture. I was too tired to haggle, so paid him the three broad pieces he wanted, and bid him get me some candles. He returned after a little delay with what I needed, and I may say at once that under a rough exterior I found this man, with all his faults, was capable on occasions of displaying true kindliness of heart.

I would like to pay him this tribute, for subsequently, as will be seen, we had a grave difference of opinion which ended in disaster for him. At the time this happened I could not but condemn him strongly, for in order to further a plot in which he was engaged, he tried to induce me to crime, and when, by a happy chance, I was able to frustrate his design, joined in an attempt to murder me. I fully believe, however, now that I can look back on affairs coolly, that, in common with others of his age, he thought it no wrong to adopt any means to further a political plot, whilst in the every day observances of life he displayed, in an underhand manner, much virtue.

When he was gone I sat down to count my money, and found I had but ten crowns in all the world. With prudence however this would last some time. Still it was gall and wormwood to me to have to weigh each item of my disbursement. It would be necessary as well to renew my attire, which, with the exception of the leather buff coat, was almost ruined by the hard wear it had been exposed to on my journey. I sat down to rest, but now that I had reached Florence a reaction set in, and assailed by a full sense of my position I gave way to despair. In a little time I became more composed; but it was impossible to keep still with the fire in my heart, and I sallied into the street, taking care to note landmarks, so as to find my way back. In this manner I must have gone for about a quarter of a mile, when I was brought to a standstill by the coming of a gay party down the street, in the direction opposite to mine, all marching by the light of many torches, to the music of a band. The musicians led the procession, which was flanked on each side by a number of flambeaux bearers, and a retinue of servants, all bearing swords despite the law.

The merry-makers walked in pairs, each lady resting her fingers on her cavalier's arm, and all laughing and talking with the utmost good-humour. I was compelled to draw myself to the wall to admit of their passing, and whilst thus giving them the road, the light fell brightly on me, and I became an object of alarm to some of the fair, who gave utterance to pretty little exclamations of terror, with the result that I came in for haughty looks from the gallants.

In the middle of the promenaders were two ladies, who, apparently not having partners of the opposite sex, had linked themselves together, and the attention of the taller of these was bestowed upon me for a moment, and it was not flattering. As she wore a mask, I could see little of her face beyond the half contemptuous look in her eyes which were dark as night, and a short curl of the upper lip, with which she no doubt intended to express the same sentiment as her glance. I waited calmly until the whole party passed on, admiring the grace of the demoiselle who had favoured me with her scornful survey. I watched them until they turned off into another street, and then went on, idly wondering who the people were, and more especially the dark-eyed lady.

The street behind me was in gloom, a few yards in front of me a lamp hanging from a wall threw a dim radiance; beyond that there was gloom again. Through the darkness before me I heard the sound of hurrying feet, coming in my direction, and almost before I was aware of it, the new-comer and I fell into the circle of the light, and met face to face.

It was D'Entrangues! He knew me as if by instinct.

"You!" he exclaimed, and on the instant his sword was

out. I said nothing. I was blind, mad with anger. My whole soul hungered for his life as I thrust at him, and in doing so slipped my foot over the edge of the narrow pavement and fell heavily. He was on me at once; something flashed in his left hand, and I felt a stinging sensation all over my side. He did not wait to see the result of his blow. Perhaps he made too sure, and springing over me, ran into the darkness beyond. I scrambled up at once, and made an attempt to follow; but my brain began to reel, and I was compelled to lean against the wall to support myself.

The clash of steel had however aroused some of the inhabitants, and hearing footsteps approaching I pulled myself together with an effort, and making across the road, turned back to my lodging. Here again I felt too weak to proceed without help, and sank to the ground, knowing I was bleeding freely. By this time two or three men came up, and after surveying the spot under the street-lamp, crossed over in my direction. The rays of a lantern held by one of them discovered me, and they hastened up. I begged the favour of their assistance to my abode, saying I had been stabbed, and this the worthy citizens readily accorded: and not content with that, when I reached my room, gave me all help in dressing my injury. The dagger, which I had to extract, had gone through the folds of my cloak, but was turned by a steel buckle on the strap of my buff coat, and had cut through the coat and down my side, inflicting an ugly flesh wound. This in itself was not dangerous; but I had lost much blood, and when the kind citizens had gone, in making an attempt to rise from my chair, I had only just time to reach my bed before I became unconscious.

CHAPTER VI.

BERNABO CECI.

I CANNOT say for what time I lay thus bereft of sense; but on coming to myself I saw the candle in my room was all but spent, and the wick flaring in a long flame. I looked to see if my wound had broken out a-bleeding afresh, and was glad to find this was not the case, and that the bandages were in their position. The small effort, however, nearly set me off once more. The room swam round, the bright flame of the candle dwindled down to a little star, no bigger than a pin point, and then began slowly to increase in size as the faintness passed off, and I was able to see clearly again. Any attempt to move gave me agony, and, closing my eyes, I lay still. I heard the candle expire with a splutter, and leave me in darkness. Then I began to get light-headed, and unable to control my thoughts. Somehow my mind travelled back to the days of my childhood, and the figure of the only living relative I can remember, my father, came before me, standing just as he was wont to stand, when about to give me a lesson in the exercise of the sword, and repeating a warning he never ceased to din into my ears. "Learning," he said, "is of little use to a gentleman. You need not know more of books than a Savelli should, but in horsemanship, and in the use of the sword——" he finished with a gesture more expressive than words. And truly old Ercole di Savelli was never a bookworm, although he ended a stormy life in his bed.

He was the son of that Baptista di Savelli, who was ruined with the Prefetti di Vico, and other noble houses during the time of Eugene IV. Such estates as Baptista had, were transferred with the person of his sister Olympia, who married into the Chigi, to that family, and with them the custodianship of the Conclaves. Baptista di Savelli left his son nothing but a few acres. The latter tried to woo Fortune in the Spanish war, but did not obtain her favours. He returned to Italy, and poor as Job though he was, hesitated not to marry for love, and engage in a lawsuit with Amilcar Chigi. What between the one and the other, Ercole was ruined in a hand turn. His wife died in giving birth to me, and disgusted with the world, he retired to a small estate near Colza in the Bergamasque. There he devoted himself to a pastoral life, and to bringing me up as a soldier, until, one fine day, having contracted a fever, he received absolution and died like a gentleman and a Christian.

I followed the profession for which I was intended, joining the levy of the Duke of Urbino, and sharing in all the ups and downs of the times, until Fortune did me a good turn at Fornovo. Subsequently things went well with me, and although I had to mortgage my narrow lands, to raise and provide equipment for the men, with whom I joined Tremouille, I was in expectation of a full reward, when I was so suddenly stricken down.

Thinking of these things in the dark, tormented by a devouring thirst, which I was unable to quench, haunted by the impression that my last hour was come, and that I should die here like a dog, without even the last rites of the church, I fell into a frenzy, and began to shout aloud, and rave as in a delirium. D'Entrangues came before me, wearing a smile of triumph, and I strove impotently to reach. Then the whole room seemed to be full of my enemy, from every corner I could see the white face, the red hair, and the smile of successful malice. The figures, each one exactly like the other, floated over me, stood by my side, sometimes brought their faces within an inch of mine, until I imagined I felt a flame-like breath beating on me. Finally they flitted backwards and forwards, rapidly and more rapidly, until there was nothing but a mass of moving shadow around me, which gradually resolved itself again into a single form. I strove to reach for my sword to strike at it, but my arms were paralysed. So through the livelong night the phantom stood at the foot of my bed, until the white morning came in at my window, and I fell into a sleep.

When I awoke, I found the old intendant of the building bending over me. The fever had abated but the thirst still remained. "Water," I gasped through my parched lips, and he gave me to drink.

To cut a long story short, I arranged with this man for such attendance as I should want, and to do him justice Ceci—for that was his name—performed his part of the contract, getting me my food, attending to the dressing of my wound, to which he applied a most soothing salve, and such other offices a helpless person must expect. He did not trouble me much with his presence during the earlier part of my illness, but came as occasion required him, and, when he had performed his work, left me to my reflections.

I may note here that I never again saw the people who helped me when I was wounded. Having assisted me to my lodging, and aided me to dress my hurt, as I have said, they departed, and apparently gave me no further thought. This I am persuaded was not due to unkindly feeling, but to prudence, and a wish to avoid being mixed up in an affair such as mine appeared to be; for the times were such, that it was better for a man's head to be unknown to the Magnifici Signori of Florence.

Subsequently, when things changed with me, I caused public cry to be made, requesting the worthy citizens to come forward; but my attempt was of no avail, beyond producing a half-dozen or so of rascal impostors, who swore to helping me, under circumstances that never occurred, on the off chance of hitting a nail on the head, and obtaining a reward. But this was long after my illness, and the block in the Bargello may have, since that time, been a resting place for the heads of the good Samaritans for all I can say. I took a longer time in mending than I thought I should, for an inflammation set in, the fever came back, and when that was passed I recovered strength but slowly. It was at this time, however, that I discovered the advantage of reading, having up to now borne only too well in mind my father's saying on that subject.

I began with Poliziano's Orfeo, a poor affair, and then procured, to my delight, a translation of Plutarch's Lives. Both these books were obtained with the greatest difficulty, so old Ceci, the attendant said, from the library of a great Florentine noble, in which a nephew of his was employed in copying manuscripts, and the old man charged me an entire double florin for the use of the latter alone; an expenditure I grudged at first; but which I would have willingly paid twice over before I finished the volume. I inquired the name of the nobleman; but Ceci was not inclined to tell me, and I gathered that the owner was probably unaware that his books were taking an airing, and enabling his library-scribe to turn a dishonest penny. On the binding of the Plutarch was pricked a coat-of-arms, a cross azure on a field argent, with four nails azure; but I could not, for the life of me, remember this device, although I had served in every part of Italy except Rome. Finally it came to my mind, that the bearings, no doubt, belonged to some merchant prince of Florence, and would therefore be unlikely to see anything more of fighting than a street riot, and therefore I dismissed the subject.

I did not neglect, whilst lying in enforced idleness, to take such steps as I could to discover the whereabouts of D'Entrangues, and specially instructed old Ceci to make inquiries of the followers of La Palisse. He brought me news in a couple of days, that the Frenchman had left Florence a fortnight ago, and it was understood he was going to join the army of Cesare Borgia, that cursed serpent who was lifting his head so high in the Romagna. This was ill news indeed, for I had been lying helpless for close upon a month; but I was on the mend at last, and resolved to follow him as soon as I had strength to travel.

During my illness I had frequently thought of madame, and with the thoughts of her, there mingled recollections of the dark eyes of the lady who had looked at me through her mask, on the night I was stabbed. I could think of madame in no way but with a kindly feeling; but strange as it may seem, any recollection of the other made my heart beat, and I would have given much even to have obtained another glance at her. In the meantime, however, my first business was to try and replenish my funds, for my supplies were almost exhausted by the drain made upon them during my illness.

Old Ceci, the intendant, had in his way formed a sort of attachment for me, and now that I was better, generally spent an hour or so with me daily in converse. One day I let out some hint of my condition, and Ceci, after a little beating about the bush, approached me with a proposal.

"Signore," he said, "there are those in Florence who would like things changed. We want our Medici back;

but we want also a few good swords, and I could tell you of a way to fill your purse."

"Say on," I replied, and the old man having first bound me to secrecy, informed me that certain notables in Florence wanted a good sword or two, to rid them of a great political opponent, in order to pave the way for the return of the Medici; and without mentioning names in any way, which, he said, would be given to me later, proposed that I should undertake the task.

I realised at once that his suggestion meant nothing short of assassination, and saw that my old acquaintance was apparently up to the ears in a political plot. My first idea was to spurn the suggestion with indignation; but reflecting that it would be better to know more, and by this means, if possible, save a man from being murdered in cold blood; I affected to treat the matter seriously, and replied that I was as yet unfit for active work; but that as soon as I was better I would discuss the subject again. He then departed.

Perhaps the time will come when the minds of men will shrink with horror from crime, even for the sake of a good object, and however much I loathed the proposal made to me, I could not but recollect that the noblest names of Milan were concerned in the Olgiati conspiracy, and that a Pontiff had supported the Pazzi attempt on the Medici. This being so, there was excuse for Ceci and his leaders, whoever they were; but my whole soul was wrath in me at the thought that I had been deemed capable of doing the business of a common bravo, and if it were not for the reason stated above, I would have flung the old conspirator out of the room. This insult also had to go down indirectly to D'Entrangues, and as I grew better, my desire to settle with him rose to fever-heat. The question, however, was my resources. Turn which way I would, there seemed to be no way of replenishing them. The idea presented itself to me to join the Borgia, who with all his faults was ever ready to take a long sword into his pay. But the man was so great a monster of iniquity, that, even to gratify my vengeance, I could not bring myself to accept the gold of St. Valentino.

There were others to whom I could apply, such as Malatesta or De la Rovere; but amongst them I would be known, and the burden of my shame too great to bear. After all, it would perhaps be better to seek to fill my purse in Florence, and let my vengeance sleep for a while. It would be all the sweeter when it came.

With these ideas in my head, I was sitting one afternoon at the little window of my room, putting a finishing touch to the edge of the dagger, which D'Entrangues had left with, or rather in me, and congratulating myself that the blade was not a poisoned one, when I heard, as from a distance a hum of voices, which gradually swelled into a great roar, and above this the clanging of a bell with a peculiar discordant note. Almost at the same time old Ceci bustled into my room, evidently in a state of high excitement, and called out—

"Messer Donati—Messer Donati! It is to be war—war!"

I should add here that I had judged it prudent to take another name on entering Florence, and adopted the first one that struck me, although I afterwards thought that Donati was not quite the name to win favour with the Florentines, amongst whom the memory of Messer Corso was still green, although so many years had passed since he was done with. Whether I let my own name out or not during my illness I am unable to say; at any rate, Ceci never gave me any such hint. The news the old man brought was not unexpected by me, yet I caught a touch of his excitement and answered—

"War—where? Tell me."

"It is this way, signore; Naples has risen, and the Great Captain has driven D'Aubigny out of Calabria, all the Romagna has gone from Cesare as that," he waved his hand as if throwing a feather in the air.

"The Holy Father has cast his interdict on Florence, and Pisa is burning the Val di Nievole."

"The devil!" I exclaimed, "this is more than I thought. The interdict is bad, Messer Ceci."

He grinned as he answered, "Bad for the Pope. Medici or no Medici we will not have a priest interfering in Florence."

"I see," I said, "you are Florentine first, and conspirator afterwards; but how do the French stand?"

"With us, for we pay. It is said, however, that things are uncertain with them, that Monsignore d'Amboise, who is now Cardinal of Rouen, has gone to Rome, and that Tremouille is awaiting the king."

"The king! Louis is at Mâcon."

"Yes, Louis himself, and the Lord knows how many barons besides, with pedigrees as long as their swords, who will eat up our corn, and pillage our vineyards from the Alps to the Adriatic. But I came here to ask, signore, if you will come with me to see. It is hurry and make haste for I cannot wait. The Carroccio has left St. John's."

I had almost recovered my full strength, and was accustomed to walk out daily at dusk in order to avoid observation, whilst at the same time I could by doing so exercise my muscles; yet at first I felt inclined to decline Ceci's invitation, alleging weakness as my excuse, for my anger was still warm against him on account of his proposals to me. Reflecting, however, that if I offended him, it would probably fatally injure any prospect I had of saving the person whom the conspirators intended to kill, I thought it best to affect a friendliness I did not feel, and changing my mind in regard to accompanying him, slipped on my sword, and followed the old man downstairs. We hastened as fast as we could to the great square. The people were swarming out of the houses, and the streets were full of a hurrying throng, all directing their steps to the point, whence we could hear the bellowing of the mob, echoed with answering cheers by those making towards the place of assembly. Around us there was a murmur like that of millions of bees, as men, women, and children, jostled their way to the Palace of the Signory. My companion, who stopped every now and again to open his jaws as wide as the mouth of a saddle-bag, and give forth a yell, hustled along at a great pace, and I made after him with scarcely less speed.

By good fortune, and a considerable amount of pushing, we made our way through the press, which appeared to me to be composed entirely of elbows, and at last reached the market-place. Here the crowd behind us slowly drove us forwards, and finally gave us the advantage of a good position. The square was lined with men-at-arms and stout citizens, with boar-spears in their hands.

All at once there went up a shout louder than ever, the crowd swayed backwards and forwards, then opened out, and admitted the Carroccio or war-car in Florence. It was painted red, and drawn by oxen housed in red trappings. The great beasts had dragged the car slowly from the chapel of St. John's, where it stood in times of peace, and laboured along under its weight. From the car itself projected two poles on which hung the banner of the Commonwealth, a red giglio on a white field. Immediately behind this came another car, bearing the Martinello or war-bell, which was incessantly clanging out its angry notes. It was to ring now for a full month, without ceasing.

Around the cars were the principal nobles of the city, and the oxen being guided to the "bankrupt stone," were there unharnessed. Pietro Soderini, the brother of his eminence of Volterra, who was then Gonfaloniere for life, raised his hand. In a moment there was silence, and the vast audience listened to the brief oration that fell from the lips of their chief magistrate. He painted in stirring words the dangers of the times; he called to the people to forget party hatreds in the face of the common crisis; he appealed to their past, and then concluded: " Therefore," said he, " for the safety of the State, have we to whom that safety is entrusted put our hope in God, and our hands to the sword. Citizens, we give to our enemies, to Rome, and to Spain, war, red war—and God defend the right!" With that, he drew off his glove of mail and flung it on the pavement, where it fell with a sudden crash.

The silence of the crowd continued for a little, and then, from forty thousand throats rang out cheer after cheer, as the sturdy citizens roared out their approval of the gage thrown down.

In the midst of all this some partisan of the Medici, hysterically excited, raised a shout of *Palle! Palle!*

"Blood of St. John!" exclaimed Ceci, "who is that fool? He will die."

It was the well-known cry of the exiled Medici, and it drove the crowd to madness. Instantly there was an answering yell.

"*Popolo! Popolo!* Death to tyrants!" I cannot tell what happened exactly; but in the distance, I saw a man being tossed and torn by the mob. For a moment, his white face rose above the sea of heads, with all the despair in it that the face of a drowning man has, when it rises for the last time above the waves; then it sank back, and something mangled and shapeless was flung out into the piazza, where it lay very still. I stood awestruck by this vengeance.

" Yet the Medici *will* come back, signore !"

Ceci whispered this in my ear, as he stood with his hand on my shoulder.

CHAPTER VII.

THE GARDEN OF ST. MICHAEL.

On our way back Ceci was somehow separated from me, whether by accident or design, I cannot say. I did not quite regret this, as I had made up my mind to see as little as possible of him for the future, thinking he had repaid himself for his kindness, by the proposals he had made to me. Indeed, I may say I never sought his society, although, until he showed his hand, his visits and conversation gave me some pleasure, for notwithstanding his position, he was a well-informed man, who, in the earlier part of his life, must have seen better days, and perhaps hoped to see them again, if his plot succeeded. The words he had let drop, to the effect that the Medici would come back, had given me a hint as to what that plot was. It was evident that my old friend was an active member of the Bigi, or Grey Party in Florence, that were then working secretly for the restoration of Lorenzo's sons. It seemed clear too, that the attempt to be made, was to be directed against some very eminent member of the State—perhaps the Gonfaloniere himself, and I began to wonder if it was not my duty to lay the information I had before the Signory. I could not, however, reconcile this with my promise of silence, and therefore my tongue was tied. Still I could not sit tamely by, and see a man murdered in cold blood, and I decided therefore, to remain in Florence somehow, and if possible avert the crime, although it would interfere, no doubt, with my own business. But one cannot always be thinking of one's self. Perhaps also, though not quite conscious of it then, I had some idea of again meeting the unknown lady of the gala procession, in whom, in spite of myself, I felt I was taking too great an interest.

During the night I had but little sleep, for the affair of the mad partisan of the Medici, and the declaration of war, had roused the citizens to fever heat, and all night long, crowds thronged the streets, their hoarse shouts of *Popolo! Popolo!* mingling with the incessant clanging of the warbell, which itself was loud enough to wake the dead. The next day, however, I resolved to take the bull by the horns, and with a view to fill my purse, determined to present myself before La Palisse, and offer him my sword. I sallied out, therefore, finding the streets fairly empty, the all-night indignation meeting of the Florentines having wearied them a little. Still, however, there were knots of people here and there, all in a more or less excited condition. I was in no particular hurry, and taking a lesson from the snail, went at a leisurely pace, and eventually reached the headquarters of La Palisse, which were in the Medicean palace, in the Via Larga. The courtyard and entrance-hall were full of soldiers, and evidently active preparations for the campaign were in progress, for there was a continuous stream of people going in and out. No one took any notice of me, and holding my cap in one hand, and straightening the feather on it with the fingers of the other, I advanced unquestioned through the crowded rooms. In this manner I proceeded until I came to a gallery, on one flank of which there was a series of windows overlooking the street; at the end of the gallery hung a purple curtain, covering, as it happened, an open door. On the curtain itself was embroidered a crimson shield, bearing the *palle* of the Medici. Before this I was stopped by a young officer, who asked me my business, and I replied it was with La Palisse himself.

"Impossible!" he replied; "you cannot see the General."

"Why not, signore?"

"Tush, man! You look old enough to understand that orders are orders."

"What is it, De Brienne?" a sharp voice called out from within. The officer lifted the curtain, and went inside. I was determined to gain an interview with the great man, and had therefore said my business was of importance. The leanness of my purse is my excuse for the subterfuge, which I subsequently regretted, as will be seen further on. Shortly after De Brienne came out. "Well, messer—messer——"

"Donati," I said.

"Well, Donati, the General will see you. You may enter."

I accordingly did so, and found myself in the presence of a short, thick-set man, seated at a small table, on which was spread a map, over which he was looking intently. In a corner of the room lay his helmet and sword, and he himself was in half-mail, wearing a Milanese corselet, on which was emblazoned the red dragon of his house. As his head was bent over the paper, I could not at first make out his features, and remained standing patiently. Suddenly he lifted his face, and looked at me with a quick "Well—your business, sir?"

I was accustomed to strange sights, but for the moment was startled, so horribly disfigured was the man. The sight of one eye was completely gone, and half his face looked as if a red-hot gridiron had been pressed against it. The other eye was intact, and twinkled ferociously under its bushy grey eyebrow. I recovered myself quickly, and made my request in as few words as possible. He became enraged as

I finished. "Bah!" he said, "I thought your business was of importance. I can do nothing for you, my list is full. You have gained admission to me under a pretence—go!" and he resumed his study of the map. I would have urged the matter, but all my pride was aroused at his words, and so, with a short good-day, I turned on my heel and walked out. Passing through the gallery, I saw De Brienne, leaning against an open window, talking to another young officer. They both looked at me, and burst into a loud laugh. At any other time I might have treated this with contempt, but I was sore all over at my reception, and approaching the two said, "You seem amused, gentlemen—it is not well to laugh at distress."

They stopped their laughter, staring haughtily at me, and De Brienne said, "Your way, signore, lies before you," and he pointed down the corridor.

"Perhaps the Signor de Brienne would care to accompany me—unless," and I looked him steadily in the face.

"Unless what?" De Brienne flushed angrily.

At this moment we heard a hasty footstep on the marble floor, and La Palisse advanced. "Still here," he said to me, "did I not tell you to begone?"

"My business is with the Signor de Brienne," I replied stiffly, for my blood was hot within me.

"I am quite prepared," began De Brienne, but the free-captain interposed.

"Not in the least. I cannot allow my officers to go fighting with every *croque-mort*, who comes here with a long sword and a lying story. Look at him, De Brienne—every inch a bravo! Harkee, Donati! Begone at once. Not another word, or by God, I will have you hanged from the nearest window!"

It did not require me to carry my perception in my right hand, to be aware that La Palisse was capable of fulfilling his throat, and although I was inclined to draw on him there and then, I knew what the ultimate results would be. So swallowing my pride as best I could, and regretting the ill-humour which had subjected me to this insult, I stalked into the street.

I made my way to my ordinary, and sat there to cool, which took some time. I was able to see, that the rebuff I received was due in great part to my own mismanagement; also that there was no hope for me from La Palisse, and that my steps must turn elsewhere if I wished my purse to show a full-fed appearance. I dined sparingly, drinking but a half measure of Chianti, which I mixed with water, and it made but a thin fluid. When I finished my slender repast, there was nothing left but to kill time. It was useless to go back to my lodging; for want of funds had compelled me to discontinue, until better times, my newly acquired habit of reading, and Ceci, despite the kindness he had shown me, was precise in the exaction of payment for offices performed by him. No more indeed could be expected from a huckstering mind such as his, inherited no doubt from a line of bargaining citizens, whose hearts were in their bales of wool. So I strolled towards the garden of St. Michael, passing on the way the piazzi, where there were still numbers assembled, and wondering at the implacable hatred of the Florentines towards their noblest blood, a hatred they carried so far, as to build the walls of the Palace of the Signory obliquely, rather than they should touch the spot where the Uberti once dwelt. And this set me reflecting on the unreasoning stupidity of the *canaille*, in their enmity towards gentle blood. Perhaps I was a little influenced in these thoughts, from the fact that the Uberti were connected by marriage with the Savelli, a daughter of Maso degli Uberti having wedded that Baptista di Savelli who upheld by force of arms his right to attend the Conclave of Cardinals. It was sad to think that of the Uberti not one was left, and of the Savelli—I alone. I will not include the Chigi, for they come through the female line, and although Amilcar Chigi, the son of my father's old enemy, subsequently made advances of friendship towards me, I felt bound to explain to him that I was the head of the house, despite the broad lands his father got with his mother Olympia, by an unjust decree of the Chamber of Lies. This, however, is a family affair, which does not concern the narration in hand. Having reached the garden, I sat myself to rest on a stone seat, set against a wall overhung by a large tree. At the further end of the walk were two ladies in earnest conversation. Their backs were to me at first, but on arriving at the end of the walk, they turned slowly round, and came towards me. As they approached, I was almost sure they were the two I had seen in the gala procession, and my doubts were soon at rest, for, on passing, they glanced at me with idle curiosity, and in a moment I recognised them by their air and gait. On this occasion they wore no masks, and I saw they were both young and passing fair. The face of the shorter of the two, whose figure had a matronly cast, was set in a mass of light hair, and looked brimful of good-humour. The other, who, in marked contrast to her companion, had dark hair and dark eyes, possessed a countenance of exceeding beauty, marred perhaps by its expression of pride. Be that as it may, my blood began to tingle as I saw her, and an indefinite thought of what might have been rose into my mind. When they had gone a few yards, the one, whom I took to be a married woman, said something to her friend, and glanced over her shoulder; but the other appeared to reprove the remark, increasing as she did so the pride of her carriage. I wondered to myself that two ladies, should be out unattended, in so sequestered a spot, at a time too when the city was so full of excitement, and watched them as they turned the corner of the walk, and went out of sight beyond the trees. I began in a useless manner to speculate who they were, and to weave together a little romance in my heart, when I was startled by a shriek, and the next moment the fair-haired lady came running round the corner of the road, crying for help. It was not fifty yards, and in less time than I take to write this, I whipped out my sword, and was hurrying to the spot. I saw, when I reached, the taller lady struggling in the arms of an ill-looking ruffian. She called out on my coming, and the man, loosening his hold, was about to make off, when, unwilling to soil my sword with the blood of a low-born scoundrel, I struck at him with my fist, and the cross handle of the sword clenched in my hand, inflicted an ugly gash on his forehead, besides bringing him down. I stood with the point of my sword over him, and the affrighted women behind me.

"Hold, signore!" he cried, "enough! I yield—what! Would you draw on a friend?"

"A friend?" I said in astonishment, as he slowly rose to his feet.

"Yes, Signor di Savelli, were you on Monte San Michele now, you would sing a different tune."

"Piero Luigi, then it is you," I said; "well, scoundrel, I am not on Monte San Michele, but you are here, and will shortly be before Messer the Gonfaloniere, unless you restore at once what you have doubtless robbed from these ladies and beg their pardon. Stop! if you attempt to move, I will spit you like a lark."

"I have taken nothing," he said, "let me go; I am punished enough."

"That is true, sir," said one of the ladies, "and we pray you let the man go."

"Not till he has begged your pardon," I replied.

Luigi did as he was bid, and humbly apologised; but as he left, he discharged a Parthian shot: "Ah, ladies! I sought but a kiss. I am but a poor thief—a crow—but the Signor di Savelli is no better, though he flies with hawk's wings."

I took no notice of the remark; and, lifting my cap, begged permission to see the ladies to a place of safety.

"We thank you for your kindness, sir," said the shorter and elder of the two, "but I see our servants approaching, and we will not therefore trespass on you. Believe me, however, we are grateful—my cousin and I."

Even as she spoke her lackeys came up, and one of them, in an alarmed tone, asked what was the matter, and turned on me fiercely.

"Be quiet, Gian," said the lady who had just spoken, "it is we who have to thank Signor di Savelli for rescuing us."

"Your pardon, signore; but we heard the ladies cry out, and seeing you here——"

"Where you should have been," I interrupted, "you lag too far behind your mistress."

The dark-haired girl, who had up to now not spoken, but, with her face very pale, was playing with a bracelet on her wrist, now looked up.

"I think we had better get back, we will not trouble this—this gentleman further. He has already done too much for us."

She dropped me a proud little curtsey, and turned away, but her friend frankly held out her hand. "Believe me, Signor di Savelli—I heard you so called—my cousin Angiola and I are both very grateful. She is a good deal upset by what has happened, and I speak for her. My husband," she went on hurriedly, "has much influence, and if any word——"

She stopped a little helplessly, and seeing she had observed my appearance, and anxious to end the affair, I cut in—

"Madam, I did nothing but drive off a cur—you thank me too much. Good day!"

I stood cap in hand until they turned the elbow of the walk, and then retraced my steps to my lodging. As I went back, I could not help railing at my luck. I was enabled to do a service, which, for no reason I could assign, I would rather have done to this particular woman than any other—a service which should have made her look kindly at me, and yet by a cruel stroke she was made to think me nothing else but a thief, for Luigi's charge was definite, and it was clear I knew him. My name was also known to her, and perhaps the rest of my story, as it was understood by the public, would be told to her, and then, adieu to my little romance, if it was not adieu already. Then again what business had I to have any such thoughts? I had yet to learn that these things come unbidden, and when they come, take no denial. Thinking in this way as I walked on, I was surprised to find I had reached the old Albizzi Palace. This building, like all the other houses of the nobles of Florence, was fortified with braccia or towers, joined to each other by bridges. These towers formed refuges during interurban wars, and stood many a siege from the people. The Albizzi Palace had four such braccia, but the two towards the Ultrarno quarter had been half demolished in some forgotten riot, and never restored. The others were however intact, although the bridge between them had long since given way. It was in one of these that I had my abode, and reaching it about sundown, began to slowly ascend the dark stairs which led to my chamber. Occasionally I stopped and rested, and it was during one of these rests that I looked up to the landing above me. It was still in light; for the setting sun shone through a giglio shaped window in the western wall. As I glanced up, a figure suddenly appeared at the head of the stairway, and leaning one hand on the balustrade, peered down into the dim light below it. I recognised the extraordinary dress at once, and a moment's survey of the face assured me it was my host of the hovel, he who had so strangely disappeared with the girl, when I fought with Brico at Perugia.

"A good day to you, friend!" I called out, "and well met."

"Who calls? Who is there?" he answered.

"One moment, let me climb up these stairs," and I made my way to the landing, and held out my hand.

He took it in silence, but his grip was warm.

"Signore," he said after a moment, "I do not know your name; but whoever you are, Mathew Corte owes you much, and will some day show himself grateful."

"My name," I said, "for the present is Donati, and as for gratitude there is no need to speak of it."

As he mentioned his name, I remembered that there was a madman so called, who had come into notoriety years ago, by asserting that he had discovered the secret of prolonging life to a hundred and twenty years. He had, I heard, written a book in which this was fully described, and presented it to the Cibo pope, with the inscription, *videbis dies Petri et ultra*. Long after, I heard Cardinal Bembo tell, in his witty way, how this same Corte presented his book to three successive popes, ending with Innocent of Genoa, adding that he took care on each occasion to substitute a new title-page and dedication. "But," the cardinal was wont to add, "it is against the canon, for our Lord the Pope to go in any matter, even in life, beyond the Holy Apostle, and therefore, no doubt, the worthy doctor's prescriptions were not followed. Such are the sacrifices the church has to make."

THE GARDEN OF ST. MICHAEL. 79

"How long have you been here?" I asked.

"Some days."

"And we have never met!"

"Ah! The place is like a rabbit-warren. There are hundreds here. But it is odd that I have never seen you."

"Not so very odd when I come to think of it," and I looked down at my shabby attire. "It is generally late when I go out."

He held out one leg, clothed in its fantastic dress.

"I too am on the rocks," and he laughed bitterly, "and feed with the goats."

Wishing to change the subject, I inquired about the girl. He turned away to the window, and when he looked back the man's eyes were full of tears.

"Would you care to see?" he asked, with a shake in his voice.

I bowed gravely, and he conducted me upstairs, fully two flights beyond my room, and then stopped on a small landing. Through the half-open door that faced us, a little dog came out, and looked wistfully at Corte. He stooped to stroke it, and then rising, passed into the room. When he had gone beyond the door, he looked back at me, saying "enter."

I did so with gentle footsteps, and he pointed to a bed in the corner of the room, on which was the figure of a woman, lying so still and motionless, that she might have been an image of wax. Her plentiful brown hair was spread over the pillow, and out of this frame, the pinched white face, with all its traces of past beauty, looked out in a pitiful silence. One thin hand was turned palm downwards on the coverlet, and, as we stood, the fingers began to work convulsively.

Corte bent over her forehead and touched it with his lips. "Little one," he said, "do you sleep?"

The girl opened her sightless eyes, and a faint smile, that lightened her face, making it wondrous beautiful, passed over her countenance.

"Not yet." She spoke so low I could hardly catch the words, "but I shall sleep soon."

I knew what she meant, for in her face was already that look which comes to those who are going away. Corte was however unable to judge. "She is better," he said, "I will give her some more wine—all that she needs is strength—my little one." With this he turned to a cupboard, and opening it, took thenceforth a bottle of wine; with shaking fingers he tried to fill a glass; but the bottle was empty.

"I forgot," he said, and looked hopelessly around him. There was that in the man's face which made me read it as an open book.

"Stay here," I whispered, "I will be back soon—very soon."

He looked at me in a dazed sort of manner, but I waited for no reply, and, slipping out of the room, ran as fast as I could downstairs, and through the darkening streets to the nearest inn. Calling the landlord I asked him what was his best wine.

"My best wine, signore! All my wines are good. There is Chianti from our own Tuscan grape, Lacryma Christi from Naples, Barolo from Piedmont, Roman Orvieto and White Vernaccia of the same brand that the Cardinal Ippolite d'Este——"

"Fool," I interrupted, "answer my question. What is your best wine? Have you any of the wines of France?"

"Wines of France!" he exclaimed, "*Corpo di Bacco!* Does not your excellency know that La Palisse and his French cut-throats have been here for a month? Think you there is a bottle of red Roussilon or Armagnac left in

Florence? There lie, however, in my cellar, two flagons of Burgundy."

"Fetch one at once—run, man!" and I flung him a crown.

After a short delay, which seemed ages to me, messer the padrone reappeared with the flagon of Burgundy under his arm, and seizing it from him, I ran back to the Albizzi Palace, and hurried up the stairs to the room occupied by Corte. Although I had been away barely half an hour, that was sufficient time to make a change for the worse in the sick girl, and I became aware that the end had begun. We tried to force a little of the wine between her lips; but she could not swallow, and now instead of lying still, kept tossing her head from side to side. Corte was undone. He could do nothing but stand at the head of the bed, in mute despair, as he watched the parting soul sob its way out.

I went towards him: "Shall I send the intendant for a priest?"

If ever words changed the countenance of a man, mine did. His eyes fairly blazed with anger, and he hissed out, " No, signore—this is a priest's work—pray if you like, but no priest comes here."

I had, as all other men have, frequently called upon God, sometimes in idle blasphemy; but never on an occasion so serious as this. Pray if I liked! I had forgotten what real prayer was. Impelled by a power I could not resist, I knelt down and tried to form some words to reach the Most High. But they would not come, I could only feel them, and I rose again and took my stand by the dying girl.

She began to talk now in a rambling manner, and with that strength which comes at the point of death from somewhere; her voice was clear, but with a metallic ring. It is not for me to repeat the last words of one who is now with her God; but I gathered from them a story of trusting love, of infamous wrong and dastardly crime. And Corte shook like a branch in the wind, as the words came thick and fast from the lips of his dying child. After a while she became still once again. So still that we thought she had passed away; but she revived on a sudden, and called out:

"Father—I cannot see—I am blind—stoop down and let me whisper."

"I am here, little one—close—quite close to you."

"Tell him—I—forgive. You must forgive too—promise."

Corte pressed his lips to her damp forehead, but spoke no word.

"It is bright again—they are calling me—mother! Hold me up—I cannot breathe."

Corte sank on his knees with his head between his hands, and passing my arm round the poor creature I lifted her up, and the spirit passed. In the room there was now a silence which was broken by a heart-rending sob from Corte. He staggered to his feet with despair on his face.

"She said forgive!" he exclaimed. "Man, you have seen an angel die. This is the work of a priest, of a pontiff, of him who calls himself Vicar of Christ! Go now, and leave me with my dead."

I took his hand, and pressing it, turned to the door. As I closed it behind me, I saw Corte bending over the still face of his child, and the little dog, throwing up its head, howled piteously.

CHAPTER VIII.

TEMPTATION.

I HAD looked upon death before; I had seen the plague strike down its victims in an hour; I had been in the hell of a sacked town, when men, women, and children, were given to the sword. On the breach at Arx Sismundea, dead, dying and wounded, were piled breast high, when we stormed our way, through the fog of battle, into Malatesta's stronghold. Stricken down at San Miniato, I saw, in the dim night, the death hunters at their fearful trade, and heard the dull blows of their daggers, as they murdered some helpless wretch, sometimes for the prize of a tag of gold lace, sometimes for the sheer pleasure of slaughter. Lying unable to move, by good luck concealed in a hollow, amidst grass which stood a yard high, I saw a man killed not ten feet from me. He rose to his elbow as the fiends approached, and called for water. But it was not water he got. How he struggled! He cried for mercy, and I can still see the wretches as they held him down. A foul-looking hag placed her knees on his chest, she looked towards the sky for a moment, as if invoking a spirit to a sacrifice, and the moonlight shone on a face that was hardly human. Then she stooped down, and with a relentless hand, plunged the knife she held into her victim's throat. But all this, which should have hardened my heart, did not affect me as the scene I had just quitted. After all, what I had passed through was done when the blood was high with excitement. Here, however, was another thing. I had watched the end of a being beautiful and pure, who was born to adorn life, and yet what was her story? Fallen into the hands of an incarnate devil, outraged, and then cast forth blinded, to die like a reptile! It was too horrible! Surely God must have slept whilst this was done. Surely the after life ought to be to her, in an inverse proportion to her sufferings on earth. But why any such infliction on one so helpless? Mystery of mysteries, and I cannot solve it. And yet she was able to forgive. At the last she could condone. What were my wrongs to those she had endured? After all I had health, strength, and the world was wide. Why waste my time in running after the morbid shadow of revenge? If I got it, would it satisfy? Would it heal my wounds! Thinking in this way, I called to mind a sermon of the Prior of St. Mark's—I heard when last in Florence. I came in the suite of Paolo Vitelli ag Citta del Castello, and at the time Savonarola had left the Duomo, and was preaching at St. Mark's. His subject was forgiveness, and his text, "Vengeance is mine, saith the Lord," came back to me with a vivid force. I rose from my seat and paced the room, my whole soul was on the cross; I had all but resolved to forego my scheme of revenge, when I heard a knock at the door. At first I did not answer, but it was repeated.

"Come in," I cried, and Ceci entered. In the state in which I was in, I had half a mind to bid him begone there and then, and only controlled myself with an effort. I could see however that, in his way, he had formed a friendly feeling towards me, and remembering my plans, forced myself to greet him with civility, and offering him a seat began the conversation.

"That was a strange finish to the Gonfaloniere's speech,"

I said, in allusion to the death of the man at the hands of the mob.

"He was a fool, and deserved to die."

"Do you know his name?"

Ceci hesitated for a moment, and I saw he was lying when he said "No."

"I gather," I added, "that you are of the Bigi, the party that favours the return of the Medici."

"Signore, I spoke words in my excitement that may well be buried. An old tongue like mine should have known to be still; but it is not that I have come to speak of. Do you know we have a death in the house?"

"That would be no new thing to you."

"True," he said, stroking his white beard, "they die here like rats in their holes."

"I suppose so; but as a matter of fact I did know there was a death, and a very sad one. I know Mathew Corte, but how have you found out so soon?"

"It is simple. I came back but a few minutes ago, and although it was late, thought I might call for the rent of the room Corte occupies, as he has not paid anything as yet. When I came in, Corte simply pointed to the body of his daughter, that was all the reply I got. She was very ill when she came; I wonder indeed she lived so long. Of course I did not press him, and if it is a loss, Messer Nobili is rich enough to bear this. But it is dreadful the way these people owe."

I winced a little, thinking of my own diminished purse, and Ceci continued: "I thought I would come and see you as I went down. It is on my way. The body must be removed to-morrow."

"You will find some difficulty in persuading him to give it a Christian burial."

"How! Is he a heretic, or a pagan—if so!"

"I did not say that. I believe the man to be mad."

"I will see him to-morrow," said Ceci. "I think he will yield to reason. Poor child! She might have been saved."

"Saved!"

"Yes, when they first came, I begged Corte to let me call the Doctor Maffeo. He would not however listen to the idea. Then I told him what to do, being a family man, who has had children to look after. All gone into the world now, and never even a message for Bernabo Ceci."

"I thought the case hopeless when I saw it."

"When you saw it, perhaps; but, signore, not at first. See! the sun is not in the Lion, and medicines should have been freely given. I would have placed the diaphragm of a sheep on her chest, had her bled, and administered theriaca of Venice; if that failed, there is bezoar."

"Messer Ceci, you are as learned as a doctor yourself."

"I have had experience, signore," he answered, as he rose to go. "Yes, do I not know? The life of my poor wife was saved twice by this treatment, and on the third occasion, if it were not for the poison which originated internally within her, as Messer Maffeo stated in a learned discourse he read to the Academy, she would have been saved again. A good night, Signor Donati, and peace to dreams—remember, it should have been as I said—either theriaca or bezoar—or both combined—a good night!"

He went out, and down the stairs, with the step of a young man, and I marvelled at the contradictory nature, which could show the kindness it had towards affliction, and at the same time coldly plan to remove a fellow-creature from the world, as one removes a bud from a tree, with a touch of the knife. But Ceci's words had also reminded me again of Corte's need. I stood at the door listening until his footsteps died away, and knew he was gone for the night. Then I pulled out my purse, and looked at its contents; there were two gold crowns left, and a few pauls. I hesitated for a little; but the need of the man upstairs was greater than mine. Drawing off my boots so that there may be no sound, I stole up softly, like a thief, and gained the landing of Corte's room. The door was partly open, and I stood before it for a short while, half afraid to enter. Plucking up heart, I crept in gently. The dead girl lay with her hands crossed on her bosom, still as if cut out of marble, and on her face was fixed a sad little smile. Corte sat on a stool near the table; his head was buried between his hands, and he had given way to silent despair. The dog lay asleep in a corner. I meant to have proffered the gold I had with me, as a loan to Corte; but I did not dare to address him in his grief. So placing the coins quietly on the table in such a manner that when he raised his head he must see them, I withdrew as noiselessly as I came, and reached my room without attracting any attention. It was not until the small hours of the morning that I sought my couch, for my mind kept working on the thoughts which agitated me after witnessing the death of Corte's daughter. At the same time, I was able to see that this consideration of the suffering of others was of the greatest benefit to me. It took me out of myself. It showed me that my own were not the only sorrows in the world, and that there might yet be others who had reached a deep of misery as far below that of Corte, as his was below mine. This led me on to consider my own position, and I began to think there was some mysterious power that was preventing me carrying out my plan of reprisal against D'Entrangues. I had come to Florence red-hot on his track. At our very first meeting he had won the hazard, and the long illness that followed gave him chance to put a distance between us; then my resources diminished whilst yet nothing was done; then came the doubts as to whether I was justified in my action; and finally, and not least, there was in me a haunting desire to see Angiola, as I called her to myself, once again. I was pulled by different strings. There was that I called conscience, urging me to give up my schemes of revenge; there was the wild animal in me, telling me to go on; there was a feeling towards a woman, which I had honestly never experienced before, which, despite my struggles against its apparently hopeless folly, was entirely overmastering me, until I did not know which way to turn, and to escape from it all decided to leave Florence at once; and then altered my mind again, when I thought of the plot I wished to thwart, and determined to make a last effort to do this, and, if possible, to see Angiola once more before I left. At last I went to sleep, waking very late in the morning. So sound was my slumber, that when I awoke I thought at first that the events of the night were nothing more than a dream; but they soon forced themselves on me in their reality, and the fact was emphasised, by the sight of the odd pauls, which were now my all, lying on the table. I gathered these up, and proceeded in search of Ceci to ask if he had made any arrangements for the burial; but he was nowhere to be found; and, as I could not bring myself to see Corte then, I resolved to breakfast on fresh air, a diet which however wholesome, was, I found, certainly not satisfying. I went to the Oricellari Gardens, which were at that time the property of the Rucellai. Here, within the city walls, one found a forest, and under the shade of the huge trees, a more miserable being than myself could have spent pleasant hours, and perhaps gained contentment of mind by observing the beauties of nature. It was here that, after the death of Il Magnifico, the Platonic Academy moved its sittings. But the gentlemen who composed it discussed their philosophy with a good dinner, and even the unfortunate who wishes to gain peace of mind in sylvan shades, should have a full belt. This fact obtruded itself more and more strongly on me, and I could obtain little relief by the expedient of tightening my sword-belt by a hole or so. Therefore, in despair, I left the beauties of nature to be so good as to look after themselves, and disbursed a half-paul in something to eat; after which I felt able to face the prospect of future starvation with a more serene mind. On return to my lodging I found Ceci was not yet come back, and still thinking it would be an intrusion to make inquiry after Corte, disposed of my time by repairing my attire as best I might, and watching the pigeons on the eaves of the roof opposite my window, with a little envy in my heart at their simple happiness, and a doubt if, after all, man was so fortunate in possessing a soul, and being cast after the image of his Maker. If our faith is to be believed there is nothing for man but heaven or hell, and perhaps the worst form of hell-torment would be to be born again in the lowest form of a dumb brute, with the faculty of fully appreciating all that the highest of mankind can. Picture to oneself a Raphael, who has slipped into the abyss, and is sent back to earth again, an obscene animal, with all the grasp of the beautiful he had in life. I do not know any punishment that would be more cruel. On the other hand, there has never appeared to me any definite realisation of the joys of heaven. It is no doubt their vagueness that is their charm. Be these things as they may, all speculation into the future is useless, and I have found my comfort in a simple faith in our religion, which has served me through this life, and will, I trust, do the same office in the next.

Thus reflecting, I passed the day quietly, and in the afternoon Ceci came to tell me all was ready for the burial. He gave me to understand that Corte had listened to reason in the matter of a priest, although I never knew what arguments he had used to effect this. The funeral was much as other pauper burials, and when it was over we walked back together. On our return a man accosted Ceci, who, he said, was his nephew, and they went off together on some business. Had I only known what I was to be indebted to this gentleman for, shortly, I should have observed him with greater attention. As it happened I gave him but a passing glance, catching a glimpse of a pale face, with strong, clear-cut features, and keen, bright eyes. Corte and I were now alone, and, respecting his grief, I said no word, nor did he speak, as we threaded our way back. Near St. Mark's, Corte suddenly seized my hand, raised it to his lips, and then turning, fled down a side street and was lost to view. I attempted to follow, fearing that sorrow had totally unhinged his mind, already a little off its balance, and that he would come to injury. My attempt however was without avail, and I returned home to disprove the proverb which falsely says that he who sleeps, dines.

The next day I was again favoured with a visit from Ceci, and after some allusion to the funeral, he once more broached the subject on which he had sounded me before, and asked for a definite reply. I gave it to him without hesitation.

"Messer Ceci," I said, "whatever my condition may be, you are in error if you think I am a bravo. In short your proposal is an insult, and you owe it to my consideration for your years that I do not fling you out of the room. I have promised you secrecy, and therefore cannot do as I would, and that is, lay the matter before the Signory; but I tell you plainly that if I can I will upset your plan, and now you had better leave me."

I had by this thrown everything into the fire; but it was not possible to control myself longer. As for Ceci, he sat for a moment, his eyes staring out of his head with rage, and his white beard fairly bristling. He rose from his seat.

"So, Signor' Donati, this is your answer, is it? Look to yourself, most noble excellency, for those I serve have a long reach. There is, however, another thing we have to settle before I go. I shall be obliged by your paying me the sum of three crowns for rent, and other services due to the excellent Messer Nobili."

I was overcome with shame, for I had not the money.

"You can take this furniture," I said, "it will pay my dues."

Ceci smiled grimly.

"I do not wish to be hard on you, and you know the punishment for debt. I will take the furniture back for two pieces, although it has deteriorated by wear and tear to the value of a florin, and you will still owe one piece. See, signore," and he suddenly changed his tone, "pocket your pride, as many a better man than you has done to fill his purse. It is but a stroke of your sword we want, and here are ten gold crowns."

"Begone!" I cried in a rage, and starting up laid my hand on my sword. Ceci instantly drew a dagger from his girdle and faced me with the highest courage. We stood before each other for a second, and then with a laugh he put back his poniard.

"I will give you time," he said. "A whole week—and now leave you to cool. Adieu, most noble excellency!"

CHAPTER IX.

THE MARZOCCO INN.

I TRIED every possible means I could think of to obtain employment, to no avail, and, in the intervals of my fruitless search for work, haunted the streets and gardens, with the hope of obtaining another glimpse of Angiola, but without any success. Inch by inch my resources diminished, until they became so small that a blind beggar would have hardly thanked me for the gift of them. I lived in constant dread of Ceci reappearing to demand the sum I owed for my rent, but he did not come. He was evidently giving me time, starving me out to surrender to his terms. I used to see him as I went in and out, sitting in his office like a spider, yet he never even lifted his head as I passed. I hated, almost feared, going by that door. Bitterly did I regret not having left Florence when I was able. It was now impossible to do so, unless as a defaulter, and the weight of that paltry debt oppressed me, as if a cannon-ball were slung around my neck. I could not leave until I paid it, and of doing this there seemed no prospect. I had parted with my cloak for money to buy food, but the last copper of that was gone, and I was now penniless. For two days I had not eaten anything but a morsel of bread, and on the morning of the third day I rose desperate with hunger, and prepared to go any lengths to satisfy it. I ate my self-esteem and made another attempt to see La Palisse, but was denied admittance, and when I came back I actually hesitated before the door of Ceci's office, and almost made up my mind to yield, and say I would do his business for him. It required an effort, so low had I sunk, to rouse my pride. At last it flared up, and with a cheek hot at my weakness, I sought my chamber and there passed the day. The pigeons that lived under the eaves opposite my window, and to whose soft cooing I so often listened with pleasure before, now aroused other thoughts within me. If I could only lure one within reach! But it was impossible, and I glared at them as they fluttered and flirted with each other, with the hungry eyes of a cat baulked of her prey. At last I gave it up, and with a curse flung myself on my bed. Fool that I was! Five-and-thirty years should have brought me wisdom. I had stayed on in Florence, allowed my chances of revenge to get more distant, in fact, reached a stage of mind when I was doubtful if I could rightly exact vengeance, drifted into abject poverty, and worse than that, was continually thinking of a woman, who, when I had rendered her a service, treated me with contempt, who had no doubt forgotten me by this time, amidst her duties, if she had any, and her pleasures, of which I doubt not she had store. So the evening came amidst my reflections and self-reproaches, and, it being dusk, I decided to go forth again, and snatch a purse, if necessary, to obtain food. As I rose, an impulse I could not control made me unfasten my money-belt, and search if by chance there was a coin within it. Of course there was not a brown copper, but my fingers, in running up the belt, touched something hard, and I pulled forth, attached to its tag of red ribbon, my cross of St. Lazare, which, it will be remembered, I had placed therein for safety the night I was imprisoned in the Villa Accolti. I had clean forgot it in my troubles, and now it lay in my open palm, with the diamonds in it winking in my face.

My whole frame trembled with excitement. Here was the means of freeing myself from debt at once, and of obtaining funds to quit Florence, nay Europe. At the lowest computation its worth could have been no less than forty crowns, and this at present was wealth to me. What with the effects of the want of food, and the sudden discovery of the cross, I began to feel weak all over, and flinging the badge on the table, sank down into a chair before it to compose myself. The room was almost dark, and I sat staring at the jewels and at the diamonds on it, which sparkled through the gloom. That little trinket was linked with the one great event of my life. All the past came vividly before my excited brain. I was again in that desperate retreat of Charles of France up the valley of the Taro, with the army of the League in full cry behind us. The old boar Trevulzio commanded the rear guard, disputed every inch of the road, and now and again stood boldly at bay, and gave a taste of his tusks to the Duke of Bari, and the fine gentlemen of Venice. It was at this moment that Roderigo Gonsaga made his dash for the heights above the junction of the Ceno and the Taro. Trevulzio saw the movement; he was powerless to help, and knew that if it succeeded all was lost. At the time I was at his bridle hand.

"Ride for your life," he said, "and tell the king—that." He pointed to the black line of the infantry of Spain moving towards the heights. I was off at once, waiting no second bidding.

I found Charles mounted on Savoy, his one-eyed black charger, one of the finest horses I have ever seen. The king grasped the situation at a glance. He gave a sharp order, closed his vizor with a snap, and in five minutes a thousand lances followed him down the long slope, up which the Spaniards were advancing. It was an absolutely silent charge. Not a cheer went up, and the only sound was the

thunder of the horses' hoofs, and the clink of mail as we
sped on after the king. Then there was a sullen crash, and
a sea of struggling men and horses. The veteran troops of
the Great Captain maintained their high reputation, fighting like dragons to the end.

Charles, whose horse had carried him far in advance of
us all, was in great danger. His helmet had fallen or been
struck off, and he was recognised. Gonsaga, seeing all was
lost, made a despairing rush at the king with a half-dozen
men at his back, and had it not been for the way Savoy
kicked and plunged, would have surely slain him. Urging
my horse to its utmost speed, I reached Charles just in time
to ward off a furious blow aimed by the Spaniard at the
king, and riding full tilt against him, brought down both
horse and man. The next moment others came up, and we
were safe. Philip de Comines reproached the king respectfully for running himself into peril; but Charles, wiping
his sword on the mane of his charger, said with a laugh:

"All is well that ends well, my Lord of Argenton; but
it is thanks to this good sword here," and he turned to me,
"that our cousin of Orleans must exercise his patience yet a
little longer. Come closer, sir."

I dismounted and approached helmet in hand. The
king detached the Cross of St. Lazare he wore, and bending from the saddle, slipped the loop of the ribbon round
my neck.

"Wear this for the sake of France," he said with a
gracious smile.

And now the patience of Orleans had come to its end,
and Louis XII. was king, and of my hopes and dreams, all
that remained was the cross of the order blinking at me.

It had to go, and there was no help for it. With an
effort I rose and, thrusting the cross into my pocket, hurried into the street. My way led to the ward of San Spirito,

and it took me some little time to reach the place where I meant to dispose of the jewel. When I reached it, I was so overcome with weakness that I had to halt for a moment to rest. It was during that halt, that hesitation of a minute, that my courage came back to me, and I pulled forth the cross and held it in my cold fingers with a heart tossed by conflicting emotions. I could not do it. Death would be preferable. Well, I had faced death before, and there was no reason why I should not do so again with an equal mind. The Arno was deep enough to hold me, and God would perhaps be kinder in the next world than in this. I placed the cross back slowly, my honour was still white, and death that was coming would give me a full quittance for all my troubles. I turned my back on the pawnbroker's, and went towards the Arno; but I had miscalculated my strength, and near Santa Felicita I felt a sudden giddiness and sank downwards on the pavement. I struggled to rise, but the faintness increased, and dragging myself close to the wall I leaned against it in a sitting posture, and a kind of stupor fell upon me, through which I still felt the intolerable pangs of hunger. In a little time I felt better, and as I saw the flash of torches, and heard voices in laughing conversation, I made an effort to rise, gaining my feet just as two ladies, with their attendants, came opposite to me, and then I staggered back again.

"Poor man! He is hurt."

"I am starving," I said in the bitterness of my agony, and the next moment could have killed myself, for I recognised the ladies whom I had rescued from Luigi in the Garden of St. Michael. I had my desire and had seen her again; but how?

Madonna Angiola made a hurried search for her purse, and not finding it, with a hasty movement tore something off a bracelet, and thrust it into my hand. Before I could recover from my astonishment they had gone on, and although I called after them, they did not stop. The shame of having received charity, and from her, was all but unbearable; but with it I felt the hand of hunger knocking at me in a manner that would take no denial. My courage was gone, and urged by the fierce pangs of my hunger, I resolved to utilise the gift, and obtain some food to give me strength to die. I smile as I think of this now. Then it was no laughing matter. I plucked myself up sufficiently to go back to the pawnshop. Entering it, I placed the article, which I judged to be a jewel, but which I had not even examined, before the man in attendance, and asked for an advance thereon.

"It is one of the gold tari of Amalfi," he said, poising it on his finger, "and of full weight. Do you wish to sell it?"

"No," I replied, "I merely wish to pledge it."

"I will give you two crowns," he pushed the money to me, and with it a receipt. I gathered these up, and staggered rather than walked to the Marzocco Inn, which lay hard by. There were half-a-dozen people supping there; but I had no eyes for them, all I could think of was the pasty, the roll of white bread, and the ruby Chianti, which I ordered. It is a common belief, that those who have not eaten food for any length of time, are unable to do so when it is placed before them at first. Whether I am constitutionally stronger than the generality of men, I do not know, all I can say is, that I formed an exception to the rule, if a true one, and demolished my supper, gaining strength with every mouthful, and feeling my chilled blood warmer with every drop I drank of my goblet of wine. My courage came back to me, and I banished all thoughts of the Arno. At last I was done, and leaning back in my seat, viewed with complacency the huge orifice I had made in a most excellent pasty, and the whiles slowly sipped my wine. That feeling of sleepy comfort, which attends like a good angel on a full meal, possessed me, my sorrows had for the moment taken themselves off, and I grieve to say I did not even bestow a thought on her, to whose charity I was indebted practically for my life. I sat for the moment, lapped in a dreamy comfort, forgetful of all things. I dozed for about half an hour, and opened my eyes with my head clear again, and my pulse beating firmly. I had, somewhat recklessly, it is true, enjoyed a crown's worth of happiness, there was another fat crown still in my pouch; with care it would last some days, and during that time luck might turn. With these thoughts running in my head, I let my eyes wander over the room. It was now somewhat late, and only the night-birds were left. Of these, a party of five was seated at a table a little removed from me, and were conversing in low tones. It needed but a glance to see they were not honest men, and from the suspicious manner in which they looked around them, I gathered they were here for no good purpose. One of the party rested his eyes on me, and then whispered to a companion, who was seated with his face from me. I caught the answer, which was given in somewhat loud tones. "Even if he does, what does it matter? Cannot a few gentlemen enjoy a glass in peace at their ordinary? If he gives trouble we can quiet him."

Could it be? Yes, it was no other than the ancient Brico, who had, I perceived, got out of the clutches of his friends, the catchpolls of Montevarchi. I made certain, therefore, I would have business shortly, and leaning back again, pretended to doze, keeping my ears very wide open, and holding a watch on the scoundrels from the tail of my eye.

"He tarries late," said one, "perhaps your information is wrong."

"I have it from a sure hand, from the younger Ceci. Buonoccorsi and he will both be here. The former, however, as you know, we do not want."

I almost started at these words. Was it possible that I had stumbled on the bravos who were engaged in Ceci's plot? If so, stranger thing never happened to me, and chance was probably throwing in my way what otherwise I would never have been able to discover. Even as the last speaker finished his sentence, two persons, evidently of consequence, and a woman entered the inn, and set themselves down at a table close to mine. The men both wore masks, but the lady did not, and let her glance run with a free look on us all. One of her two companions, a very stout man, put down his mask, disclosing a jolly rubicund face, and roared out for a flagon of wine. The other, still keeping his features covered, engaged in lively badinage with his fair friend, and as he moved his hand slightly, I caught the flash of a valuable ring.

The five at the table all had their heads together now, and I saw the one nearest to me stealthily draw his sword. With an apparently careless movement I so placed my own weapon as to be at hand on the moment. Presently Brico arose, and swaggering across the room with a glass in his hand, deliberately stopped before the lady, and drained it to her health. She laughed back her appreciation, and Brico called out, "Blood of a King! Madonna, but you waste yourself with His Corpulence there," and he jerked his hand towards the stout man, who sat speechless, his cheeks purple with rage. "Come and join us good fellows here," he added, and attempted to pass his arm around her waist; but the masked stranger flashed out his rapier, and Brico only escaped being skewered by an agile retreat. This was, however, the signal for an instant assault, and with a shout of "A Medici—*palle*—*palle*," those at the table rushed on the smaller party. As they rose, I jumped up, and pushed my table with great violence in their direction. Two of the men fell over it, and this gave me time to draw my sword and join the weaker party. The lady rushed out with a scream, and the stout gentleman bellowing lustily for help followed suit, and made his exit, no attempt being made to hinder him, the attack being solely directed against the masked man, who with his back to the wall, and the table between himself and his assailants, defended himself with great spirit and skill.

Slashing one of the ruffians across the face, which put him out of the fight, I ranged alongside of the stranger, and a very pretty set-to ensued. At this juncture the innkeeper entered with half-a-dozen others, and kept dancing about, adjuring us to stop, but offering no help. I made for Brico, but could not reach him, having to engage with a better swordsman than I had met for many a day; but I saw we were now three to two, for the ancient was more bent on executing flourishes with his sword, and in cheering on the attack, than on real business. My opponent was a left-handed man, so anything like a time-thrust was out of the question. He played the usual game of left-handed men, namely, a cut over, and disengagement in tierce, but remising, I forced him to a straight riposte, and pinked him through the ribs. He fell with a howl, just as my companion ran his man through. We were now two to two, if Brico was included, but the others waited for no more and fled, no attempt being made to stay them by the host. The innkeeper, however, began to make a great to-do; but the stranger thrust his purse in his hand, and lifting his mask spoke a few words in mine host's ear. The effect was magical, and the padrone was now all civility. We had a look at the two men who were down, the one who was slashed across the face being nowhere to be seen. They were both quite dead, and an ill-looking pair of corpses did they make.

"Have these carrion removed, padrone—and beware how you say a word of what has happened, signore," and the masked man held his hand out to me, "I thank you heartily, and you will find I have a long memory. Do me the favour to accompany me to my house."

I had no reason to refuse, and bowing my acknowledgments, we left the inn.

CHAPTER X.

NICCOLO MACHIAVELLI.

As we reached the street, I expressed the hope that the lady and her stout companion were in safety. The stranger laughed: "Oh, Buonoccorsi, he and La Sirani are no doubt shivering in security by this time; but let us hasten, for although we have barely more than a couple of cross-bow shots to go, our bravos may return and have better luck. St. John! but it was a narrow affair."

Our way led back by Santa Felicita, past the Ponte Vecchio, and at length we came to a halt before a small side door, let into, what seemed to me, nothing but a vast blank wall. My new friend opened this door noiselessly, with a key he drew from his pocket, and invited me to enter. Pleading ignorance of the way, however, I gave him the pass, and followed him up a narrow and very dark stairway, which opened into a long gallery, likewise in semi-darkness. Up this gallery we went, then there was another small passage, and lifting a curtain at the end of this, we stepped past an open door into a large room, evidently a study, for it was filled with books all but the side near the passage, which was covered by a heavy tapestry. In the middle of the room was a large table, littered with papers in much confusion, and eight tall candles burning in a pair of grotesque candelabra, threw a bright but soft light over the chamber.

"Sit you down there," said my host, pointing to a chair, "and we will have something to drink. *Diavolo!* You are wounded! Why did you not say?"

I looked at my left arm, and sure enough the coat-sleeve was red, with an enlargening patch. It was only a trifle, however, as we found on examination; but my companion, who still kept his mask on, insisted on bandaging it, which he did with deft fingers, and then turning to a curiously inlaid cabinet let into the wall, brought thenceforth a flagon of green crystal and two long-stemmed Venetian glasses.

Whilst he was thus engaged my eyes rested on a book on the table, and I saw at a glance that it was the copy of Plutarch's Lives which Ceci had lent me on payment, so that it was most probable that I was in the presence of the noble, against whom the Medici plot was directed, and in whose library the intendant's nephew was employed, partly I guessed as a spy. My hand was on the book as my host placed the glasses on the table, and observing the movement, he said with a smile:

"I see, Signore, you not only carry a sharp sword; but know a book as well."

"As for books, Signore," I answered, "I know but little of them. This one, however, I thought I had seen before."

"Indeed," he said, "that is odd, for I believe this is the only rendering of Plutarch into Italian which is in existence. Strange, too, as for over a week I could not find it anywhere."

"Very," I answered shortly, and my host, pouring out a glass for me, helped himself, and settling comfortably in a chair opposite to me, slowly removed his mask and laid it aside. I saw before me, a man in the prime of life, of middle height and slender figure, with however a great dignity of carriage. His head, covered with short dark hair, was small, but well-shaped, his dark eyes sparkled with intelligence, and a slightly aquiline nose curved over a pair of thin, sarcastic lips, which were however now smiling at me with as much good-humour as they could express.

"Books," he said, "are the delight of my life, without them all would be stale. Here," and he held up a volume, "is a priceless treasure. It is a manuscript copy of Cicero's De Gloria. I obtained it from my friend, poor Angelo Poliziano." .

"I am afraid," I said, "I could only look at it, for I have not studied the ancients."

He laid down the book: "Of a truth, men were giants in those days—but hark! That is too loud for a rat." At this moment we heard a distinct rustling behind the tapestry, which hung on one side of the wall. My host sprang up, and with his drawn rapier in his hand, lifted the arras. I followed him; but we observed nothing but a door, which was concealed behind the curtain. "This is a private door leading to the corridor, and confound it—it is open. How the devil did this happen? However, this will make things sure." He turned the key which was in the lock, and removing it, placed it carefully aside in a drawer, and his face was shaded a little with anxiety. This however he brushed off like a fly, and resuming our seats, he poured out some more wine for both of us, and said:

"Signore, now that I observe you closely, it appears to me that your sword, good as it is, has not helped you to fill your purse."

"It was able to save your life, Messer—I know not your name," I answered with a little heat, and rose as if to take my leave. He laughed cheerfully, and putting his hand on my shoulder, pressed me back into my chair.

"Sit down, signore, I meant no offence, and my name

is Niccolo Machiavelli. Will you give me yours in return?"

I was then before the Secretary of the Council of Ten, the crafty politician who at that time held Florence in his hand, and with whose name all Italy was full. I now understood Ceci's plot at once, but the question was, should I give my right name? Sooner or later the Secretary would find out, and I accordingly answered him as honestly as possible.

"I pass under the name of Donati, your excellency, will that do?"

He leaned back reflectively. "I like confidence when I give it," he said, "and yet perhaps it does not matter. You had no idea who I was when you helped me?" he added with a quick look.

"Not in the slightest." I did not feel justified in adding more.

"Well, Signore Donati, I have work for which I want a brave man, and if you care to accept it, I offer it to you."

"Your excellency, I will plainly say that I hardly know where to turn for employment, in fact, I am in such straits that I cannot afford to look for a hair in any egg that may fall my way; at the same time your business must be such as I can take with honour."

"With honour of course," he smiled sarcastically, and then added, "I suppose I can trust you?"

"You need not give me the employment, signore, if you do not think you can trust me—and pardon me—it is getting late."

"Sit down, man, I did but try you, and you are the man I want. Where do you lodge?"

"In the Albizzi Palace, in the street di Pucci."

"Could you leave Florence at a moment's notice?"

"It is a matter of funds."

"They will be provided."

"Then, yes."

"Enough! To-morrow a man will call on you, precisely at noontide, with a letter. I want that letter delivered into the hands of the Cardinal of Rouen at Rome. It is a secret matter, and if you fail in it you may forfeit your life. If you succeed, his eminence will give you further occupation. Do you accept?"

"Yes."

As I said this we again heard the creaking noise, and Machiavelli jumped up as agilely as a panther, and sprung to the door behind the arras. It was open; but no one was there.

"*Maldetto!*" he exclaimed. "Signore, there are spies in my own house—help me to tear down this tapestry."

I did so, and in a few minutes we laid bare the side of the room, and piled the tapestry in a heap against a bookshelf.

"That is better," Machiavelli said, "you see—the spy, whoever he is, must have a master key. There is no use going into the passage after him; but for the present I fancy we are safe. I must have a bolt put on and keep a watch. To resume business however. You say you accept, and only need funds."

"Exactly so."

He pulled from a drawer a bag, which chinked with a pleasant sound to my ears.

"Here," he said, "are a hundred crowns. It is your fee for the task I set you."

"It is ample."

"And now, Messer—Donati—farewell! You will always find a friend in me. You know your way—I have left the side door open—and bear a loose sword."

"A word, your excellency."

"Say on."

"From what has happened to-night, I see plainly that the plotters against your life have friends very near you. If they failed this time they may not fail again. One of the men who made the attack to-night I recognised. He is called Brico, formerly an ancient, perhaps still so, in the army of Tremouille."

"I will attend to the Signor Brico."

"Yet a little more. If your excellency's movements are known it is probably from within your own house. I would keep an eye on your library scribe."

"*Per Bacco!* Signor Donati, but you know too much. I am more and more your debtor."

"The hundred crowns have repaid me," I replied as I took my departure, having said all I dared say of the plot without breaking my pledge of secrecy to Ceci.

Now it happened that as I gained the corridor, I saw in the dim light a figure retreating hastily before me; but with noiseless footsteps, and having in mind the strange attempt to play the spy on us, I made no doubt but that here was the culprit, and followed up. I saw the figure turn at the end of the corridor and enter another gallery, then another, and yet another, finally vanishing as it were against the wall. Owing to my not knowing the way properly, and to the semi-gloom, I was unable to follow fast enough to overtake the spy, who flitted before me like a ghost, but in a very human hurry. When at length I came up to the wall, I looked to see if there was a door of any kind; but could discern nothing, and was so astonished that for a moment I felt a little chilled, thinking that it may have been a spirit after all. Fortifying myself, however, with the thought that if it was a spirit, it seemed in no way anxious to meet me, I went to a closer examination, and saw by the moonlight that I was before a door, painted in exact imitation of the marble wall. This settled my doubts, and putting my shoulder to it, I made a trial, with all my strength, to force the passage, but in vain. I therefore gave up the matter, and turned to find my way back. This was, however, easier said than done. I could not find the gallery I wanted, and after groping about hopelessly for a little time, thought that I had best give a shout, which would no doubt summon some one to my aid. I was just about to carry this into execution, when, on further reflection, it struck me that I might be landed in other difficulties thereby, and that I might make another try to free myself, without bringing the house about my ears, and perhaps compromising the secretary, who had, I saw, an active and enterprising enemy under his own roof. So I stilled my tongue and made further exploration, with the result that I found myself before a stairway, that led to the floor below me, and determined to see where this would take me. Accordingly I descended as softly as possible, and arrived in a few steps at a small landing, covered by a carpet so thick, that I felt as if I was treading on the softest of moss. At the end of the landing, and opposite to me, was a half-opened door, the room inside being in light. Stepping noiselessly up to the door I peered in, and saw a chamber furnished with the utmost luxury, and apparently just vacated by its occupants. In a corner of the room stood a harp, lying on a table close to a low luxurious seat were some articles of dainty feminine embroidery; soft silken curtains shrouded the walls, and the ceiling was painted, apparently with some representation of the history of the house. A white marble figure of Cupid held out at arm's length a lamp, whose opal shade softened its bright light; and on a gilded triangle, set in an alcove, swung a blue and scarlet macaw—a rare Eastern bird—who, with his head tucked under his wing, slept in a position which would be intolerable torture to any other created thing except a bird. It was clear that I had invaded the private sitting-room of the ladies, or lady of the household; and I was about to beat a hasty retreat, when the screen of an inner room was swung aside, and I saw before me my two unknowns of the Garden of St. Michael, and the giver of the tari which had saved me from death. It was too late to go back now, as the sound of my feet on the marble stairs would certainly reach, and perhaps alarm them, tread I ever so softly; so I resolved to stay where I was until they retired again, and then go back. This I judged would be very shortly as it was late. I had not however sufficient experience then, of the lengths to which those nocturnal confidences, in which the fair sex indulge with each other, extend. In the meantime I could not but admire the graceful figures before me, and especially of her, who had given me the tari. Clad in a soft clinging robe, clasped by a jewel at her throat, and a silver girdle round her waist, with her pale proud features set in a mass of dark hair, she seemed to me an embodiment of pure womanhood, and I thought how lucky the man would be who could have such a companion to help him through life. I guessed also that the other was the wife of Machiavelli, being aided thereto by her statement, when I drove Luigi off, that her husband was one who could help me much. At the same time I could not but feel some pity in my heart for her, when I thought she was wedded to a man of a character so contradictory as that of the Secretary, who could leave a fair wife for the sake of indulging in low dissipation, and come back after a narrow escape with his life, to bury himself in matters of state, or in the perusal of the ancients. However there was no sign of sorrow on her fair and mirthful face, as with all the teasing nature of a kitten, she walked up to the macaw and stirred him up with her white fingers, an attention he did not appear to relish, for he ruffled his plume, and let forth an ear-piercing shriek.

"Heavens!" she laughed, "how that bird screams! He is almost as cross as you, Angiola."

"Thanks," replied the other; "I do sympathise with the bird though, for you never leave off teasing. It is enough to make a saint cross, Marietta."

"Well, I won't tease any more," and Marietta put her hand on her friend's shoulder. "I am sure though it was he, and I will have that last word."

I wondered to whom the reference was made, as Angiola replied: "I really do not care if it was; but there is a draught, and I must shut this door."

She came up so quickly that there was no time to retreat, and in a moment I was discovered.

She gave a little cry, and stepped back.

"Who are you, sir? How dare you——!"

I saw that the other was going to scream out, and burst forth: "Madam, I implore you to be still. There is absolutely no danger. I have had business with his excellency, and missed my way. Pardon the intrusion," and I stood with my cap in my hand.

"Well, sir," said the Lady Angiola, "as you have found out that you have missed your way, had you not better turn back?"

"Why, Angiola, it is the gentleman who rescued us in the gardens!" called out Madonna Marietta, with a sudden recognition.

"Who looks as if he were here now, to make up for it by cutting our throats. According to you he should have been dying of starvation at Santa Felicita."

"Madam," I cut in, "I wish I had died of starvation rather than heard this. I will however restore what I have received. If you can only show me the way out of this house I shall be grateful, and I again seek pardon for disturbing you."

" I suppose you are speaking the truth. Come, give me that candle, Marietta."

The other handed her a candlestick, and refusing my proffer to bear it, and with a curt request to walk in front, she directed and led me along the interminable galleries until I recognised the corridor from which I entered. I was again about to thank her, but she simply pointed to the door.

" Your way lies there, sir."

I opened the door and stepped on to the stairway without another word. In shutting the door behind me I glanced once more in her direction. She was already on her way back, the single candle throwing its soft light on her loose robes and graceful figure.

I made my way down the stairs, at the end realising the sensation of suddenly finding my foot meet the ground after the last step. I thought there was yet another and was brought up with a nasty jerk. Stepping out softly into the street, and holding my drawn sword in my hand, I hurried towards my abode. When I had gone about fifty paces, I heard the sound of a door opening and shutting behind me, but thinking it was the wind playing with the door I had left unlocked, having no key, I took no notice, and went on; but soon became aware I was being followed. I stopped therefore, and deliberately faced round. The footsteps behind me instantly ceased, and I could make out through the moonlight, the shadowy figure of a man, stooping as if to search for something. This was of course nothing but a pretence, and I had half a mind to go back and question him. Reflecting, however, that it would be wiser to avoid any further adventures for the night, and that after all it was but one man, I went on, and my pursuer did likewise, but at a greater distance than before, until finally apparently gave the matter up seeing I was on my guard. Crossing the square of Santa Felicita, however, I saw some one running swiftly a little ahead of me, and then disappear behind the shelter of the small casino of the Medici which stood there. I felt sure it was my shadower. He had passed me by some short cut, and was now probably intending to bring matters to a head. Keeping well in the middle of the road I went on, and to my surprise saw nothing, but in a short time again became conscious that I was dogged, and dropping into an artifice quickened my pace to a run. The sound of rapid footsteps behind me, showed that my curious friend was doing likewise, and not to deprive him of the exercise, I kept up the pace, until we reached the street di Pucci and were close to my lodging. Here I faced about and ran back full speed at my pursuer, feeling sure that the burst I had given him would try all his speed to get away. He so little calculated on my change of front, that he ran on about twenty yards, before realising what was the matter. Then he turned round and was about to make off, when I reached him, and driving him against the wall held him there, with the point of my sword at his breast. Imagine my surprise on seeing before me the young man with whom Ceci had gone away on our return from the funeral of Corte's daughter. He was doubtless also the spy of the evening, and now, with a face white with either terror or anger crouched against the wall, holding a dagger in his hand; but any attempt to use it would have been useless.

"Well," I said, "have you had enough of this?" and I emphasised the question with a sharp prick.

"Mercy!" he called out, thinking his last hour come, and scrabbled on to the pavement.

"Be off with you then!" I said, and assisted his departure with a hearty kick as he rose. He needed no second bidding, but made off at a good pace.

When his figure mingled up with the haze, and was lost to view, I proceeded on my way wondering a little at the incident. I could not help connecting it with the affair in the Secretary's room—the man I had chased up the endless galleries of his house, and the attempt at murder in the Marzocco Inn. Why was I followed? I could not make this out; but thankful that I had escaped with a whole skin, climbed up the winding stairway of the tower which led to my chamber. Carefully shutting the door, I lit my candle, and emptied out the contents of the bag I had received from Machiavelli on to my bed so that the coins might make no sound.

CHAPTER XI.

THE LETTER TO D'AMBOISE.

I COULD have thrown my cap over the housetops, I could have shouted for joy, as I saw the coins spread out before me. I stooped over them, holding the candle aloft in one hand, whilst I ran the fingers of the other through the clinking metal. There they lay! broad, shining pieces of silver, flecked, here and again, with the mellower light of gold. At one stroke, when my luck was apparently at its lowest ebb, it had turned again, and was coming up in high tide. Not only this, I was to go to Rome, the very place of all others where I was likely to meet D'Entrangues; and I breathed an impious prayer, that good angels might see he came to no hurt until we met, and even as I prayed the vision of that dying woman who forgave with her last breath, came before me. My hand shook so that I could barely hold the candle, and turning away, I placed it on the table and went up to my window. Midnight was long past and we were touching the morning. The only sound that broke the stillness was the distant clang of the martinello, keeping up its insistent beat; but the wind was from me, and the chime came softened to my ears. Already the east was whitening, and the moon was sinking to rest. All the old half-formed resolutions I had made, to let my enemy's crime pass, to leave vengeance in the hands of God, came up and fought with the fierce desire that the apparent opportunity of meeting D'Entrangues again, had fanned into life. What had not that man done to me? How could I forgive? We are all not framed in the same way. A tender woman might condone what man would never pass over. Why should I not be the instrument of God's punishment on that man? Without Him nothing was possible, and if I succeeded in killing D'Entrangues would it not mean that the deed had his sanction? On the other hand, there were the words of Savonarola's text, and the forgiveness I had seen with mine own eyes. Tossed by doubt, now resolved, now wavering—at one time certain I was right to be my own law, at another encompassed by a terrible fear of sin—I did what all men have to do at some time or other: I sank down on my knees, and wrestled with the temptation. I do not know what words of prayer I used, or how long I was there; but I can say this, that when I rose, my mind was at rest, and I had won a fight with myself. I would leave D'Entrangues to the justice of God. And for my honour? I would win it back again, not in distant lands, but here—here, where it was taken from me, and then—what a fool I was! When my shield was white once more, I would sheathe my sword, rebuild our old castle in the Sabine Hills, and there, perhaps—oh! I dreamed mad things when that peace fell upon me. But there was such a prosaic matter as sleep, and I had work for the morrow, so I pulled myself together, and with a mind more comfortable than for many a day, swept the coins into the bag, saw again to the fastening of the door, and, seeking my bed, slept a dreamful sleep until aroused by the cooing of my friends the pigeons. It was with a very different air that I went down the stairs that morning, and I realised, from contrast, how brave a heart a full purse can make. I meant to have paid Ceci at once, but he was not in his office, so I breakfasted in a leisurely manner, at the sign of the Double Florin and then returned.

As soon as I reached the Albizzi Palace, I went straight to Ceci's office, and found him engaged in conversation with a man. The latter started when he saw me, and hurriedly took his departure; but not before I recognised in him Ceci's nephew, and my shadow of last night. He gave me no friendly look as he went out; perhaps he was sore with the memory of the end of my boot, and I had a mind to give him the day, but prudently held my tongue between my teeth. Ceci was looking much disturbed and annoyed, and I laughed secretly to myself as I thought that, after all, I had been the instrument of upsetting the political plot to murder, in which the old conspirator had a share.

"A good day to you, Messer Ceci," I said. "I have come to settle my account."

"It is of long standing," he replied, somewhat brusquely; but I was not going to lose my temper, as I had things to find out.

"All the more pleasure in receiving it," and placing a couple of gold pieces on the table, I received my quittance and change.

"Messer Ceci," I went on, "I leave Florence to-day and there has been ill blood between us—your making entirely. I cannot forget, however, that when I was ill you helped me much, and that in other ways you were kind. Let us part friends—and, Messer Ceci, you are old. I would advise you to let matters of state alone."

He looked at me, and the corners of his mouth hardened, as he said, "Leave me and my age alone, Messer Donati. If it was not for you, there would have been a deed done last night at which all Florence would have rung again."

"So your precious nephew brought the news to you this morning?" I answered with a question, hazarding a shot.

Ceci remained silent, and drawing my conclusions, I went on, "Had what you plotted succeeded, you would have been in a fair way to taste the arms of the rack. Even now you are not safe. You see, Ceci, I know too much, and it would be wise to be civil."

"Not safe," and he laughed scornfully—"who says I am not safe?"

"I do—remember the Secretary has long arms."

"There are others who have longer, Messer Donati, and a dead tongue can tell no tales."

"I take your warning," I replied, and, turning on my heel, sought my chamber to await Machiavelli's messenger. I could not help thinking I had been wise to force the conversation with the intendant as I had done, and was sure, now that Ceci and the other conspirators were aware who had spoiled their soup, they would devote a little attention to me. It behooved me therefore to wear a loose sword for the future, and look well into corners before I passed them. I was not sure moreover whether I should still consider myself bound by my promise of secrecy, now that I had been as much as told that the conspirators were likely to include me in their plans, and turn their knives on me. I could well see that the Secretary would not be able to retaliate by the open process of the law, against the attack made on him, considering the circumstances under which it took place. That he would do so, however, under the mask, I felt sure, and he had received sufficient warning. Whilst thus reflecting I heard the gong in the yard below me strike twelve, and shortly after heavy steps ascended the stairs, with the sound of much puffing and blowing. The new arrival stopped at my landing, and knocked firmly at my door. Thinking it best to be careful, I unsheathed my sword, and letting down the bolt, stepped back a pace before I called out, "Come in." The door opened, and in walked my stout friend, who had retreated so rapidly from the bravos at the Marzocco,

"Messer Donati?" he said with an inquiring look.

"The same," I bowed, and offered him a chair.

"The devil!" he exclaimed, sinking into it, "but it is like an ascent to heaven for a sinner to reach you," and he mopped his face with a large handkerchief, "that curmudgeon downstairs, the intendant, flatly refused to inform me where you were, until I mentioned I came from the Secretary."

"You mentioned that!"

"Yes—or *diavolo!*—how was I to find you? Let me tell you, sir, your consequence was much increased thereby," he puffed rather than spoke.

"I do not doubt it," and I marvelled at Machiavelli having selected this garrulous fool to be the bearer of his letter.

Subsequently I discovered that the Secretary did this deliberately, in order, if complications arose, to be able to deny that he had any hand in a transaction, in which an obscure soldier like myself, and a notorious old scamp like Buonoccorsi had borne part. In fact he very often adopted an artifice such as this, namely first sending public despatches solemnly by a known official of state, and following them up at once by a secret letter, which either confirmed them, or put quite a different complexion on their meaning; taking care to choose his messengers in such a manner that he would have nothing to fear from failure of theirs.

"I have come with a letter for you," Buonoccorsi continued, and pulling from a breast pocket a sealed but unaddressed packet, he handed it to me. "His excellency," he said, "tells me you know what to do with this."

"I do," I gave answer, and examining the seals carefully, put the letter in the pocket of a vest, which I wore under my buff-coat.

"Then that is done," he replied, "and now, signore, have you anything to drink—my throat is like a lime-kiln?"

"I am sorry I have not, but if you will accompany me to the Marzocco."

"The Marzocco! Blood of St. John! No more Marzoccos for me," he burst in, as the red went out of his cheek at the very thought of last night's affair. "Man alive! if Florence only knew what happened last night, the whole place would be in an uproar. It was lucky for the Secretary that you came to his aid, as I had to protect La Sirani —ladies first, you know—and could not help his excellency in any way."

"I see," I replied.

"Oh!" he went on, "there were three others in the street, but *presto!* I disarmed one, pinked another, and the third would have met a like fate, had not La Sirani hung on my arm in her fright, so he made off. I would have pursued, but, hampered with the lady, what could I do?"

"And is not Florence to know what happened last night?" I asked.

He winked his eye, and replied—

"Between you and me, Messer Donati, I think not. You see the Secretary has a fair wife, and they say Madonna Marietta possesses a tongue as well as beauty. Apart from this, you must be aware, as a man of the world——"

"Quite so," and I rose with a smile, "but you must allow me to see that you cool that lime-kiln of yours. I am only sorry I must ask you to come a little way with me."

"Oh! I would go a long way for a can, Signor Donati, and will drink one gladly to your health."

So saying he got up, and we went down and out into the street. I took him to my ordinary, "The Double Florin," and he took a long time in quenching his thirst. When at last he had done, he wished me good day, and we parted, not deeming it desirable to be seen too much together in the streets, and besides I had much to do to get off by the evening. I made up my mind to recover the gold tari I had pledged, and after that to buy a horse and quit Florence at once. The tari itself I should have liked to have returned, as I had promised, or rather said in my anger last night that I would; but I could see no way of doing this without attracting too much attention. On my way to the pawnbroker's I kept my eyes well open, and caught a glimpse of the library scribe, walking on the other side of the road, engaged in conversation with a man, who, despite his common dress, had an air of rank. The latter parted from Ceci's nephew almost as soon as I saw them, and the scribe kept on in my direction. I saw he was again following me, and regretted the mercy I had shown last night, resolving, if opportunity afforded again, to quiet his curiosity for some time to come. I duly redeemed the tari, somewhat to the surprise of the pawnbroker, whose pledges did not as a rule pass so swiftly back into the hands of their rightful owners. On coming out of the shop, my follower was nowhere to be seen at first; but he soon appeared, always keeping on the opposite side of the road. I resolved not to go back to my lodging, but to quit Florence the moment I had secured my horse. It was necessary however to provide some change of attire. I did not intend to substitute a steel corslet for my buff-coat, having a mind to fight my way back to fortune with no defence but that over my heart, and contented myself with purchasing a light steel helmet, a pair of stout riding-boots, a cloak, and some other articles which could go into a small valise, capable of being fastened on to the back of a saddle. These I left at the vendor's, promising to call for them in an hour or so, and hurried towards the horse market, my shadow still keeping behind me, in his accustomed place. Opposite the Baptistry I heard, to my surprise, some one shouting my name, and looking in that direction, saw a man running across the pavement towards me. I recognised at once one of my lances, Jacopo Jacopi, a Lucchese, whom I had every reason to believe devoted to me. He had served with me at Fornovo and after; and although he subsequently left me for a little time, on my joining the Venetian fleet against the Turks, he returned to my banner once more, when it was spread on firm ground, and had always proved a devoted follower. He came now to me with joy on his face, shouting out, "Ah, excellency! It is I, who am a glad man to see you."

"Jacopi," I exclaimed, "but my name is no longer Savelli. It is Donati now—and what do you here?"

He looked a trifle embarrassed, as he replied, "I am seeking service—I left the army when your excellency left."

Knowing the man to be a stout soldier, I decided on the instant what to do.

"See here," I said, "I have no time to lose. Will you follow me once more? I am bound to Rome on an urgent affair, and leave to-day."

"Will a dog sniff at a bone? Will a cat pass by cream? Will an ass turn up his nose at a carrot? I will follow to the devil, let alone Rome, excellency, and at once if you will."

"Have you a horse?"

"Nothing, signore, but an arquebus and my sword, which I have at my lodging."

"Then come with me, we must buy two horses, and leave at once."

"I am ready, your worship," and taking his place a little behind me we hurried on.

"We will have a hard task to get at Rome, now that the whole country is up, signore," said Jacopo as we walked along.

"I have thought of that," I answered, "I propose to go by Leghorn, and taking ship there, proceed to Rome by sea."

Jacopo gave such a groan at this, that I turned round in surprise, and became at once aware that my shadower had crossed the road, and come so close up to us that he must have overheard every word of our conversation. This was most annoying, and a disaster of which the future consequences might be most serious. I determined however to be rid of him for the rest of my stay in Florence at any rate, and addressed him sharply—

"Signore, I seem to have excited much curiosity in you. May I ask what it is you want?"

He stood for a moment, at a loss for reply, and then said, "The road is as free to me as to you."

"I admit that," I said; "but I object to your stopping to listen to my conversation, and therefore will be obliged by your passing on, unless you want a more severe punishment than you received last night."

He turned pale with anger, and slipped his hand into his vest; but as suddenly pulled it out again, and without another word hurried past us.

"Mark that man, Jacopo;" I said, "wherever he is, there is danger for us."

"Your excellency has only to say the word," and Jacopo put his hand to his belt.

"Not so, my friend. Florence is not a safe place for a man to use his dagger in broad daylight, unless covered by the cloak of a great man. Besides it is not to my taste. Merely keep your eyes open, and if you see him anywhere, tell me at once."

"It shall be so," he answered; "but who would inquire about a mere citizen like that?"

"Never mind, Jacopo; rest assured I know what I am about, and now tell me some news of the army."

"The duke is in full march on Perugia, and means to drive Cesare thence. The whole country is awake, as you know. The general, Ives d'Alegres, is come on a mission to Florence."

"Ives d'Alegres here!"

"Yes, excellency, and the Lord of Bayard has hurried to Rome."

"Then this means something that I cannot follow."

"Nor can I explain, excellency."

"And tell me, has the Duchesse de la Tremouille gone back to France?"

"Yes, by sea from Leghorn, with a great train of ladies, just before war was declared again. It is said she has gone to the court of the king at Maçon, and the escort was commanded by the Count Carlo Visconti."

"Do you know any who went with her?"

"Nearly all the ladies who were at Arezzo, for the duke, it is said, would have none of them, now that war was begun again."

I had to come to the question direct, "Was Madame d'Entrangues in the train of the duchess?"

"I am sure of that, excellency. I was with them as far as Siena, when I took my leave."

So she had gone, and I felt a relief at the news. Once in France, she would be safe with her family, and I was honestly glad she was out of the dangers of the time.

We now reached the horse market, and with some search discovered two likely-looking animals, whose price was within the measure of my purse. I could not afford to pick and choose to any great extent, but for forty crowns became the owner—after a little trial, which showed they were as sound as I could see—of two nags, one a bay, and the other a russet, with an off foot white above the pastern, an unlucky colour, and the white marking denoted devilty. But he was a shrewd-looking beast, and I kept him for myself, giving the bay to Jacopo. Having paid on the spot for these, together with the necessary saddlery, we rode to the shop where I had left my purchases, and collected them. It was here that the idea struck me that there was an opportunity to keep my word, and return her gift to Madonna Angiola; therefore asking messer the shopkeeper for sealing-wax and some parchment, which he willingly supplied on a small payment, I carefully folded up the tari, and sealed up the packet. Taking it in my hand, I went out to Jacopo, who was holding the horses, and said—

"See here, Jacopo. Take this packet to the house of the secretary Machiavelli. It lies in the ward San Spirito, near Santa Felicita, and cannot be missed. Deliver it into the hands of the Lady Angiola, say nothing, and come away. There is no reply needed, you follow?"

"Excellency."

"Right. Then after doing this you may dine, collect your arms, and meet me in an hour and a-half at the San Frediano Gate. And you might as well bring a feed for the horses with you. Stay, here are two crowns."

"It shall be done, your worship. I know the Secretary's house, and the rest is simple."

He mounted his horse, and trotted off; and reflecting that a chaffinch in a cage is better than a mavis in a bush, and that I might as well dine now whilst I had the chance, I swung myself into the saddle, and proceeded at a smart pace towards the Double Florin.

I had to cross the piazza of the Signory on my way there, and whilst doing so came face to face with a riding party. It was composed of several ladies and gentlemen, and amongst them was Machiavelli, who glanced at me with a friendly twinkle in his eye, and gave me an imperceptible nod of approval. Almost immediately behind him was old Ives d'Alegres, riding with a bolt upright seat, and making himself agreeable, in his bear-like manner, to the Lady Angiola, who rode beside him. There was no avoiding them, and yielding to a sudden impulse I saluted as they came up. A look of contempt spread over the features of the general, who made no response, and Madonna Angiola kept her eyes fixed before her, as if she had seen nothing. They passed by in a moment, leaving me speechless with anger, for owing to my failure to preserve a disguise, I had allowed my beard to grow again, and D'Alegres without doubt recognised me. There was some excuse perhaps for him; but none, I could think of, for her, and to add to my chagrin, I thought that Jacopo would probably waste hours in awaiting her return. I let my horse out to a hand gallop, notwithstanding the pavement, and luckily doing no injury to any of the passers-by or to him, pulled up in a few minutes at the door of my ordinary. Here, although I tried to eat, I was so angry that I could only trifle with my food, and raging within myself, I drank a full measure of wine, swallowed such morsels as I could, and went to see after my horse. By my directions he had a light feed, and was being rubbed down. As provision against accidents, I purchased a bottle of Chianti, together with a roast fowl and a loaf of white bread, and these I placed in my saddle-bags. Then, seeing to the saddling of the horse myself, I exchanged my velvet cap for the steel helmet, and drawing my sword-belt in by a hole, sprang into the saddle, and went on at a leisurely pace towards the San Frediano Gate. There was still plenty of time, so I made no hurry, and indeed, when I reached the gate, the gong there boomed out five o'clock, leaving a half-hour still to spare before Jacopo was due. I pulled up therefore at the side of the road, and dismounting, led my horse up and down. It was whilst thus engaged, that I noticed a priest, mounted on a smart cob, trotting in the direction of the gate, and knowing that a misfortune and a friar are seldom apart, I observed him narrowly as he passed. He drew his cowl, however, over his face, so that I could make nothing of him; but on reaching the gate he stopped to ask some questions of the sentry there, and the man, in raising his hand to salute, slightly startled the horse, which threw back its head. This sudden movement made the hood the rider wore fall back a little, but it was enough to enable me to see it was the library scribe, old Ceci's nephew; and I augured no good from this, resolving nevertheless to be on my guard more than ever. The pretended priest received an answer to his inquiry, and giving his benediction, in true sacerdotal manner, rode off at a pace that showed his seat on the library stool had not interfered with his seat in the saddle. It was now fully the half hour, and yet Jacopo did not come. I waited until the gong struck six, and was just about to ride off, leaving a message with the guard, when I saw him approaching.

"Make haste," I cried as I mounted, "you are late."

"Pardon, excellency! But the lady was not there. I had to wait a full hour before she came back from riding, and the General d'Alegres was with her."

"Did you give the packet?"

"I did, excellency. I rode up, asked who the Lady Angiola was, and presented the packet, saying it was from the Cavaliere di Savelli, my master."

"Oh, glorious fool! Did I not tell you my name was Donati? Did I not tell you to say nothing, but merely give the packet into the lady's hands?"

"Body o' me, excellency! But there were so many about, my wits almost went a wool-gathering. I gave madame the packet, however, and she took it."

"Said anything?"

"Nothing, excellency—never a word."

There was no use crying over spilt milk, and cursing Jacopo in my heart for a muddle-headed fool, we started off. On reaching the sentry, I thought I might as well try and find out what the sham friar was looking after. The man raised his hand in salute as I came up, and flinging him a crown I bade him drink to the health of the Signory therewith.

"Marry! I will with pleasure, and yours, too, excellency," he said, as he pocketed the money, evidently stirred by the amount.

"Instead of mine, drink to the health of my good friend the monk, who has just gone on. Can you tell me if he inquired for any one here?"

I relied on the simplicity of the man, and on taking him by surprise with the question, and as it happened I hit my mark.

"In truth, excellency, the reverend father did inquire about a party of five horsemen, who took the road to Leghorn about four o'clock this afternoon. He doubted much if he could overtake them ere nightfall he said, and would have to ride hard."

"I poised another crown on my finger absently. "Do you know any of the party who went ahead?"

"No, excellency; but their leader was an old man with a long white beard, and I think I heard him addressed as Ceci. Excellency, the wine will flow to-night—a hundred thanks."

I dropped the crown into his palm, moving him to his closing words.

"Come on, Jacopo. It grows late," and setting spurs to our horses, we rode out at a gallop.

CHAPTER XII.

THE AMBUSCADE.

It is good to go through the air, with the strength of a brave horse under one, to know that his strong muscles are stretching with an enjoyment as keen as his rider's pleasure, to hear the air whistle as one cuts through it, and to feel the blood fairly dance in the veins. After those weary weeks of illness, of inaction, and of mental despair I had passed through, it was as if new life was poured into me, to know that I was once more in the saddle, with a prospect, however faint, of regaining all I had lost. As the landscape on each side of me melted into a green grey streak, it seemed to carry away with it my suffering; as the true horse answered willingly to the touch of my spur, I forgot the past, and was once again Ugo di Savelli, with a spirit as high as the days before the black sorrow fell upon me. To the left of the road was a broad stretch of springy turf, crossed by a fairly wide water channel. I could not resist giving the beast a burst over this, and followed by Jacopo, galloped over it with a free rein. Both the horses took the jump like bucks, and carried away by the moment, we held on, until we reached the stony and boulder-covered incline which led to the valley of the Greve. Here the turf came to a sudden end, in a line such as the edge of a calm sea makes in a bay, and then began a steep descent of gravel, and loose stones, whose many colours of grey, ochre, and brown, were splashed here and there, by masses of short thick shrubs, which gradually increased in denseness, until they spread before us, a sea of sombre green, that stretched to the clear blue line of the Greve. Here on the crest of the slope I drew bridle, thinking the horses had enough of it for the present, and that it would be well to husband their strength. Jacopo pulled up alongside of me, and stooping to pat the neck of his mount said—

"Excellency, the horses are in good condition; they will carry us well to Leghorn!" He spoke the truth, for although they might have been in better training, as the few clots of yellowy white foam, on the part of the reins which had touched their necks showed, still we should have been content with less, from new and practically untried purchases, such as we had made, and I congratulated myself mentally on our luck, for Barabbas himself would have had much to learn from the horse-dealers of Tuscany. Thinking in this way, I replied:

"Yes, Jacopo, they seem to be a cheap forty crowns' worth, and we have been cheated as little as possible. As you say, they should carry us well on our journey, and we can either dispose of them at Leghorn, or take them on to Rome if necessary."

"If I may speak, excellency, I would advise taking them with us. But oh, signore, is that not superb?"

With an Italian's inborn love for the beautiful, he pointed to the view around us, and although not a Florentine, I could feel why it was that her citizens so loved the City of the Lily. The sun was setting in opal and rose, and as we turned to give a last look behind, we saw that this light was reflected from the west, on the great fleecy masses of clouds that were slumbering in the pure blue of the sky, and was again thrown back, or rather downwards, on to Florence itself, bathing in its glow the campaniles of the churches, the grim palace of the Signory, and the towers of the houses of the nobles. Where the light did not fall, the shadows were in soft greys, that deepened to a purple black, and a yellow band marked where the walls clasped the city like a girdle. To the east, as we looked, the hills of the Prato Magno rose in a heavy solid outline, with the jagged peaks, trying as it were to stab at the sky; to the north, covered with a heavy pine forest, lay Senario, shutting from sight the upper Voldarno, and the Mugello; whilst, as we faced slowly round by our left, we saw the silver ribbon of the Arno, and the heights of Monte Orlando, the landscape being closed in on the west by San Miniato, over whose cypress crowned heights the sun now hung like a soft ball of fire. As I gazed upon this, a sadness came upon me, and my mind filled again with the image of the woman, whom I began to realise that I loved in spite of all; and I almost laughed in the bitterness of my heart, when I thought that this burden of a hopeless passion was added to the weight I already had to bear. I began to fairly despise myself for my weakness, in that for the moment I felt inclined to turn my horse's head and ride back to Florence. It was gall to know, that if she but lifted her finger, I would go back like a beaten dog, and it required me to summon all my pride to rescue myself at the time. It was such hopeless folly, such madness, that I began to think I must be little short of an idiot, and cursed myself with such hearty good will, that Jacopo, who was always a trifle free with his tongue, began to let it wag.

"If your excellency is so liberal with curses on yourself, methinks you will have none to spare for your enemies," he said.

"True, Jacopo," I answered, "but the word enemies reminds me, that you should keep your arquebus ready for instant use, and now I think we had better jog on."

Jacopo's answer was to unsling his arquebus, which he rested crosswise on his thigh, and we began to slowly descend the slope towards the river, the loose gravel crunching under our horses' feet.

"It is loaded," said Jacopo, somewhat irrelevantly, as we came to the banks of the stream; but I understood he was speaking of his piece. "It is loaded, excellency," he repeated, "with three balls, which I have had dipped in holy water, and on each of which I have cut a cross for luck. I lay my life on it, that if discharged, it will bring down whatever it is aimed at—saint or sinner."

"Heaven grant that it may be the sinner, Jacopo; but only take care you are ready to discharge it when the time comes."

"Never fear, signore. Jacopo Jacopi is too old a soldier to be caught napping," with these words we plunged into the Greve, and after much careful stepping on the part of the horses, for the animals found their foothold an uncertain one in the smooth round stones under the water, we reached the opposite bank, and trotted on with the horses' noses in a line towards San Miniato. The sun had now sunk behind the hill, which was so full of memories for me, and although there would be a moon later on, we had for the present to face a rapidly increasing darkness.

"By keeping at this pace, excellency," said Jacopo as we trotted on, "we shall reach the Resa shortly before it gets quite dark, and I submit that we stop there to feed the horses. As your honour commanded, I have brought a meal for them, and there was space enough in the sack for a snack for me, which would do at a pinch for two, if your excellency would but condescend to taste of it."

"You say well, Jacopo; but I also am an old soldier, and my saddle-bags are full. A fasting body makes but a faint heart, whether for man or beast—on the other bank of the Resa then, we shall call a halt. There is a little light still, enough to increase the pace—so onwards!"

We broke into a hand gallop, keeping one behind the other, and following the windings of a cattle track, for I had purposely avoided the road after receiving the information I had extracted from the sentry at the San Frediano Gate. It was evident, that the party of men, followed by Ceci's nephew, had left Florence to carry out some desperate design. I had been dogged all day by this man, and now he had galloped off in disguise to join the men who had left Florence before he had, and amongst whom was his uncle. Ceci's words at our last interview, and the persistent manner in which I was followed, left me no room to doubt that I was the object of their attention, and that it would be necessary to keep well on the alert. I did not apprehend danger at once, but thought that if an attack were made, it would be in the narrow valley between the low hills to the north of Montespertoli, or at Ponte a Elsa, each of which places was particularly suited for an ambuscade, although of course, considering their numbers, the attempt might be made anywhere, and openly, without very much danger. So with another hurried word of warning to Jacopo, and holding my sword ready, I galloped along, increasing the pace as much as possible, whenever we went past a clump of trees, and both of us keeping as sharp a look-out as the light, or rather darkness, permitted. We avoided the regular ford of the Resa on the Montespertoli road, crossing higher up in the direction of Montelupo, and here got a good wetting, for the water was deeper than we anticipated. Had Ceci and his friends only lain in wait for us at this point, we should have had no chance. As it happened, however, we had taken a zig-zag route, which had either thrown them off the track entirely, or we would meet them further on, either at one of the two spots mentioned by me, or in some other equally convenient locality. At any rate, we were safe for the present, and that was something to be thankful for, even if we were in darkness. So my thoughts ran on, as we scrambled somehow to the opposite bank of the Resa, and groped our way up until we felt soft grass under our feet, for we had dismounted on fording the stream, and led our horses by their bridles up the steep left bank. Here we called a halt, determined to await the moon, and Jacopo managed somehow to tether the horses; fastening the halters to the stump of a tree he discovered by stumbling against, and on which he wasted some of those curses he was so anxious for me to reserve for my enemies. After giving the horses their feed, which they nosed out readily enough, despite the darkness, he joined me where I sat on the grass trying to dry, and wrapping up the lock of his arquebus in a woollen cap, which he produced, to keep it from damp, he took his seat beside me at my invitation.

"It is too dark to eat now, excellency," he said. "I for one, like a light of some kind, even if it be my Lady Moon, with my meals, and we have some little time to wait—illluck to it! Do you call to mind, signore, it was just such a night as this when we lay outside the breach at Arx Sismundea, waiting for the signal rockets?"

"I do, Jacopo."

"Ah, that was a fight! We have had nothing like it since then—not even Fornovo—but good times are coming, excellency, and maybe we will see them again."

"How comes it, Jacopo, that with this prospect before you, you left the army?"

"There was trouble, excellency, big trouble at Siena, and I left to avoid the attentions of Messer Braccio Fortebraccio, whom your worship doubtless remembers."

I could get no further explanation from Jacopo, but afterwards found out that he had fought with and grievously wounded a man who had spoken disparagingly of me; and fearing lest the swift discipline which D'Alegres maintained might overtake him, had immediately deserted, making his way to Florence, where a lucky chance threw him in my way. I thought it well, at this time, to explain to Jacopo, the danger I feared of an ambuscade, and he, knowing the road as well as I did, agreed with me in regard to the spots most likely to be chosen for the attack.

"Would it not be prudent, excellency, to await daylight, and, keeping out of the beaten track, avoid these gentlemen?"

"You see, Jacopo," I answered, "we have not time for all this, and must take some risk. I mean, therefore, to go as far as we can to-night."

"As your worship desires. It is not that I fear the danger, but I do not like putting my head in a bag. *Buono!* There is the moon, and I already begin to taste my supper, after which, excellency, I have no care which way we travel, either by broad daylight, or through the teeth of these brigands."

As he spoke the stars began to pale, and the moon rose slowly above the horizon. In a few minutes, so bright and clear was the light, that one may have easily read by it, and I was glad to see, moreover, that the shifting clouds were gone, and there was every prospect of a fine night. It was fall-to, now, to our supper, and adding my store to my faithful follower's supply, I sunk distinctions of rank, and we enjoyed a meal, with a hearty contentment that had been a stranger to me for many a day. When the last drop of wine in the bottle was finished, and we had picked our last bone, Jacopo arose with a sigh.

"Before supper, excellency, I was ready to eat and then

fight my way through an army; now beshrew me, if a sound nap of an hour or so is not much to my taste!"

I could not forbear smiling, but did not rise to the hint, and when our horses were saddled again, and every buckle and strap examined with the minutest care, we mounted and set off. As although we both well knew the direct road to Leghorn, but were not acquainted with the district so as to correctly pursue our way by moonlight, I decided to run the gauntlet of the ambuscade, if there was any, and take the risk of coming off with a whole skin, to the certainty of losing our track by chancing short cuts, which might lead to, Heaven alone knew where! Now that we were once more on the road, we trotted along at a fairish pace through the silent night. The way led for some distance over an uneven plain, covered with a multitude of white stones, that shone in the moonlight like water. The plain gradually narrowed to where it was intersected by a chain of low hills, and it was in crossing these that we should have to ride through a narrow gut, and possibly meet our danger. As we approached the hills, the short, stunted foliage that tufted the plain, changed to a half-grown forest, in the midst of which the road wound, and here we halted for a second, whilst Jacopo examined his piece to see that all was aright, and gingerly blew at the match thereon, to give the fire a little strength. This being done, we proceeded with the greatest caution, riding one behind the other, and going slowly, as we feared a pitfall of some kind among the trees. Luckily there was none, and at last we got out of the immediate presence of the forest, and into the gut, where the precipice rose high on each side of us. All was rock and stone, but the road was fairly even, a trap could have been seen, and going slow a mistake here, so we clapped spurs to the horses, and sent them along, and although momentarily expecting to see the flash of an arquebus, we were agreeably disappointed, and got out of the passage without mishap of any kind.

"*Animo!* Signore, we are out of this, and to-night will not be bread for the teeth of these brigands;" and Jacopo, whose horse had carried him a little in advance, drew rein to let me come up, as we rode out of the tail of the pass.

"I hope so, but we are not out of the wood yet," and I pointed to where a dip in the ground showed there was a small stream, and on the opposite bank the road again led into forest land.

"And I was just going to beg your worship's leave to troll a catch," said Jacopo; and as he uttered these words we plashed into the shallow stream before us. Almost at this moment my horse neighed shrilly, and an answering neigh from the wood before us rang out into the night.

Crack! Crack! Two red tongues of fire licked out from the darkness of the trees, we heard the loud report of firearms, and a brace of balls sang past, unpleasantly close to my head.

"Quick, Jacopo—follow me," and driving my spurs home, the good horse plunged forwards, topping the bank almost on the instant that the ambuscaders, who rushed out with a shout, reached it. The man to my left, who was riding a white horse, pulled up in an unaccountable manner, and making a point at the one on my sword side, I ran him through the throat, my blade twisting him clean round in the saddle as I dashed on. The attacking party, coming at a great pace, were carried by their horses down the slope into the stream, and before they could turn I had gained a fair start, and to my joy heard Jacopo swearing as he galloped behind me.

"*Maldetto!* I could not fire, signore—you were right in front of me—but here goes." He turned back in his saddle, and would have let off his piece had I not shouted out :—

"Hold! hold! till I tell you," and fortunately he heard my words, or the chances were there would have been a miss with no opportunity of reloading.

We gained a full hundred yards before the others recovered themselves, coming after us with yells of anger, and I distinctly heard Ceci's voice—

"Two hundred crowns for them, dead or alive!"

Now commenced a race for life. We had the start and meant to keep it; but their horses were the fresher, and it became a mere question of who could last longest. We made the pace as hot as we could, in the hope that if we came to close quarters again some of our pursuers would have tailed behind. For a little time things went well, and I was beginning to think we should be able to show our friends a clean pair of heels, when I suddenly felt my horse puffing, stretching his neck forward and holding on to the bit, in a manner which left no doubt to my mind that he was done. Jacopo, too, called out—

"We had better fight it out, excellency; my horse is blown."

Before giving a final answer, I slung round in the saddle to see how the enemy were getting on. The only two who were at our heels was the man mounted on the white horse, who had pulled aside in so strange a manner when charging me, and another, whom I could not make out. The rest were well behind, but riding hard. We could probably account for these two, and turning back I shouted to Jacopo—

"All right; fight it out."

As I said this my horse stumbled and rolled clean over, killing himself on the spot, but fortunately throwing me clear of him and without doing any damage to me. I had just time to scramble to my feet, when the two foremost of our pursuers were upon us.

Jacopo had been carried some yards on by the speed of his mount, but as the men came up he turned sharp round in his saddle and fired. The report was followed by a yell of pain, and the leading horseman fell; the other, who bestrode the white horse, again sheering off from me. Here he met with Jacopo, who was coming back at a gallop, and, it seemed to me, fairly flung himself from his horse, doing this in so clumsy a manner as to be immediately ridden over by my knave.

"Mount—mount, excellency—mount behind me!" and Jacopo steadied his horse. But there was no time, and three of the remaining horsemen dashed up. Two of the horses shied past the body of my animal, but the third came boldly up, and the rider immediately engaged Jacopo. I could not give my brave fellow any aid, for my time was fully occupied in dealing with my own adversaries. Their horses were too fresh, or not well in hand, by great good luck, and so they could not manage to come at me together. Seeing this, I made a dash across the road into the wood— it was but a few feet—and both my adversaries followed, with the result that the horse of one of them put his foot in a rut, and stumbling forwards unseated his rider, and the other, in aiming a cut at me, got his sword entangled for a second in an overhanging bough. This second was, however, enough for me to give him six inches of cold steel, and he pulled round and rode off, dropping his sword, and swinging from side to side in his saddle like a drunken man. The man who had fallen from his horse was nowhere to be seen. Indeed I did not look for him, but rushed back to the assistance of Jacopo, and this time, having opportunity for observing, if only for a twinkling, saw his opponent was my friend, the sham monk. He, however, had as quick an eye, and taking in the situation, made a sudden charge at Jacopo, and as suddenly wheeling his horse to the left, shot past him and fled on ahead, leaving us masters of the situation.

"Are you hurt, excellency?" called out Jacopo.

"Not in the least. How are you?"

"Nothing but a scratch, excellency, which I received from his reverence, who, for all his monkish cowl, wields a good weapon."

"Well, jump down and let us see who our friends are, but first let me look to your wound."

"It is really nothing as I said, signore," and Jacopo sprang lightly to earth. I did not, however, listen to him, and taking from him his flint and steel, lighted a piece of dry wood, which I converted into a torch. With the aid of this and the moonlight, I examined Jacopo's wound, which after all was but slight, and had just bandaged it up with my kerchief, when I became aware that the man whom Jacopo had ridden over, had arisen on his hands and knees, and was crawling off into the brushwood.

"Steady, friend," I said, and running up to him, gave him a prick with my sword as a hint to stop. He made a little outcry, but had the good sense to take the hint, and casting the light of the torch on his face, I recognised my old acquaintance the ancient Brico.

"So, signore," I said, "I have again to be thankful to you."

Jacopo too came up and recognised the man at a glance.

"*Cappita!*" he burst out, "but it is the ancient Brico! Shall I beat his brains out, excellency?"

"Mercy, most noble cavalier," exclaimed Brico, "I yield me to ransom."

"Ransom forsooth!" called out Jacopo, "such ransom as a noose will give you. Prepare to die."

"Be quiet, Jacopo," I said, "the ancient has yielded to ransom, we will leave him to discuss the terms with the moon. Fetch me the bridle from my poor horse yonder, and bind this knave firmly."

Jacopo needed no second bidding, and in five minutes the ancient, securely bound, was sitting like a trussed fowl in the middle of the road, alternately cursing and weeping.

"Perhaps, excellency, we had better look at the other," and Jacopo pointed to the man whom he had shot, who lay on his face. "Perchance," he added, "he too might turn out an old acquaintance."

We did so, and as we bent over him I saw it was Bernabo Ceci gone to his last account. He was shot through the heart, and lay quite dead, with a frown on his forehead, and his teeth clenched in the death agony. I looked at him in a sad silence which Jacopo broke.

"I never knew a cross-marked bullet to fail, excellency. He is stone dead."

"May he rest in peace," I answered; "he was a brave man, although my enemy."

"He is still enough now, your worship—and see! There is his horse grazing quietly. It will do excellently to replace the lost one."

He ran forward and secured the animal, whilst I had a final look at my dead beast. His neck was broken, and there was an end of him. Whilst Jacopo at my request was changing the saddles, I stirred up the ancient, who had lapsed into silence, and begged the favour of his informing me to whom I was indebted for the excitement of the night. Brico at first would not answer, but an inch of steel removed his sulkiness, and he told me all that I believe he knew, which was to the effect that he and some others had been hired by a great Florentine called Strozzi, to stop me at all hazards on my journey to Rome, and that the party was commanded by Ceci, who was to pay them two hundred crowns for their trouble. More he evidently did not know, and disregarding all his entreaties to loosen him, we rode off, wishing him a good night. Nevertheless I am afraid he suffered considerable discomfort.

"That rascal monk," said Jacopo as we jogged along, "has gone on ahead of us, and to-morrow, perhaps, will rouse the country in advance of us."

"Never fear, Jacopo," I answered, "he is no monk, as I well know, and his only chance was to escape as he did. He will hark back soon enough to Florence. Such hawks as he do not fly far from their eyries."

And in this I proved to be right, and the library scribe was never seen by me again.

So we kept to our way, deciding to rest by day on the banks of the Evola, to which we came in the early morning. Here we concealed our horses in the forest which fringed the banks, and the tireless Jacopo, leaving me to watch the cattle, proceeded on foot to a small hamlet he knew of, returning in about an hour with the materials for a substantial meal, and a small skin of wine. In order not to be taken by surprise by the neighing of our horses, which would assuredly discover us if other riders passed, we hobbled them in a secure place, and sought a safe retreat for ourselves, almost half way up the low hill which bounded the river at the point where we halted. Here we spent a restful day, the only incident being the passing of a fine body of men-at-arms across the Evola. From the double-headed lion on their standard I perceived they were part of the *condotta* of Colleoni, a devoted adherent of the Borgia, and it was fortunate that we did not meet them or it would have gone hard with us, for I was known personally to Colleoni and most of his officers, the free-lance having changed sides after Fornovo, ostensibly because he said it was against his conscience to war with the Pope; but in reality being bribed by an immediate present of a fief in the Campagna, and the promise of the lordship of Bergamo, which, although his son obtained it, he himself never enjoyed. So much for the two-headed lion which crossed our path as we lay hidden in the shade of the trees. Our horses also being actively employed in cropping the rich turf in the hollow where they were tethered, behaved themselves excellently, with the result that the long line of men-at-arms passed on and out of sight, without doing us any harm.

In this manner we continued our journey, halting by day and travelling by night, and finally reached Leghorn in safety. Here we took passage in a ship bound for Rome; but were compelled to wait two days in Leghorn, as the master was not ready to sail at once. At last, all things being arranged, we got our horses and ourselves aboard, and put out to sea with a fair wind. The master of the ship had sailed with Messer Columbus to the New World, and lost no time in giving us the history of his adventures, which were in truth marvellous beyond imagination. I listened with a smooth face, and the good man no doubt thought that I believed his stories. In this, however, he was mistaken, nevertheless they were diverting in the extreme. Jacopo was overcome by the sickness of the sea, and flung himself down in a corner on the deck of the ship from which spot nothing would induce him to move. At every lurch he threw out a prayer which ended in a groan, and so great was his distress, that as he afterwards stated, he would have sold his soul to Satan for a paul, if only to obtain an hour's relief. As for me, I was well, having had some experience of the ocean before, when employed by the Most Serene Republic for service against the Turk, and found contentment in the master's stories, and in pacing up and down watching such things as came under my view. I had plenty of opportunity for reflection on the voyage, and came to the conclusion that on delivering my letter to the Cardinal at Rome, I would seek out Bayard if he were there, lay my story before him, and beseech his help to enable me to recover myself.

At last, one fine day, we reached Ostia, and there disembarked after bidding farewell to the master, and set out on our way to Rome. Jacopo recovered his spirits as his foot touched land, and though the ruddiness of his cheek had paled a little, he was quite himself again by the time we crossed the Stagno di Ostia. Finally we came in full view of the Eternal City, and towards the afternoon, having pressed along at a good pace, our jaded horses brought us before the Gate of St. Paul.

CHAPTER XIII.

ROME.

As we rode up to the ruinous stretch of the battered wall, and saw before us the gate, lying open against the mottled green and grey high-ground of the Aventine, that old hill, covered with straggling and unkempt vineyards, and studded with the walls of monasteries, I was moved more than I can tell, for I was about to realise a dream of my life, and put foot once again in the place of my birth, a spot not only bound to me by that tie, but sacred with the hundred legends of my forefathers' history, men who had for centuries played so great a part in its fate, until our house was cast forth by the mother-city, to wander as exiles over the land. It is true that since the days of my childhood I had not seen Rome, it is true that such memories of it as I had were dim and misty, and that to recall them was like trying to bring back before one's eyes, when awake, the vague but pleasant visions of a delightful dream; nevertheless my heart filled with a strange joy, and my pulse began to beat more rapidly, as each stride of my horse brought me nearer home. In short, I was a Roman come back to Rome, and in these words sum up my feelings.

Filled with such thoughts, I tightened the reins half unconsciously, and my horse, doubtless upset by his voyage, and the hard going from Ostia, very willingly slackened his pace to a walk. Jacopo, as in duty bound, followed my example, and immediately began to buzz into speech.

"It is nearly six years since I last saw that gate, excellency, when with Count Carlo Orsini we rode up, just as it was closed behind Cesare Borgia."

"That was when you left me for a time, on my taking service with Venice."

"True, your worship; I had no mind for the galleys," and Jacopo shuddered at the recollection of his recent voyage. "My courage," he continued, "is firm enough on firm ground, but when the sea plays cup and ball with me, I have no soul to think of my own salvation, let alone fighting. *Ohime!* But on that villainous craft we have left, there were times when I was only too anxious not to live."

I smiled as I inquired, "And after your service with the Orsini where did you go?"

"Well, your worship, no sooner did Count Carlo drive those scorpions of the Colonna and Borgia back to Rome, than the Most Serene Republic must needs step in and cause peace to be made. This threw me and sundry other honest fellows out of employment, and on to the edge of starvation, so we boldly rode into Rome, and changing from the bear to the bull, tendered our services to the Borgia, and they were snapped up I can tell you. I was lucky enough to find a master in the Duke of Gandia."

"Lucky, you call it."

"Ay, your worship! for Giovanni Borgia had an open purse and a free hand. I was with him until he was murdered, and then, affairs being warm in Rome, and hearing you had come back from the sea, why, I came back to the old banner."

"It is said that Gandia was murdered by the Cardinal Ascanio Sforza."

"Indeed no, your excellency! I saw the deed done. It was in this way: the Duke and his brother Cesare, then Cardinal of Valencia, supped at the house of their mother, the Lady Vannozza. After supper they must needs walk home together; I was the Duke's sole attendant, but Cesare was accompanied by his cut-throat Michelotto and half-a-dozen others. On the way some mention was made of Donna Sancia, Don Giuffré's wife, and the brothers came to blows. The Cardinal stabbed the Duke with his own hand, and he gave a great cry and fell down dead. Seeing it was no use trying to help a dead man, and being in no hurry to trouble St. Peter myself, I knocked down the strangler Michelotto, and making a run for it, escaped with a whole skin. The body of the Duke was flung into the Tiber, and was discovered by a charcoal monger of the Ripetta, whom Cesare hanged at Tor di Nona, as a reward for his intelligence. They buried the Duke, as you know, signore, in Santa Maria del Popolo—poor man!"

"And you mean to say that this was never known to the Pope?"

"I never said anything about that, your worship; a secret cannot be kept by half-a-dozen, and I dare swear our Lord knows all about it or else the Cardinal Ascanio would hardly be in the Cesarini as he is. These things, however, must not be spoken of in Rome. Men's tongues should be weighted with lead when the Borgia's name crops up."

We had by this time come opposite the Monte Testaccio, that curious mound made of old pottery, which lies towards the river, south-west of the Ostian Gate, and so engrossed were we in our talk, that we did not observe a large party of riders of both sexes, with an escort of men-at-arms, coming at a hand gallop from our right, straight in our direction. Our attention was however sharply drawn to the fact by the cry of an equerry who was riding well in advance of the others, and this man shouted:

"The road! The road! Way for His Holiness! Way! Way!"

We drew off at once to the side, Jacopo dismounting and sinking to his knees. I however contented myself with uncovering, and watching with no little astonishment the party as they came up. They were evidently returning from hawking, and at the head of the clump of riders were two men in full Turkish costume.

"Who are those Turks?" I asked Jacopo, and the knave still kneeling, and holding his hands up in supplication, answered hurriedly—

"One is the Soldan Djem, excellency—O Lord, I trust we may not be hanged as an afternoon's amusement—the other, the fair one, old Alexander VI. himself—O Lord! What cursed luck! Kneel, excellency; it is our only chance."

"Tush!" I replied, and remembered at once that the brother of Bajazet, the Grand Turk, was a hostage in Rome, practically a prisoner in the hands of Alexander, a legacy he had inherited from the Cibo, and which brought him forty thousand ducats annually. I could understand Djem in Eastern costume, but the Pope masquerading in broad delight as a Moor! It was as wonderful as it was disgusting to me. And then the remembrance of Corte's daughter came to my mind, and as they approached, I could hardly refrain from making a dash to rid the world of the monster who sat in St. Peter's chair. I barely saluted as they passed, but Jacopo roared out for a blessing, and the papal hand airily cast a benediction at us. Alexander was apparently in a high good-humour, for, turning in his saddle, he made some joking remark to a lady who rode a trifle behind him, whereat she laughed loudly, a harsh unmusical laugh, and glanced at me with a half-amused air, from under her heavy lashes as she went by. The rest of the party, spurring, laughing and chattering were a few yards behind; and as they clattered on to the road, Djem, giving a wild shout of *Allah! Allah!*

threw the reins on the neck of his barb, and galloped through the gate at full speed, followed by Alexander and the rest of the riders, who urging their mounts to a racing pace, and, both men and women, yelling in imitation of the Moor, vanished through the gate after him in a whirlwind of dust. So quickly did all this happen, that I had hardly time to observe the faces of those who passed me, and indeed, so astonished was I, that I had scarce room in my mind for any other feeling. I had of course heard wild tales of the Vatican, and strange and horrible stories of the Borgia himself, indeed there was one crime that should have brought down God's lightning on the man, for all that he was the Vicar of Christ; but I never for one moment conceived it possible that Alexander could so far forget his place as to appear in public robed as a heathen, and gallop through the streets of Rome like a drunken madman.

When they had gone, Jacopo arose from his knees, and dusting them with his hands whilst he looked up at me, said: "*Corpo di Bacco!* But I gave up all for lost. I vow a candle to St. Mary of—I forget where—but to the shrine nearest to the place we dine, for this lucky escape."

"Come, sirrah!" I said, a little annoyed, "mount. There never was any danger."

"Your excellency is pleased to say so," he replied, swinging himself into the saddle, "but if you saw two old men and a half-dozen old women strung up for merely blocking the way, as I did at Tor di Nona, perhaps your worship would think as I do."

I made no reply, allowing Jacopo the run of his tongue to relieve his feelings, and we went on slowly until we reached the gate. Here I spoke, "As you know Rome better than I do, Jacopo, you had best lead the way; but I want to pass by the two houses of my family before we make for the Strangers' Quarters, where we must find a lodging for the night."

"Very well, your worship!" and Jacopo drew a little to the front. "There they go," he said, shading his eyes with his hands, and turning to the left, where a dun cloud of dust on the Via della Marmorata marked the progress of the Borgia. "The best way, signore," he continued, "is over the hill; we will get a view from there, and then passing by the places you want to see, make for a quiet hostel I know of in the Strangers' Quarters."

Following him, we rode up the Aventine, until we reached the old wall of Servius Tullius, here we stopped to observe the view. To the west and south-west we could see the green of the Campagna merging into the distant grey of the Roman Maremma, whilst beyond that a clear blue line, below the flush of the coming sunset, marked the sea. Beneath us lay the Tiber and the Island, the yellow water of the river stirred into ripples by the breeze, and looking from the distance like hammered brass. Beyond the Tiber rose Monte Gianicolo, behind which the top of the Vatican Hill was just visible. To the north the view was a little shut in by the Palatine and the church of St. Prisca above us, and far off rose the cone of Soratte. North-east and east lay the Palatine, the Esquiline, with the campaniles of Santa Maria Maggiore and San Pietro in Vincoli. Over Monte Coelio we could see the heights of the Sabine Hills, and running our eyes along the Appian Way, we could almost descry the Alban Lake, the mountains being distinctly visible. We stayed for a few moments drinking in the view, and then going onwards, turned north-west, past St. Prisca, and began the descent, by a winding way, held in by vineyards. Coming down we caught a glimpse of the three churches of the Aventine, namely S. Sabina, S. Maria Aventina, and St. Alessio, which was held by the monastery of St. Jerome, whose walls rose hard at hand. A look to the right showed us the Circus Maximus, above which towered a huge obelisk surrounded by four lions. At length we came to the Vicola di San Sabina, and at the corner of the street rose the grey walls and square tower of the castle of the Savelli. I drew rein, and looked at it with a bitter heart, and a sigh I could not control escaped me, as I saw the breeze catch and spread to the wind the silken folds of the standard of the Chigi, who bore quartered on their shield the star of the Savelli and the tree of De la Rovere. It flaunted there, in all the insolent pomp of a new house, whose moneybags were full, and the sight of it was enough for me. Jacopo must have caught the look on my face, for he said kindly—

"Who knows, excellency—luck may turn."

Well meant as the words were, they jarred on me, and without replying I moved on, silently raising my sword to the salute, as I passed the grim gates from which my ancestors held the road as far as the river, and almost held Rome itself.

As we went past the Island, I did not even raise my head to see the Theatre of Marcellus, within which lay another and the oldest of our family houses, having come to us through Pierleone towards the close of the eleventh century.

Jacopo was for going straight on past the monastery of the Aracoeli, on the Capitol; but unluckily I discovered that my horse had cast a shoe, and this was a matter not to be neglected. So we turned to the right, and entered the Campo Vaccino, formerly the Forum of Rome. It being now sunset, here were collected hundreds of oxen and buffaloes, and from the height of Monte Caprino we could hear the bleating of the herds of goats which were pastured thereon, and the tinkling of their bells as they moved slowly down towards their shelter for the night. A hundred fires were blazing cheerfully, and served to dissipate the blue vapour which began to hang over the place. Round these fires were groups of people, mostly countrymen, who seemed in the best of spirits, as they listened to songs, or watched numbers of their party, who danced merrily to the tune of a pipe. Hard by were a number of sheds, used by mechanics, and the blaze, which showed a forge in work, soon attracting our attention, we made there at once, and had the horse attended to.

Whilst the smith was beating out a shoe, I sat down on a rough bench, my horse being fastened to a wooden post, and Jacopo holding his nag by the bridle paced up and down, occasionally stamping his feet on the ground to free them, as he said, from the ants. In other words he was suffering slightly from cramp. To my right was a large crowd, evidently enjoying a show of jugglery, and from their cries of wonderment and pleasure, they seemed to be having their money's worth. So I rose and elbowed my way to a good place, unfortunately only in time to see the end of the affair. The juggler was robed in a doctor's gown, and after performing a trick, he distributed nostrums for various ailments, free of payment. Imagine my surprise, in recognising in him no other than Mathew Corte; and as I came up, he placed a tambourine in his little dog's mouth, and bade him carry it round for subscriptions. Coppers were freely flung in, and as the little animal stopped before me, I dropped in a florin, and stooped to pat its head. As I rose I caught Corte's eye, and saw he knew me, but as he made no sign I stayed quiet. Collecting his money, the doctor bowed his thanks, and began packing up the instruments of his trade. I went back to my seat, and watched the smith at work on my horse, thinking that Corte must have somehow come into funds, and wondering how he had managed it. After a little time I felt a touch on my shoulder, and turning round saw him beside me. I invited him to a seat, inquiring after his health.

"It grows better day by day," he answered, "now that my work is begun. And you, signore?"

"I can say the same," I answered; "I grow better day by day, now that my work is begun."

"There is a favour I ask, Messer Donati," he went on.

"What is it?"

"It is this, and do not think me ungrateful. I am here playing a part. We will meet again, perhaps, under different surroundings. All I ask is that if we do, you will make no sign of recognition, nor mention to anyone that you know me."

"As you wish, Messer Corte."

"A hundred thanks, and yet another thing—short reckonings make long friends," and he pressed into my palm two gold pieces, the amount of the sum I had left with him the night his daughter died. I had no desire to take them back, not knowing how Corte stood; but he assured me he would be deeply offended if I did not, and that he was well provided with the sinews of war. Where he had got them I know not, and of course I had no option but to receive back the money I had given him, though I did this most unwillingly. When this was over, he pressed my hand once more, and, wishing me good night, hurried off.

By this time the blacksmith had completed his task, and we delayed no longer, but went off at once. It was fortunate that Jacopo knew Rome as he did, or we might have been hopelessly lost in the labyrinth of streets, some of them in total ruin, some of them entirely uninhabited, for at the time so hideous was the misgovernment of the city, that all who could do so had fled from Rome, and those who remained could not have exceeded thirty thousand in number, of whom at least ten thousand, men and women, were beings who had lost all claim to the respect of mankind, and were capable of almost any crime. These are hard words, but true, nor indeed have I ever seen a place where all that was bad was so shamelessly exposed, as in Rome when Roderigo Borgia was Pope. At length we reached the Strangers' Quarters, but Jacopo's hostel was not to be found, and after searching for it in vain, we were content to pull up before the door of a small inn built on the lower slope of Monte Pincio, barely a bow-shot from S. Trinità de' Monte, the church erected by Charles of France in 1495, and a little beyond the convent of the Dames du Sacré Coeur. I cannot say that the hostel was an inviting-looking place; in fact it was little better than one of the common *osterie* or wineshops with which Rome abounded; but it was too late to pick and choose, and for the night at least, I determined to stay here. Our first duty was to attend to the horses, which we had stabled in stalls, immediately below the room to be occupied by me, Jacopo having to put up with lodgings in the stables for the night. After the beasts had been fed and groomed, I set myself to a plain dinner, washed down with the contents of a straw-covered *mezzo fiasco* of Frascati. Jacopo waited on me, and when I was done, contentedly devoured the remainder of the *manzo* or boiled beef, and cooled his throat with a bottle of Marino, which I presented to him. Whilst he was thus engaged, I went down and had another look at the horses, and as I patted their necks, and they whinnied at me, I thought regretfully of the good beast who lay dead on the Leghorn road, and wondered what had become of Brico, of whom, notwithstanding his villainy, I could hardly think of without smiling. It was in truth strange that a man, so arrant a poltroon at heart, should desert his natural occupation of a lackey, to play the bravo, and pose as a soldier. How he had ever even obtained the rank of ancient was a matter of surprise and wonder to me. At length I dismissed him from my mind, and coming back, found Jacopo at the end of his meal and his bottle. It was late enough now, and giving him warning to sleep lightly, and to arouse me at once if necessity arose, for I liked not the look of the place, I climbed up the ladder leading to the loft above the stables, which was to serve me as a chamber for the night.

CHAPTER XIV.

GEORGE OF AMBOISE.

I SHOULD mention that before retiring I had obtained from the landlord a good-sized lanthorn, which I had carefully filled with oil, and trimmed under my own eyes. Holding this in my hand I ascended the ladder leading to the chamber, or rather loft I was to occupy, and on gaining my point I placed it on the floor, near the opening by which the ladder led into the room, and so directed the light that its glare passed downwards, and up to the entrance of the stables, leaving the sides of the stables in darkness, although my own room was bright enough. This was a precautionary measure, as it would discover any one attempting to come in by the stable entrance, which had no door, and would enable me at any time to see to rush down quickly to the aid of Jacopo, should he need it. I debated a short while as to whether I should undress for the night; but so little did I like the looks of the place, which was more like a house of call for bravos than anything I had seen, that I did nothing beyond removing my boots, and flinging myself as I was on the vile truckle-bed in the room, I placed my drawn sword by my side, and sought to sleep, struggling resolutely to get this, despite the legions of inhabitants the bed contained, who with one accord sallied forth to feast upon me. But sleep I was determined to have, as I had work for to-morrow, and knowing Jacopo to own sharp eyes and quick ears felt no scruple about getting my rest, determining however, to make it up the next day to my knave for his vigil, which I was sure would be faithfully kept. Finally, despite the attacks of my enemies, I dropped off into a light slumber, which lasted for two or three hours, when I was startled by hearing a shrill whistle, the clash of swords, the kicking and plunging of the horses, and Jacopo's voice shouting out my name. I woke up at once, with all my wits about me, and on the instant ran down the ladder, sword in hand, parrying more by accident than design, a cut that was made at me by some one as I descended.

As I touched ground, two men darted out of the door, and ran across the half-ruined yard in front of the stables. A third, whom I recognised as Jacopo, was about to follow, but I held him back by the shoulder, having no mind to run risks around dark corners whilst I had my letter to deliver. Jacopo yielded to me very unwillingly, and in answer to my hurried inquiry, gave me an account of the affair which had been as brief as it was noisy.

"When your worship retired," said he, "leaving the lanthorn to so to conveniently light up the stable entrance, I had another look at the horses, and then settled myself down on that heap of straw yonder, my back to the wall, and my sword in my right hand. So an hour, or may be two, passed, and then I heard voices outside, and some one swearing at the light. Oh ho! says I to myself, there's a night-hawk about, and I remained on the alert, not thinking it worth while to give tongue then. After a while the voices dropped away—and, excellency, I am sorry, but I must have slipped off into a doze, and beshrew me! if I did not dream I was aboard that cursed ship again, and being made to play pea-in-the-drum once more. I therefore made haste to awaken, and as I opened my eyes heard a crackling noise outside. I rose slowly and crept towards the entrance, and just as I reached within three feet of it a handful of pebbles was thrown in, and one of the horses started a bit. The stones were clearly flung from outside to see if any one was awake; but of course I made no sign, and the next minute two men appeared at the open entrance. I gave a whistle to rouse your honour, and went at them at once—and your excellency knows the rest. I think however I touched one—see there!"

He held the point of his blade to the light, and placed the end of his finger on a stain on the sword.

"Three inches at least," he exclaimed, and with a satisfied air, stooped down to clean his finger on the straw at his feet. I thanked the good fellow for his zeal and the fidelity he had shown.

"As for that, excellency," he said, "there is no need to praise me, for I expect to be made a cavaliere when your worship wins back the lordships of the Savelli!"

"You are brave enough for a cavaliere," I laughed, "the point however for you at present is sleep. Go up to my room and get what you can. I have done for to-night, and will watch the horses. It was after them that our visitors came."

But to this he would not consent on any account, nor was I so anxious to go back to that bed, so bringing down the light from above, we passed the rest of the night close to the horses. In the intervals of dozing Jacopo related to me, twice over, in the minutest detail, the story of the hanging of the two old men and six old women which he had seen at Tor di Nona, and finally sank off into sleep. I did not make any attempt to arouse him, and kept on the watch myself until the lanthorn burned with a sickly glare, and the crowing of a cock told us the morning was begun. In a few minutes it was light enough to see, and Jacopo rising, shook himself like a dog, and stepping up to the lanthorn extinguished it; after which, with much whistling, he set himself to water the animals, give them their morning feed, and groom them.

Leaving him thus engaged, I strolled out into the courtyard, where there was already a figure or two moving, and stepping through a gap in the ruined wall, climbed up a portion of the slope of Monte Pincio, following a narrow lane, on each side of which was a half-deserted garden, and bending my steps to where, from amidst a clump of trees, I could hear the song of a *caponera d'edera* or blackcap, who was in full tune. Attracted by the music of the bird, I went on until I heard the plashing of water, and found myself at the basin of a deserted fountain, which was hemmed in with vines and creepers, and from which a thin stream of water was pouring, and bubbling down the hillside in the direction of S. Trinità di Monte. The basin was made of grey stone, cracked with age in many places, and from these fissures sprouted masses of white serpyllum, the flowers in full bloom. In the centre of the basin was a much damaged figure of Ceres, and from her horn a stream of water fell with a melodious splashing, which, mingled with the song of the bird, had a pleasing effect upon my ear. I took advantage of the solitude of the spot to enjoy the luxury of a bath, and when I had dressed again, climbed a few feet higher, and facing round ran my eye idly over the view. Through the grey mist rising over the houses and vineyards, the Tiber lay, like a yellow snake at rest; one could see no motion of the waters. Near the Ripetta, long spirals of dark smoke curling up to the sky marked the quarters of the charcoal-burners, and the sunrise, which was behind me, cast a glory on the colossal statue of the archangel Michael, where it stood on the gloomy keep of St. Angelo, like a triumphant god alighting upon earth. A dark rolling mist, bright at the top with the sunlight, blue-grey beneath, covered the city below me; but I could make out the octagonal dome of the hospital of San Spirito, the vast walls of the Vatican, then in course of construction, and the dark stretch of cork trees that filled the Valle dell' Inferno, beyond the Vatican hill. Monte Mario was all alight, and I could distinctly make out the Villa Mellini on its summit. There were landmarks that even a stranger, such as myself, who had the barest knowledge of the place, could not miss; and as I watched the heaving mist below me, I saw a sudden flash from the bastion of St. Angelo, and a moment after the boom of the morning gun reached my ears. I did not wait to observe more of the scene, but retraced my steps to the albergo, where I found that Jacopo had ordered a little table to be put out into the portico, and on this my breakfast was set. As I attacked this, Jacopo asked the order of the day, and I informed him that when he had breakfasted we should settle with the host and seek other lodgings, after I had attended to the business I had with Monsignore d'Amboise.

My henchman was also anxious to know if I meant to take any steps with regard to the attempt at robbery last night. I was well enough inclined, but determined to let the matter rest until my business was done, and for the present said I would remain content with the satisfaction that we had saved our steeds and throats. By the time I finished breakfast, Jacopo, who had already taken a meal, had saddled the horses, and was holding them ready for our departure. I summoned mine host, but at first could obtain no view of him. Finally on my threat to depart without settling my score, he appeared with his arm bound up in a sling. As he was unwounded the evening before, I made no doubt but that he was one of the two who had visited us last night, but said nothing, merely remarking, as I paid my account, that the love of horseflesh frequently brought people into trouble. He did not seem to appreciate the remark, and scowled at me, at which I bade him begone, and to thank his stars that his house was not pulled about his ears. He did not attempt any reply, but slunk off, and inwardly resolving to clear out this nest of scorpions from Rome at the first chance, I rode out of the gate, followed by Jacopo, and we directed our way towards the Ponte S. Angelo. I had not the least idea where his emienence of Rouen was staying; but made certain it would be somewhere in the Borgo, and that once I had reached the papal quarter, I should find no difficulty in my search for D'Amboise, and in delivering to him Machiavelli's letter.

As I went on, I began to feel nervous in spite of myself, as to what the results of my interview with the cardinal would be, and whether it would end in the further employment, which the Secretary had distinctly said it would. I had no reason to doubt, however, and it was with a hopeful mind that I trotted up the Lungo Tavere, and was brought to a halt by a gruesome spectacle at Tor di Nona. There was a crowd assembled, watching an execution, and Jacopo, sidling up to me, remarked as he pointed to a body swinging in the air—

"What room there would be for Messer Braccio Fortebraccio here, signore—see that pear, of the kind he loves, growing there? *Barta!* But there is another one——" and, even as he spoke, another wretch was hoisted into the air, and then another and another. I did not stop to look; but Jacopo stayed behind, overtaking me at a gallop as I reached the Piazza di S. Angelo.

"It is the doctor of St. John's on the Lateran, and three of his bravos, signore. It is said he was accustomed to spend his evenings in cutting purses and throats; but, as ill luck would have it, meddled with one of Giulia Bella's friends, and no money could buy an indulgence for that."

"If true he is well served, and there are others of his kidney whom we could spare with equal pleasure."

"Mine host of our inn, excellency, for instance. But the gibbet at Tor di Nona does not always bear fruit like this. I mind early one——"

At this moment, however, I set spurs to my horse and lost the rest, being afraid that Jacopo intended to retail to me the story of the old men and women who had been hanged as a morning's diversion by Cesare Borgia, and as he had twice delivered himself of this to me as we sat up last night, I was in no mood to hear it again for the third time. Near the statues of Peter and Paul, on the bridge, was a guard-house, occupied at the time by a detachment of Spanish infantry, and to these men I addressed myself, inquiring where the cardinal of Rouen was staying. I was told, at once, that his eminence was lodging in the new palace of Cardinal Corneto, opposite the Scorsa Cavalli, and that my best way was to turn to the left on crossing the bridge, and then to the right at the junction of the Borgo San Spirito and the Borgo San Michele.

Bestowing my thanks and a largesse on the men for their kindness, I went on at a gallop, congratulating myself on the ease with which the difficulty was solved, and in a few minutes had crossed the Piazza Scorsa Cavalli, and was before the residence of the cardinal. At the time I speak of, it was not quite finished, but still habitable, and had been rented by Monsignore d'Amboise, as being conveniently near the Vatican.

On entering the courtyard, I dismounted, and giving my horse to Jacopo to hold, ascended the steps, and boldly announced myself as an urgent messenger who had business with his eminence. I was ushered by a page into a reception room, and early as the hour was, there were a considerable number of people already in attendance, awaiting the morning levée. Here I was left to cool my heels for a little time, the spruce page informing me that the cardinal was engaged at breakfast, but that he would tell him of my coming, and asked my name. I hesitated for a moment, but decided to keep the name of Donati which I had assumed, and gave that, adding that I was the bearer of an urgent despatch to the cardinal, which I must deliver with my own hands. The young man then left me, as I have said, and taking a good position near the entrance door to the adjoining room, I leaned back against the wall, and awaited my summons. The reception room was of noble proportions, oblong in shape, the ceiling being supported by two pillars of veined marble, which, although they diminished the size of the chamber, had a good effect. The marble flooring, arranged in a patchwork of black and white, was bare of all furniture, and as the room gradually filled, the constant moving of feet, the sound of which rang sharply on the stone, made it appear as if a lot of masons' hammers were at work. I let my eyes wander over the groups as they stood or moved about, wondering, if by chance I should see anyone I knew; but they were all strangers to me, mostly Frenchmen, with a fair sprinkling of priests amongst them. They were one and all trying to jostle past each other, so as to gain as close a position as possible to the entrance door, near to which I stood; and as I watched this with some little amusement, I heard a whisper in my ear, and glancing round beheld a man standing near me in a doctor's robe, holding a heavily bound missal in his hand. I saw in a moment it was Corte, and he whispered in a low voice:

"Well met again, signore, remember your promise."

"I do, and the promise I made to the juggler will not

be forgotten to the doctor. Is it wise, however, if you wish to remain unknown, for us to be seen speaking here?"

"Not very, but I wanted a word with you. Do not look round at present, but near the pillar to your right are two men, one dressed half in cloth of gold, and they are more interested in you than you think. I overheard a snatch of conversation—they are moving this way. By your leave, signore," raising his voice, he attempted to push by me, and catching the hint his last words had thrown out, I answered loudly, "First come, first served, learned doctor, and you must bide your turn."

"I am a man of peace, and therefore yield." Corte moved off, and I was free to look around me. I saw that Corte's little piece of acting, to which I had risen, was due to the fact that the man in the cloth of gold and his companion were edging nearer to us, and at the time were barely six feet off. Resting my hand lightly on the hilt of my sword I looked the two full in the face, but could make nothing of them. The one who wore a jerkin of gold cloth met my look for an instant, and then dropped his eyes, a faint flush rising to his cheek. I saw that he was a young man of a singularly handsome countenance. A short neatly curled moustache fell over his upper lip and mouth, but there was no sign of a beard on the small and rounded chin, which was cleanly shaven. On his right cheek he wore a black patch, placed as if to hide the scar of a wound, although his complexion was as delicate as if the sun had never touched it. In his ears he wore earrings, an affectation of female adornment hateful to me, and the fingers of his small right hand, which he held ungloved, were covered with rings. The hilt of his rapier too, peeping from under the folds of his gay cloak, was crested with jewels, and altogether it seemed as if I could have nothing to fear from this painted lily, who looked more fitted to thrum a lute in a lady's bower than have aught to do with the stir of the times. I therefore loosed my glance from him with some contempt, and turned to his companion, who was robed as an abbé, and evidently in a sour middle age. His features were bolder than those of his companion, but distinctly those of the canaille, and there was nothing in them in any way remarkable.

Nevertheless I thought it well to be on the watch, knowing that a dagger thrust is easily sent home, and there was the certainty, too, that the fact of my coming to Rome with a letter was known to the Medici plotters in Florence, and evidently it was their object to frustrate its delivery. What puzzled me, however, was that the look the young man directed to me was not unfriendly, and it struck me that if I could only hear his voice it might give me some clue to a recognition. The two had come a little between me and the door, and I was just about to contest the place with a view of forcing their hands if possible, when the door was flung open and the same page who had taken my name appeared and called out—

"Signor Donati, his eminence awaits you."

As the door opened there was a general movement towards it. But the cry of the page in a moment arrested the crowd, turning the look of anticipation on the faces of all to one of disappointment, and a loud murmuring arose against my being so favored. I lost not a second in stepping forward, and in doing so purposely brushed against the young man near to me, turning round as I did so with a somewhat brusque "By your leave, sir." I fully expected that he would resent my rudeness and make some speech, but he merely bowed his head with a courteous inclination, showing a set of small and even teeth as he smiled under his blonde moustache. I was a little put out by the failure of my plan, but the next instant the door closed behind me, and at any rate the letter to the cardinal was safe, and my task was as good as accomplished.

I followed the page therefore with an equal mind, and lifting a curtain, which fell in heavy folds at the end of the passage, where a couple of gorgeous lackeys stood, he called out "Messer Donati," and then stepped aside to let me pass. I entered the room with a firm step, and saw before me a large, but plainly-furnished apartment. In a lounge chair near a small table, on which was set out a light repast, was a man whom I at once guessed to be the cardinal. He wore a purple robe, and the barettina or small skull cap, which covered the tonsure on his head, allowed his short grey hair, which curled naturally, to be seen around it. Under the cap I saw a square resolute face with keen black eyes, and a full but kindly mouth. He was just putting down a glass of vernaccia as I came in, and I caught the purple glitter of the sapphire ring he wore in token of his rank, as he set down the glass. He was not alone, for, leaning against the window and caressing the head of an enormous wolf-hound, was a splendidly-dressed cavalier, who looked up as I came in, and I saw at once it was Bayard. I kept my eyes away from him, however, and advancing straight towards the cardinal, placed the letter before him without a word.

D'Amboise looked at the seals carefully, and then taking a small jade-hilted knife from the table, ripped open the envelope, and ran his eye quickly over the letter. As he did so not a muscle of his face moved to show how the contents stirred him, and when he had finished he held it out at arm's length, saying—

"My dear Bayard, what do you think of this?"

Bayard made a step forward to take the letter, and in doing this our eyes met, and he frankly held out his hand. I could hardly believe it when I saw it extended towards me. My breath came thick and fast, and the whole room swam around. The man was the soul of honour, the noblest knight in Christendom; he had seen my trial, nay, he had been one of my judges, and he offered me his hand! He must hold me guiltless, I felt. "My lord!" I rather gasped than spoke as I took his grasp, but seeing my emotion, he put in—

"Sit down, cavaliere. His eminence will forgive me for disposing of a seat in his house—we are more than old friends." He placed his hand on my shoulder and forced me to a seat, whilst D'Amboise, still holding the letter in his hand, looked at us with a puzzled air.

"St. Dennis!" he exclaimed. "What does this mean, Bayard?"

"It means, your eminence, that this is a gallant gentleman who has been most basely used; but pardon me—the letter."

He took the letter from the cardinal's hands and read it quickly, whilst I sat still, with emotions in my heart I cannot describe, and D'Amboise glanced from one to another with a half-amused, half-curious look on his keen face. Bayard finished his perusal in a few seconds, and laying the letter on the table said, "Nothing could be better. We should be prepared for action, although there is yet plenty of time. I wonder how in the world the Florentine got wind of this?"

"Oh, he has long ears. We shall, however, want a good sword, and if all that the secretary writes is true, we have got it in your friend the Cavaliere Donati. In fact Machiavelli suggests him for the task."

"My name, your eminence, is not Donati," I here put in, "but Savelli. When misfortune overtook me, I changed my name; but I see no reason for hiding the truth from you."

"Quite right," said D'Amboise, "but Savelli! Is this the Savelli of the Arezzo affair, Bayard?"

Bayard nodded assent, and the cardinal continued, turning to me. " Then, sir, I have heard your story, and you have more friends than you think. But of this, later on. Were you not at Fornovo ? "

" Yes," I replied, wondering what the cardinal's speech meant.

" *Ciel!* I made out your patent of St. Lazare myself. What could have made Tremouille act as he did I do not know, and he is as obstinate as a mule. Bayard, I know all about this gentleman, and your testimony to his worth convinces me that what I have heard is correct. I could never believe the story myself."

" My lords, you may doubt; but the world——"

" Will yet come round to you, cavaliere," said Bayard, and added, " Your eminence could not have a better sword for your purpose than that of M. di Savelli here, provided he will accept the task."

" I will accept anything from you, my lords," I said.

" Good," said D'Amboise, " now let me tell you how you stand. Acting doubtless in the advice of friends, Madame d'Entrangues wrote to me a full account of the affair, which ended so badly for you, and explained fully her husband's treachery. This she begged me to forward to Tremouille with a view of getting your sentence altered. As you have just been made aware, I have some knowledge of you, and it was a thousand pities to see a sword, which had served France well, turned away. I laid the matter before the duke, but he replied to say he could take no action. The duchess, who is my cousin, has also used her influence but to no purpose, for Tremouille stirs his porridge with his own hand, and does not care if it burn or not, as long as he stirs it himself. We could get the king's pardon for you, and as a last resource that might be done, for I like as little to be thwarted as His Grace of Tremouille; but that will raise you up a strong enemy in the duke, and it will not kill the story—you see."

"I do, your eminence. How can I thank you?"

"I do not want your thanks, cavaliere; but France wants your sword. Your only way is to do a signal service for France, and after this the matter is easy. Tremouille is generous, and it would want but a little pressure to make him rescind his sentence apparently of his own accord, provided you could do what I have said. Strange how fate works!"

I remained silent, and D'Amboise went on: "Such a service it is possible for you to do, and I will put it in your way. I cannot at present give you details as they have to be discussed with the secretary, who will shortly be in Rome. This much, however, I can tell you; get together a few good men, you doubtless can lay your hands on them, and be ready. You will no doubt want funds, but they will be arranged for. In the meantime you may consider yourself as attached to my suite—a moment," he continued as I was about to pour out my thanks, " you had better for the present call yourself Donati. I know something of the history of Roman families, and your name would not smell well to the Chigi and Colonna, and remember the Tiber is very deep."

He touched a small handbell as he concluded, and the page appeared. "Defaure," he said, "send the Abbé Le Clerc and my gentlemen to me; after that you will please inform the steward that apartments are to be prepared at once for M. Donati, who is here." The page bowed and vanished, and as I rose to await the coming of the suite, the cardinal went on with a smile, " Messieurs in the ante-room are doubtless getting impatient; we must make haste to receive them." As he said these words a grey-haired priest entered, bearing on a cushion the scarlet hat of a prince of the church, and following him, half-a-dozen gentlemen, and grooms of the chamber. The cardinal rose, and leaning on the arm of Bayard, walked slowly towards the door. Le Clerc bore the hat immediately before him, and the rest of us formed a queue behind. As we came to the door it was flung open by two lackeys in a blue and silver livery, who shouted out—

" My Lord Cardinal—way—way."

We passed into the room where the people were arranged in two rows, and D'Amboise walked down the line, bowing to one, exchanging a word or two with another, until he came opposite Corte. The doctor dropped to his knee, and presenting his book, solicited the cardinal's influence to obtain for him an audience with the Pope, to whom he desired to dedicate his work.

"*Perte!*" said the cardinal. " Why not go to his eminence of Strigonia—books are more in his line than—well, we shall see—we shall see."

He passed on, and the next group that caught his eye was that of the young stranger in the cloth of gold and his companion.

As the cardinal approached, the young man drew a letter from his vest, and presented it with a low bow.

D'Amboise tore it open and glanced over the contents. "*Diable!*" he exclaimed, " from Madame de la Tremouille herself. See here, Bayard, the Duchess writes, introducing her friend the Chevalier St. Armande—I know not the house."

" We are of Picardy, your eminence."

The voice was singularly sweet and soft, and a strange and undefinable resemblance in its tones to some other voice I had heard struck me, but I could not fix upon anything.

" The Duchess says you are anxious to serve: would it not have been easier to send you to the Duke ? "

St. Armande looked round with a heightened colour, and then replied, speaking in the same low, soft tones:

"If your eminence will kindly read the letter, you will perceive that my desire was to see something of the court of Rome before joining the duke."

D'Amboise glanced at the letter again, and an odd smile passed over his face.

"I see," he added, "the postscript—My dear Chevalier, Madame de la Tremouille's requests are commands to me. If you will do me the honour of joining my suite, I shall be delighted. Permit me to introduce you to the Cavaliere Donati, who is also a new friend."

I bowed and extended my hand, and St. Armande placed his within mine. It was small and delicate as a woman's, and as I clasped it for a moment, it felt as chill and cold as death.

CHAPTER XV.

THE GIFT OF BAYARD.

THE levée lasted some little time, as D'Amboise, who was studious of the arts of gaining popularity, listened with apparent interest to any one who chose to address him, and seemed to possess a wonderful memory for even the most trifling details. This was, in fact, an informal reception, which the cardinal, both as a prince of the Church, and the representative of France at the Papal Court, held daily, and hither came all the lesser members of the French party in Rome, and all those who hoped to gain something from the prelate by the simple process of asking; for D'Amboise was known to be generous and free, despite an occasional testiness of manner, such as he had exhibited to Corte, and shown in the first instance to St. Armande.

Corte I spoke to no more that day; but I saw him, where he had retreated to the extreme end of the room, his book under his arm, evidently waiting to make his exit. St. Armande took his place beside me, his companion, the abbé, dropping into the rear. Once he, St. Armande, hazarded a remark, which I did not catch, and therefore did not answer. In truth, I was in no mood for speaking, my mind being full of my eventful interview with the cardinal and Bayard, and I was more than grateful for the happy chance that had enabled me to draw my sword in aid of the secretary Machiavelli. I thought too of Madame D'Entrangues, and of what she had done in my behalf, and would have given much to have thanked her for her efforts, fruitless although they apparently were. But what struck me most of all was the fact, that whilst in my misery at Florence I was upbraiding fate, and all but cursing God, friends were at work, trying to help and aid me, and this taught me a lesson.

At last the levée came to an end. The last petition monger had made his request, D'Amboise had made his last pleasant speech, and, turning slowly round, we made our way back, when the cardinal retired with Bayard to an inner apartment, leaving us to our own devices. St. Armande, whose appearance attracted general attention, was surrounded by the gentlemen of the suite, who asked the last news of the court, and the last scandal of Maçon, where Louis was, holding high revelry, instead of marching, as he should have done, at once into Italy, after the defeat of Cesare at Fossombrone. The result of his action being a further truce that much delayed his success, and indeed very nearly ruined his chances, which were great at the time. As for me, I was left to myself; no one coming near me except the huge hound, which rose slowly, and approaching, surveyed me with a grave interest. Then, apparently satisfied, he wagged his tail in approval, and touched my hand with his grim muzzle. I ran my fingers over his shaggy coat with a caressing motion, and, observing Defaure, the page whom I had first addressed on arrival, begged him to show me my apartments, enquiring at the same time of Jacopo and the horses.

"The house is full, signore," he replied, "but we have done what we could for your accommodation. The horses have been attended to, and the Sergeant Jacopo awaits you in your rooms."

"Thanks, friend," and I followed him, smiling a little

to myself at the French rank which Jacopo had assumed, no doubt out of compliment to our host, my new employer. We passed out by the same entrance by which I had come in, and, crossing a courtyard, the page ushered me to a set of apartments in an outbuilding, and left me with the information that dinner would be served at noon for the cardinal as well as the gentlemen of the suite.

I found Jacopo in high glee. He had set out all my apparel, and was engaged in burnishing his sword. This he put down as I came in, and burst into speech.

"Blood of St. John! Excellency, but did I not say luck would turn? Yesterday we were anywhere," and he held up both hands with the fingers outstretched, "to-day, behold!" and he waved his arms around the room, which was certainly fitted with luxury, and struck me as all the more luxurious after my past privations.

"The horses, Jacopo?"

"Are well as might be, signore, and munching their corn as if they were never to have another feed. Does your excellency mean to stay long in this land of plenty?"

"Not for long, Jacopo. And harkee! Remember not to address me by any other name than that of Donati. Do not let a hint of my real name escape you, and avoid babbling over the wine cup."

"I will be dumb, excellency."

"A good deal depends on your prudence in this, and you must take care not to fail. Now to business, and keep your ears open and your head clear. How do we stand as regards funds?"

Jacopo, to whom I had entrusted my money, pulled out a leather purse and counted the contents.

"There are five-and-thirty crowns with me, signore, and five I gave your worship this morning, making forty in all," and he restored the purse to its hiding-place under his belt.

"Enough for our needs at present, and more will be forthcoming soon, for there is business in hand."

"I said that luck would turn," repeated Jacopo, his face showing joy at the news.

"Never mind the luck, but attend to me. I want to enlist half-a-dozen good men, men who will go anywhere and do anything. They must bring their own arms and horses, and I will engage them for a month, and pay each man five crowns."

"That is at the rate of sixty crowns a year for each man. We could enlist half Rome for that."

"Probably, but it isn't half Rome, only half-a-dozen men I want."

"Very true, your worship, and I will doubtless be able to find them; but, excellency——"

"What is it?"

"Six men at five crowns each makes thirty crowns, and——"

"Did I not say more will be forthcoming? You need not pay them in advance. Two crowns each on enlisting, and the remainder on completion of the task. Will that do?"

"It is enough surely."

"Very well, then you may set about this at once, and remember that they should be lodged close at hand, and be ready to go anywhere at a moment's notice."

"Excellency."

Whilst this conversation was going on I had effected such change in my attire as was possible, resolving to take the first opportunity the following day to summon a tailor and give him orders for things for which I stood in need. Jacopo was just about to depart when Defaure, the page, appeared, bearing with him a note and a ruleau, which he said was from his eminence. These he left with me and retired, saying there was no answer. The note was brief, merely hoping I was in comfort, and sending me in the ruleau a hundred crowns, with the intimation that if I needed them another hundred was ready for me. The sum, however, was more than ample, and giving Jacopo further directions to engage a couple of lackeys I sent him away, rejoicing at my good fortune, with a present of ten crowns for himself, which the honest fellow at first refused to take, and only accepted on my pressing the sum on him.

This being done there was nothing left for me but to await the dinner hour, and I strolled down to the stables to look at the horses, which were in truth in such luxury as perhaps the poor beasts had never enjoyed. A groom of the cardinal's establishment had attended to them, and I slipped a piece of silver into his hand for his trouble. He bit this to test whether it was genuine or not, and then settled himself on a heap of hay to mend some saddlery.

I left him to his occupation, and, with a parting caress to my beasts, moved further on to look at the other animals. And here, meeting the head groom, I had some conversation with him, admiring the cardinal's stud.

"Yes, excellency," he said, "they are good horses, notably the two barbs which the Soldan Djem presented to his eminence, but there are other two now in our stables, belonging to the Sieur de Bayard, the like of which I have never seen. They are this way, excellency, if you will but accompany me."

I readily assented, and passing by the barbs, whose slight delicate frames belied their powers of speed and endurance, we came to a couple of stalls, in which there were a pair of war-horses that fully justified the head groom's praise. They were both English, and I recognised the breed, as Hawkwood had brought three or four with him from Britain, saying, and with truth, that they were the only animals that could ever carry him when in full mail. But the two before me in the stables were as superior to Hawkwood's as a barb is to a mule. One was the great bay Bayard was riding on the day of my trial, when he accompanied the duke and his staff back to Arezzo. The other was a blue roan, whose colour did not show off his size to advantage, but whose broad chest, sloping shoulders, and lean flanks marked his power. His eyes were mild and soft, yet full of fire, and his small head was set like that of a stag upon his strong neck. Two grooms, bearing on their liveries the arms of the house of Terrail, of which the Seigneur de Bayard was chief, were in attendance, and set to work with a somewhat unnecessary zeal on our appearance to polish the coats of their charges which already shone like satin. Whilst engaged in admiring these splendid animals, I heard the deep bay of the hound behind me, and turning, saw Bayard himself who had come to visit his favourites. I complimented him on the possession of two such steeds, as who would not have done, and Bayard said—

"Yes, they are fine animals, truly the finest I have ever seen, except perhaps the one-eyed Savoy, who was also of the same breed; and yet I am not sure," and he ran his eyes over the horses. "They were given to me, along with Bran here"—he touched the head of the hound—"by His Majesty, Henry of England, when I was taken prisoner in the English War."

"A noble gift."

"Yes—from a noble prince. And you really admire them, cavaliere?"

"Yes—and I knew Savoy too, and doubt if he was better."

"What can knight want more? A good horse, a good hound,"—and his face saddened a little—"a true love. *Pardieu!* but I must see to that last. My castle on the Garonne needs a chatelaine."

I said nothing, knowing of the one great sorrow of his life, which he bore so bravely, and which I knew had bitten to his heart for all his gay words.

"Castor and Pollux I call them," he said, indicating the horses with a slight gesture. "Not that they are alike, except in speed and courage; but that they are both supposed to have been born the same day, and have never been separated. The best of friends must, however, part, and a knight wants no more than one horse; so, cavaliere, if you will accept Castor, the blue roan there, you will find that he will never fail you."

I could hardly speak for the moment, and at first stoutly refused to take so valuable a gift; but Bayard would have no denial, and the short of it was that Castor was led into one of the stalls reserved for me.

To say that I was grateful would be to say very little; but I will merely add here that the gift itself was only equalled by the manner of the giver. I accompanied Bayard into the garden, which lay to the west of the palace, and in course of conversation told him that I had received the sum sent by D'Amboise, and of the steps I had taken to get together a few men, and assured him that whatever the task was that I was to be set to perform, nothing but death itself would cut short my endeavour. Our talk then drifted to other matters, and he gave me some information of interest concerning Madame D'Entrangues. It appeared that D'Entrangues, who had a friend at court in his kinsman, Etienne de Vesci, the seneschal of Beaucaire, had forwarded a strong petition against Tremouille's decision regarding himself, and a prayer that the king would restore him to his position, and compel Madame D'Entrangues to return to him. As if he himself had not abandoned her! Owing to his influence with Cesare he had moreover obtained an order from Alexander denying madame the refuge of a convent. Louis had, however, declined to interfere with Tremouille's decision, but had ordered madame to leave the court and return to her husband. Fearing that force would be resorted to in order to compel her to return to D'Entrangues she had fled from the protection of the Duchesse de la Tremouille, who denied all knowledge of her movements, and the matter stood there. By this time it was almost approaching the dinner hour, and we separated, Bayard, followed close at his heels by Bran, going to seek the cardinal, and I returning to my chamber, where I found Jacopo who had just come back. He had been to the stables on his way up, and was loud in his praise of Castor.

"They say he is fleet as the wind, excellency, and he is as gentle as a lambkin. It is a glorious steed, and a princely gift."

"It is so; but what success have you had?"

"None as yet about the swords, signore; there has not been time; but I have engaged a couple of grooms and a lackey, and ordered plain liveries for them. The grooms are even now with the horses, and the lackey will be here to-morrow."

"Very well, there is time enough. Basta! There go the trumpets. His eminence must be served."

We made our way to the dining-hall, entering it almost at the same time as the cardinal, his guests, and the rest of the suite. At the high table on the *daïs* sat the cardinal, with Bayard, another prince of the church whom I afterwards found out was the Cardinal of Strigonia, a scion of the house of Este, and a tall, sombre-looking man, with high aquiline features, and a complexion almost as dark as a Moor's. He was plainly and simply dressed, wearing a light steel corselet over his jerkin, and round his neck the ribbon of St. James of Compostella, whilst the order itself, a red enamel sword with a *fleur-de-lis hilt*, set in an oval white enamel medallion with a red border, studded with brilliants, flashed at his throat. His short, closely-cropped hair was white as snow, but the long moustache which dropped over his mouth and short, pointed beard, was untouched by a streak of grey. Altogether a remarkable man, one whom no one could pass by without looking at twice; and in me he excited the greatest interest, for he was none other than Ganalvo de Cordova, the "Great Captain," and the most skilful general of the age. He had only a few weeks before driven Marshal d'Aubigny out of Calabria, and was marching straight on against Tremouille, when the cessation of hostilities stopped his plans, and suddenly resigning his command he had come to Rome, for what purpose no one knew, although it was said that his resignation and difference with the Spanish Court was but a blind.

Be that as it may, I had now an opportunity of seeing together, seated side by side, the dark and stern grandee of Spain, as able as he was cruel, as vindictive as he was brave; and the brilliant and polished Bayard, who seemed to have gathered in his person all the noblest qualities of knighthood, and on the white shield of whose honour there was never a stain. And how different was the fate of these two men! De Cordova, after holding the highest offices, after being practically a king, after shedding an imperishable glory on his country by his victories, and staining her memory indelibly by his perfidy, died at last, with all his fine spun webs broken. And Bayard—old as I am, my eyes grow moist when I think of that glorious day at the passage of the Sesia, when, covered with wounds, overborne by numbers, and fighting to the last against hopeless odds, Pierre du Terrail gave back his soul to God. But long years were to pass before this happened, and Bayard was at present in the hey-dey of his career.

The table for the gentlemen of the suite was placed just

below the *daïs*, and extending further down the room were other tables, for all who could obtain seats thereat, whilst at the extreme end of the room was a high stand, whence any one was at liberty to bear away as much of a meal as he could carry off on the point of his dagger.

Estimating roughly, I should say that fully three hundred persons dined daily, in this manner, with D'Amboise, and this hospitality, which he exercised in the manner of a French feudal noble, was the subject of much amusement at the Papal Court, where they prided themselves on a more refined and delicate style of living. At any rate, all that was here was safe to touch, and no one had need to fear that a dinner at the Palazzo Corneto with the Cardinal of Rouen was a prelude to a supper with St. Peter in heaven. His eminence, who was a notable trencherman, beamed down from his high seat on us all, and tried valiantly to assay conclusions with the Cardinal of Strigonia; but was compelled at last to own himself beaten, for Ippolyte d'Este was one in a thousand at table; in fact, this jovial prelate ended his days suddenly, after a prodigious dinner, which began at eleven in the morning and ended at four in the afternoon, concluding with so light a dainty as a dish of roasted cray-fish, washed down with a bottle of vernaccia, a wine of which he was inordinately fond. At our own table, there were about a dozen or more, and I found myself seated next to St. Armande, whilst opposite to me was Le Clerc, the cardinal's chaplain, and next to him an officer of the Papal Guards, a Spaniard, who spoke little and ate much. St. Armande passed by the wine, drinking only water, and in reply to a question of mine answered that he was under a vow.

"We can absolve you here easily, chevalier," said Le Clerc, who overheard the remark, "here is some Orvieto which I can recommend," and he pushed the flask towards St. Armande.

The latter, however, would not be tempted, and Le Clerc shook his head.

"A wilful man must have his way, chevalier; but that Orvieto was a present from Pierrot, Our Lord's most favoured servant."

"Indeed," said the Spaniard; "then I can safely say it is the last present you will receive from Don Pierrot."

"How so?"

"Cesare arrived last night, very suddenly, with two men only, they say. He has not, however, yet seen His Holiness—although he is in the Vatican."

Le Clerc remained silent, but St. Armande asked in his low voice—

"I do not follow, sir. Could you not explain? Unless I ask too much. You see I am a stranger to Rome."

The Spaniard smiled grimly.

"It means, chevalier, that Pierrot was found this morning with a dagger sticking up to the hilt in his heart."

St. Armande turned pale, and Le Clerc asked in a low tone—

"Are you sure of this? When did it happen?"

"As sure as I sit here. It happened an hour or so after Cesare's coming. The Pope is said to be overcome with grief," and the lips of Don Diego de Leyva took a sarcastic curve.

"Great heavens!" said Le Clerc. "Poor Pierrot!"

The chaplain rose from his seat with a slight apology, and approaching D'Amboise, leaned over him and whispered a few words in his ear. The cardinal nodded with apparent unconcern, and Le Clerc came back; but watching D'Amboise narrowly, I saw that although he still appeared to laugh and jest, his eyes were grave and his brow troubled.

In fact, shortly afterwards, the high table broke up, and we followed suit very soon. Despite his effeminate appearance, I had begun to take a liking to St. Armande, and as the next few hours were at our disposal, I invited him to ride out with me, as I had a mind to try Castor's paces. This, however, he declined, with the somewhat shy air that marked his manner, and leaving him to his devices, I ordered Castor to be saddled and took him out. When I returned, about five in the afternoon, I felt that all that had been said of the generous beast I rode, underrated his value, and that I possessed a matchless steed, who was fit to run for a kingdom.

CHAPTER XVI.

FRIEND OR FOE.

For the next few days the routine of my life was exactly the same, the morning attendance at the cardinal's levée, the daily dinner in public, and long rides with Castor in the afternoons, in which I was sometimes accompanied by St. Armande; but this was not always possible, as he was closely attached to D'Amboise's person. D'Amboise frequently asked me to accompany him to the Vatican; but up to now I had begged permission to decline his invitation, on the plea that, with the business before me, it would perhaps be well for me to live as much in retreat as possible. The cardinal said, with that good-tempered laugh of his, which entirely belied his astute scheming nature, that as I was as yet ignorant of my task, I need not be so careful. I replied to his eminence, that it was just because I was in the dark, that I was so circumspect, and he was then good enough to agree with me. I was, however, naturally anxious to see something of the Vatican, and one of my reasons for refusing, besides that of prudence, was that I was not sufficiently well equipped. This, however, with the funds at my disposal, was soon mended, but from some cause or other, I had up to now not gone. Jacopo was not so successful as he anticipated he would be, in raising his men. It was, above all, necessary to have them trustworthy, and it was difficult to get men of this class for a merely temporary employment such as I offered. At last the matter was arranged, and by the end of the week I mustered a body of six stout fellows, all of them fairly well mounted, and what was better, all of them trained soldiers. I had them lodged near the Ripetta, and the cardinal's table afforded them a free dinner, of which they were not slow to take advantage. In order to keep them employed, I took them out with me every afternoon, dismissing them upon my return, with orders to join the nightly escort of the cardinal and Bayard, to and from the Vatican. I saw a good deal of Bayard, and at times expressed myself with impatience at being kept to cool my heels. He told me he was not at liberty to mention the details of the business on which I was to be employed, and advised me to bide my time with a patient heart. Amongst other matters we spoke of was the murder of Pierrot, and Bayard told me that Cesare Borgia had left Rome the next day without seeing his father, the Pope, and that he was crushing out completely the stand made against him by my old chief Vitelli of Citta del Castello, and others.

I took Bayard's advice and held patience by the tail, although I longed for work to begin. My men were in good fettle. They had enough work to keep them out of mischief, the pay was good, they had sufficient leisure for amusement, and there was therefore no grumbling.

I used to sup alone in my rooms, occasionally asking St. Armande to join me; and after supper we diced together for an hour or so, for very small points. He was an infant at the game, and I taught him a good deal, so much so, that after a little practice, for he was very quick with his wrist, he mastered my favourite throw, and one evening after returning from the Vatican, he knocked me up in my rooms, and flung on the table a bag of gold pieces.

"Three hundred of them, cavaliere!" he said, "I won them from Fabrizio Colonna, who is looking green with rage. If your purse is running short, they are at your service. Ha! I see a flask of Orvieto—may I?" and he poured himself out a goblet, at which he began to sip, in apparent defiance of his vow.

"The devil!" I exclaimed, "but you are flying at high stakes, chevalier. Your Picard estates must be broad. Thanks all the same for your offer, but my purse is as full as I want it at present."

He leaned back in his chair, with a pink flush on his delicate features.

"I meant no offence, cavaliere; but what is the use of money unless one can share it with a friend?"

"There was no offence taken, St. Armande," I replied, "and if you will take none, I would like to have my say at you."

He looped one finger in his golden moustache, and showed his even teeth in his smile, as he said,

"Speak on."

"Then, chevalier, it seems to me a thousand pities that a young man like you should waste your time here, as you appear to be doing. I understood you to say you had never seen a sword drawn in earnest as yet—and your moustache is grown! Take my advice. Play no more for gold pieces with Colonna or anyone else. Mount your horse, and join Tremouille at once."

"Ah! that is good," he said; "and why does the grave and reverend Cavaliere Donati waste his time here, hanging at the heels of a churchman, and moping o' nights like an owl on a ruined wall, instead of stirring the times himself with the point of his sword?"

With any other I would have been annoyed; with the youth before me I was slightly amused, and at the same time a trifle surprised. Hitherto he had appeared so shy and reserved, and now, of a sudden, he had thrown this off, and had put on an air which I had not noticed before, but which became him vastly. I set it down to the fact that perhaps he was slightly warmed with wine, having apparently absolved himself from his vow; although of course I did not appear to notice this last, as he was in a manner my guest. I therefore made reply.

"My reasons for my action, chevalier, are good, and when the time comes I promise you I shall not be found sleeping."

The gentle reproof in my words seemed to bring him back to his old self, for by the light of the candles I observed him flush scarlet, and that curious look which recalled a strange resemblance to some one I knew, but could not remember, came over his features. I began to relent as I saw his confusion, almost as soon as I had spoken; and added, "I may say that the time is not far distant—that it is a matter of days only."

"Take me with you."

He asked this almost in a tone of entreaty, keeping his eyes away from me, however, and nervously twisting at his moustache.

"And your secretary, as you call him, the abbé?"

"Oh, he will come too, and we could confess to him."

I hesitated for a second, and then made answer.

"Very well. Only you must be prepared to start at a moment's notice, and there will probably be hard riding and hard fighting, and there is yet another thing."

"What is that?"

"You must come as a simple volunteer, and must make no enquiry as to what the business is on which I am engaged. I risk my life for my own purposes; if you wish to do likewise you are welcome to join me, on the condition I have just stated."

"I accept with pleasure."

"Then that is settled, and I have a new comrade."

"Hurrah!" and he raised his glass to his lips.

After that he retired, it being late. I saw him across the courtyard as far as his apartments, and then returning to my rooms, unconsciously took the chair St. Armande had vacated. The goblet of wine he had filled was before me, and I idly lifted it in my hand. It was barely touched. In fact he could but have tasted a few drops only.

Like lightning a suspicion of treachery came on me. The man had been pretending to drink. With what object? I could not make out. Was the offer of the money a blind? Perhaps so, and if then? I had been a fool to agree to his joining me, with that sour-looking abbé of his. Yes, I had been a fool, but it was lucky I discovered my own folly in time. I should keep my eyes on this silken diplomat, and if necessary pick a quarrel with him, and run him through. Somehow I did not like the idea of this, however; but determined to get rid of him in one way or the other. I would allow nothing to stand between me and the road back to honour. So musing I sat for a half-hour or so, and was startled by Jacopo's sudden entry, so lost was I in thought. He came and stood, bolt upright, next to my chair, without saying a word. I knew from this that he had some request to make, some favour to ask, as otherwise he would not have hesitated to make play with his tongue at once.

"What is it Jacopo?"

He shifted uneasily from one foot to the other, and then replied—

"Your excellency, I want leave."

"Leave! What for? You are not going to be married, are you?"

"Heaven and the saints forbid, excellency. No—no—

it is not that, it is only leave for the day I want, and also for our men."

"The devil! What are you going to do?"

"Only a little dinner, excellency, which I am giving."

"And wasting those crowns you got the other day. Well, that is your affair, not mine. Yes, you can have the leave."

"A hundred thanks, excellency."

"Mind you, there must be no brawling, no trouble."

"Excellency."

"Well, good night, and remember what I say. Here, you might remove this wine-cup as you go."

"Good-night, signore," and Jacopo, lifting the goblet, went out. The night being fairly warm, I kept my door open, and as he passed into the portico, I saw him drain the contents of the goblet with a gulp, and heard him draw his lips together with a smack of approval, and march off to his quarters, chuckling at something or other.

The following afternoon I rode out with Bayard and half-a-dozen others. It was a hawking party, and there was a long gallop to our point of operation, which was to begin a little way beyond Ponte Molle. In a short time we started a noble heron, and Bayard flinging his peregrine into the air, we rode after the birds. It was a glorious ride, and Castor and Pollux far outstripped the others, so much so that when we drew rein beside the stricken heron, and Bayard slipped the hood on to his hawk, our companions were not in sight. This, however, troubled us little, and turning rein we made backwards. On our way back I seized the opportunity to mention to Bayard that St. Armande had volunteered to aid me in my task, and that I had accepted his offer.

"It will do him good," he said; "he seems a noble youth, who has been tied too long to apron-strings."

"Do you think so?" I said; "he strikes me as being effeminate to a degree—and yet I cannot help liking him."

"He has a wonderful pure mind," said Bayard; "the boy, for he is no less, is as innocent as a child."

"The Vatican will not improve him then, especially if he plays for gold crowns with Colonna."

"Plays for gold crowns!" exclaimed Bayard; "you are surely mistaken, cavaliere."

"Did he not do so last night, my lord? I understood he won three hundred off Fabrizio?"

"Impossible," said Bayard, "I was at the Vatican last night, and the party in which Colonna was playing consisted of Strigonia, Monsignore Florido, our Lord the Pope, and Colonna himself—no more. St. Armande was standing hard at hand for some little time, but never took a wager. In fact, he passed most of the evening with Giulia Bella, thrumming on a lute, much to the annoyance of his holiness. I should say it would be well for him to quit Rome."

"Then I am wrong," I said; "yes, I fancy it would be well for him to quit Rome."

By this time the others came up, and we said no more. As we went back to Rome, I dropped a little behind, reflecting on what Bayard had told me. It was certain that St. Armande had lied to me, and I began to feel sure he had done this not for my good. In short, it seemed to me that this innocent looking boy, with his shy retiring manners and apparent want of knowledge of the world, was nothing more or less than an accomplished actor. Then again he was a Frenchman, and how came he, obviously fresh from France, to become an agent of the Medici plotters, for so I put him down to be? There were the letters from Madame de la Tremouille, his introductions were unimpeachable, the cardinal believed in him—the whole thing was contradictory. Above all, there was my strong personal liking for St. Armande. In his presence I never felt that secret warning which all men feel when they are with an enemy. I have never known it fail with me, and with St. Armande there was no such warning, no such silent signal which goes straight from soul to soul. On the contrary, I felt he was almost more than friendly towards me, and I felt, in my turn towards him, despite our short acquaintance, very nearly the same protective feeling that one has towards a defenceless child. As may be imagined, I was in no very comfortable frame of mind about this, and rode back silently, revolving the point. When we reached the palace, almost the first person I met was St. Armande, and as I dismounted he came up to me with a cordial greeting and asked—

"Well, cavaliere, good sport I trust?"

"Very," I replied shortly, and then looked him straight in the face as I added, "Do you intend to give the Colonna his revenge to-night?"

Something in my tone caught him, he met my eyes for a moment, then dropped his gaze, and looked towards the ground. We stood thus before each other for a little time before he replied, and his voice was almost inaudible.

"Perhaps—I am not sure," he added with an effort.

I was standing, holding Castor's reins; but as he spoke I handed the horse over to a groom, and, linking my arm in St. Armande's, said loudly, and with a tone of affected gaiety:

"You missed a great ride, chevalier—come take a turn with me in the garden."

He yielded passively, and in a few steps we had crossed the courtyard and were in a secluded portion of the palace gardens that was called the Lemon Walk. This I may add was subsequently improved out of existence by the architect, in the course of completion of the palace and grounds.

When we reached this spot I unslipped my arm, and turning round faced St. Armande, having resolved to end my suspicions.

"See here, chevalier," I said, "I am playing for heavy stakes, I am walking on dangerous ground, and must know where I put my feet; will you answer a plain question, are you friend or foe?"

He looked round him in a helpless sort of way, his colour coming and going, but said nothing. Was it possible the man was a coward?

"If you do not reply," I said, "I will take the risk, and treat you as an enemy, do you hear? you lied to me when you said last night you had played at the Vatican with Colonna—now draw." I pulled out my weapon, and stood before him, expecting every instant to see his rapier in his hands; but he stood absolutely still, his head hanging down.

"Man," I said, "have you not heard? Am I to think you a coward as well as a liar?"

"How dare you say that!" he burst out. "You—you of all men—Oh! what am I saying! Yes, I did not play with Colonna; but I thought you were hard pressed for money, and—and invented the fiction, thinking that perhaps——"

"That perhaps I would accept your winnings over the gambling table, rather than the offer of a friend. You do me much honour, chevalier."

"You wrong me, Savelli,—nay, start not. I know your name and story, and, before heaven, I say I am your friend."

"You know me!"

"Yes, and am working for you; come, put by your sword. Look at me! Do I look like an enemy?"

He had recovered himself, and met my gaze fearlessly.

Where could I have seen that face before? I drew my hand over my forehead as if to sweep the cobwebs from my memory, but with no avail.

"Well," he went on, with a smile, "do I look like an enemy? If I do, your sword is ready. Strike now, it will be a quick riddance, come!"

I put back my sword with a snap.

"I do not understand, but I accept your explanation."

He held out his hand frankly.

"That is right, and you will still let me be your comrade?"

I took his grasp.

"Yes, if you wish it."

We walked back together in silence, and on reaching the courtyard St. Armande said,

"I am afraid I have fallen much in your esteem."

"My esteem, chevalier, is at present of no value to man or woman."

"Do you think so?" he said, and then rapidly, "Adieu for the present; remember, I hold you to your word that you think me a friend."

I made no answer, and he ran lightly up the steps of the principal entrance.

I supped that evening for a change with the gentlemen of the suite; but St. Armande was not there, and there were a few free remarks made concerning the manner in which he was supposed to have been received at the Vatican by Giulia Orsini, and Lucrezia Borgia.

"If it goes on like this," said Le Clerc, "we will have to drag the Tiber for his body, and say masses for his soul, unless he puts the seas between himself and the Borgia."

"He never struck me as a man to run after the ladies," I said.

"No," replied the abbé, "but it is the other way. You

would stand no chance against him, cavalier, for all your long moustache—a thousand thanks," and the genial Le Clerc seized the flagon of Orvieto I passed to him, and filled his goblet.

After this the conversation changed, and I shortly retired to my apartments, and dismissing my lackey, sat down to read a book on falconry that the cardinal had lent me. I had not been occupied thus for an hour when the door opened, and Jacopo cautiously peeped in. He withdrew his head on catching my eye, and I heard him shuffling outside.

" Come in."

" Excellency," and the sound of further shuffling, but no Jacopo. I lost patience at this, and fearing at the same time that there had been trouble, repeated my order to come in sharply. This had the desired effect; but as soon as my henchman appeared in view I made certain there had been a brawl. He was very red in the face, and from under the helmet he wore I could see a white bandage.

" What the devil does this mean, Jacopo?" I asked sternly.

" I have come to report, excellency."

" You hardly appear in a fit state to do so."

" Perfectly fit, excellency," and Jacopo drew himself up to attention and saluted.

" Is the matter of importance? For if not, you had better come to-morrow."

" Yes, your excellency—matter of importance. By your worship's leave, as you are aware, I gave a dinner to-day, and we had——"

" Never mind what you had; to the point."

" Boiled meat with sause, sausages with garlic, a *risotto alla Milanese*——"

" I do not care what you had, go on fool."

"I am going on, excellency. Where was I—a *risotto* did I say? And bread made with yeast. And for drink, signore——"

"I doubt not you had store of that, Jacopo."

"But a dozen flagons or so of wine, your worship—all rosso."

"Jacopo—you will be good enough to retire at once."

"I am retiring, excellency; but my report."

"Will do for to-morrow."

"As your worship desires; but we have burnt the inn."

"What!"

"The inn, where we rested the day of our arrival in Rome, your worship. What with one thing and another, the landlord footed up his bill to four crowns. And I said to my friends, 'What! Are honest soldiers to pay like this?' Whereat there was trouble, excellency; but we came off best."

I rose without a word, and seizing Jacopo by the neck, ejected him from the room, with, I am sorry to say, very considerable violence.

Cursing myself for my folly in having been so generous, I banged the door after him, and returned to my book. I could not, however, read, for my mind was full of the consequences that might arise from this mad freak of my followers, and I determined to seek out the cardinal the next day, and obtain his permission to move out of Rome to some quieter spot, and there await his instructions. Amidst it all, however, I could not help being pleased at the thought that retributive justice had overtaken the scoundrel tavern-keeper, the memory of whose bed made me shudder. I had no doubt that Jacopo was speaking the truth, and that, even as he spoke, the flames were sputtering merrily above that den of thieves.

CHAPTER XVII.

THE VATICAN.

The next morning I sought an early interview with D'Amboise, and stated to him what had occurred, proposing that I should leave Rome at once, and await his instructions at any point he should fix. To my surprise he did not regard the matter in so serious a light, saying that a small fine would no doubt settle the matter. "My dear cavaliere," he said, "Our Lord does not desire the death of a sinner, but only his purse. Make your mind easy, but keep a tighter hand on your men."

"I shall assuredly do so, your eminence."

"Another thing. I think you will have to put aside your shyness, and attend me to the Vatican for the next few days. It is extraordinary how suspicious the Court here is. They keep a constant watch on me, and on all the suite, and your seclusion, and solitary rides out, have been the subject of remark. The ladies too are taking interest in you. In fact I have been specially asked to bring you with me, by Madonna Lucrezia, all owing to a foolish remark made by Strigonia."

"I am at your eminence's orders."

"It is a little risk, but I do not want them to think that you are anything but a mere member of my suite. If there were the slightest suspicion, all my plans would be upset, and the time is at hand now, a day or two at the outside."

"Thank God! I am eating my heart out here."

"Courage, cavaliere! It will end soon. By the way, is Bayard right in saying you have enlisted St. Armande?"

"Yes, your eminence."

"*Ciel!* I should not have thought he would have been one for your purpose. But that is your affair," and he began to laugh.

"I have seven good swords behind me, your eminence. The chevalier may or may not do well; but I could hardly refuse his request."

D'Amboise made no answer, and our interview came to a close. I would, however, add here that nothing ever came of the burning of the inn. No complaint was ever laid, as far as I could find out, and the matter might have been an every-day occurrence, so little attention did it excite. I of course did not know that affairs had reached to such a pitch of disorder in Rome, and lived in hourly expectation, notwithstanding the cardinal's speech, of having considerable worry over the revengeful zeal of Jacopo. I took care that no such thing was likely to occur again, and Master Jacopo was penitent, swearing he would never give me further cause for annoyance. At the *levée*, that morning, St. Armande was, as usual, beside me, and I whispered to him to hold himself in readiness, as the time for our business was at hand.

"I am glad of that," he answered, his face lighting up.

"I attend the cardinal to-day to the Vatican," I said, by way of continuing the conversation.

"There will be much going on this evening," he made reply. "The Florentine envoy has been here for the past two days, and the affair at the Vatican to-night is in his honour. Do you know that you have excited great curiosity in the hearts of the court ladies?"

"Indeed? It is not my way."

"Is it not? Well, Lucrezia expressed a particular desire to see you."

"I trust it may not lead to the Tiber, chevalier. The attentions of the Lady Lucrezia are a trifle dangerous."

His face became very grave.

"Be civil to her, nothing more," he whispered. "You are quite right. Oh, how I hate that place!"—and he shivered a little.

"Well, we will soon be out of it."

"Please God!"

There was no one at the high table at dinner that day, both the cardinal and Bayard having gone to dine with Sforza at the Sforza Cesarini, quite an informal business, and none of the suite accompanied them.

The conversation at our table turned much on affairs, and as there were for once no guests, speech was very free.

"The fleur-de-lis will cover our tongues," said Le Clerc, "and to-day we may let them wag."

"Then how long is this truce to last?" asked De Briconnet, the captain of the cardinal's guard. "I am sick of this idleness here," he added.

"As for that, no man knows whether it is peace or war," replied Le Clerc. "Tremouille is chafing at Passignano, swearing that the game was ours if we had only let him march on after Fossombrone, and he was right. Now Cesare has stamped out the Magione league, and the Borgia are as strong as ever."

"How came such a man as Roderigo Borgia ever to be made pope?" I asked.

Le Clerc laughed as he passed on the Orvieto.

"When our Lord, the sainted Innocent, was called away, there were three favourites in the conclave. One was Giuliano della Rovere, the other Ascanio Sforza, and the third Roderigo Borgia. His eminence of St. Sabine's was our man, and the election would have been certain had not Borgia and Ascanio joined hands and the Milanese voted for Roderigo."

"I did not think Sforza would have been so self-sacrificing," said De Briconnet.

"There were compensations, Jacques," Le Clerc went on. "Four mule-loads of gold were given to Ascanio, he was made vice-chancellor of the church, and given Borgia's own palace, the Cesarini, where his eminence dines to-day. Immediately after the elections were made I was at the rota exchanging a few words with your uncle, the cardinal of St. Malo, and he told me that as soon as the result was known, Medici turned to Cardinal Cibo, and said, 'We are in the jaws of the wolf! Heaven grant that he may not devour us!' As for Borgia he could do nothing but walk about, calling out, 'I am Pope, Pontiff, Vicar of Christ!'"

"I do not suppose it can last long," said De Briconnet.

"Heaven knows. He is close upon seventy-one and grows younger every day. He is as strong as he was thirty years ago. And there are few men who can sit a horse as he can, even now."

"That is true," I remarked, and gave the story of my meeting with the Borgia on the day of my arrival in Rome.

Shortly after this our dinner, where speech had been so free, broke up, and, finding out the hour at which the cardinal would require my attendance, I took my book on falconry, and repaired to the garden, intending to pass the afternoon in its perusal. I made for the Lemon Walk, and found a companion in Bran, who was wandering there in a disconsolate manner, evidently missing his master. I set myself down on a sheltered seat, Bran stretching out his length at my feet, his muzzle resting between his paws, and so we remained in quiet, the dog absolutely motionless, and I engaged in my book.

So an hour must have passed, when Bran gave a low growl, and looking up I ran my eye up and down the walk, but could see nothing. I then followed the direction in which the dog was gazing, and through the leaves opposite to me, saw a stretch of green, terminating in a clump of three huge chestnuts. A further examination showed two figures standing in the shade of the trees, one of them was St. Armande, and the other, his secretary, the abbé. But what surprised me, was that the chevalier appeared to be overcome with some powerful emotion, for he was leaning with his arm against the trunk of the tree, against which his face was pressed, and his figure shook as if he were weeping. The abbé stood by him, with a look of compassion on his features, and was endeavouring to pacify him.

It was clear that I was looking at something I was not intended to see, and with a low, "Quiet, Bran," to the dog, which the well-trained beast instantly obeyed, I rose, and whistling a catch loudly, walked down the avenue, with my back towards St. Armande and the abbé, Bran stalking by my side. I did not look round, and of course could not tell what happened, but I could not help wondering what it was that affected St. Armande so strongly. It was hardly the place for the confessional. Yet it was no business of mine to pry into other people's affairs. So handing over Bran to a lackey of Bayard, I went up to my apartment, and attempted to resume my interest in my book.

This, however, was not possible, for in a few minutes I found myself with the volume in my lap, my eyes staring into vacancy, and thinking of St. Armande. I began to try and analyse my feelings towards him, but beyond that I was certain he had inspired me with a strong friendship I could go no further. It was this friendship that urged me to accede to his request to be allowed to share in my coming adventure, although I was well able to see that he was anything but fitted for a desperate deed. Still somehow, I could not find it in my heart to refuse him, although I felt I was doing an unwise thing. I consoled myself, or rather tried to console myself, with the reflection that he would have to take his chance like any other man of my troop, and if he fell, well, there was an end of it, and of him. Yet I was not comfortable, and then, to give my thoughts another turn, I bent them on other matters, and it came to my mind that it was a little surprising I had not heard of D'Entrangues in Rome.

When Bayard told me of his petition to the king, I had asked whether anything was known of D'Entrangues' movements, and he said he did not know. It was curious, too, how I appeared to have entirely mastered that mad longing for revenge, which at first held me. It was a direct answer, as it were, to my prayer, and, so thinking, I began to realise how close in reality a man is to the divine power, which he often, too often, thinks far from him. And a certain feeling of satisfaction came upon me at the thought of the strength I had gained by my victory over myself. Indeed, I felt sure, that if my enemy was in my power at the moment that I would not injure him, but let him go without harm.

In this manner, attempting to read, and trying to think, without very much success in either undertaking, I passed my time until my lackey came to assist me to dress, in order to be ready to accompany the cardinal to the Vatican. After dressing, I descended the stairs, and mounting Castor, placed myself at the head of my men, and joined De Briconnet at the grand entrance of the palace. The captain of the cardinal's guard had his full force of thirty swords out, it being a reception night of some importance, and with great courtesy allowed me to place Jacopo and my six men in front of his troop, drawing his own horse alongside of mine, and discussing, with much cunning, of falconry, in which he was more than an adept.

We had to wait some little time for the cardinal, but at length he came, accompanied as usual by Bayard, and with him all the gentlemen of his suite including St. Armande. On reaching the foot of the stairs, D'Amboise enquired somewhat sharply for me; but changed his tone to one of pleasant greeting when he saw I was in waiting.

"St. Dennis!" he exclaimed, " I thought you were not coming after all."

We had but a few yards to ride, and our passage along the Via Alessandrina to the Portone Bronse, took but a few minutes. As we rode up there, we kept the obelisk in the centre of the Piazza di S. Pietro to our left, and saw before us the walls of the new cathedral of St. Peter, then about four or five feet high, the ruins of the old church still standing around it. At the time I speak of, nothing had been done for about fifty years towards advancing the work, begun by Nicholas V., and the great design, afterwards altered and put into execution by Giuliano della Rovere, when he became Pope as Julius II., was then in a skeleton form, looking more like the remains of some sacked shrine than the beginning of a new work. The fifty years of neglect having the effect of making the new work almost as ruinous as the old church founded by Constantine.

Although, as I have mentioned, there were to be great doings at the Vatican that evening, there was no crowd assembled in the Piazza of St. Peter. It was full of soldiers, but the people of Rome, who might have been expected to be there in numbers, to see the processions of nobles and their followers, were conspicuous by their absence. Men-at-arms there were in store, but no happy, jostling crowd of the commons, for a terror was on Rome, and men kept as far as possible from the Borgo. The piazza was, however, brilliantly lit up, and the body guards of the various notables were strictly confined to the places assigned to them, order being maintained by about a thousand men of the Spanish guards of the Pope, under the immediate command of De Leyva. The light from the lamps was reflected back by the glittering arms of the men, and the various ensigns of the great houses were distinctly visible. The single column of Colonna, rose side by side with the eagle and griffin of Borghese, the six lilies of Farnese trembled in the wind, near Colleoni's two-headed lion, and a little in the background was drawn up a solid looking body of cavalry, over whom fluttered the standard of the Borgia; these were Cesare's own lambs, as he called them, veterans of many a hard fought field.

At the entrance steps we halted, and were met by two chamberlains, who, with their staffs of office in their hands, ushered us to the bronze gates, by which we were to enter the Vatican. We passed through amidst a blare of trumpets, each side of the passage being lined with pikemen, standing stiff and motionless as statues. Our way led to the Torre Borgia, the portion of the Vatican occupied by Alexander, and the distant strains of music caught our ears as we went on, and shortly entered the noble reception rooms, which were crowded with people.

The Pope himself stood at the extreme end of the apartment, surrounded by a brilliant group of ladies and gentlemen, and as we came up to make our duty, I had good opportunity of observing him. Alexander was fully seventy years of age, but so hale, hearty, and strong-looking, that he might have easily passed for a man of middle age. He was dressed as a private gentleman, in Spanish costume, with high boots, a jewelled dagger at his side, and a smart velvet cap on his head. But the face itself struck me as remarkable to a degree. He was clean shaven, so that all the features were clearly discernible, the heavy sensual chin, the wide cruel mouth, surmounted by a nose almost Jewish in its curve, the retreating forehead bulging over the eyes, and the eyes themselves, in which there seemed to burn the fires of insatiable appetite, and passion without end; all these, combined together to make up a countenance which was a fitting mask for the evil soul within. I made my obeisance with the others, stifling with difficulty a sudden desire to fling aside the hand I touched, and walk out of the room.

I moved slightly aside, and watched the various groups as they wandered to and fro, or stood together conversing; and the hum of voices, the gay strains of music, and the brilliant dresses made up together a scene well worth the looking at.

The Florentine ambassador was talking to the Cardinal of Santa Susanna, a few feet from me. I caught the tones of his voice, and as he turned round our eyes met. Machiavelli, for it was he, glanced at me as at a perfect stranger, and then, slightly adjusting his purple lined robe, moved slowly onwards with his companion.

"We mount yet higher, signore—*excelsior!*"

The words were breathed rather than whispered into my ear, and Corte stood beside me.

"*Excelsior!*" I repeated with a smile, "but are you not putting your head in the lion's mouth?"

He smiled back upon me, more of a snarl than a smile. "The beast is gorged now. He will not think of me—see, there is some one coming your way—adieu!"

He turned and passed into the groups, and St. Armande touched my arm.

"You are to be presented to the Lady Lucrezia," he said, and the next moment I found myself bowing over the hand of one of the most beautiful, and certainly the most infamous woman of her age. She was barely twenty-three; had already wedded three husbands, and was to become a wife again, and marry Alfonso of Ferrara. She was seated in a low lounge, and as I came up she extended her hand to me with a charming smile. Standing before her, looking at her large limpid eyes, at the small red bow of the lips, and the clear cut features set in a mass of red gold hair, I could not imagine that the stories I had heard were true. It could not be that this fair young woman who was before me had smilingly committed crimes of nameless horror. I would not believe it.

"So, cavaliere, you have come to the court at last! I thought you were never going to do us that honour."

"His Eminence of Strigonia said you meant to take the vows," and a lady, who was leaning over Lucrezia's seat, laughed as she put in these words. I recognised the peculiar unmusical laugh I had heard at the gate St. Paul, and glanced at her with some interest.

"My sister-in-law, Giulia Farnese—Giulia Bella, is it not?" and Lucrezia touched her lightly on the arm.

"Oh, yes, Giulia Bella—and are you really going to become a hermit?"

"I might have had such thoughts until I came here," I said, "but I must now put them aside."

"Neatly turned, cavaliere—St. Armande himself could not have put it better—sit here, chevalier," and Lucrezia made room for St. Armande on her lounge.

At this moment a commotion at the entrance attracted our attention, and a man robed in black, followed by two others, walked up towards the Pope.

"Heavens!" said Lucrezia, "it is Cesare!" and a look that was not sisterly came over her face as she glanced at her brother, who moved slowly up the room, men falling away from each side of him, and greeting no one. He kept himself covered, and below his square velvet cap, I saw a resolute face, the mouth and chin, covered by a moustache and short beard, not so hidden, however, but that one could distinctly see against the dark hair on his face, the full red line of the lips, set in a habitual sneer. Bad as the whole brood of the Borgia were, this was the worst of them all. He was as far beyond them in infamy as they were beyond the rest of mankind in evil doing. The very room was hushed into silence as he entered, and I watched with more interest than I can tell, the stately figure of this wicked man, as he went up to meet his only less wicked father. It was their first meeting since the murder of Pierrot, and Alexander, who stood in dread of his son, began to tremble violently as he approached, looking this way and that, as if he would avoid him. At last they came together face to face, Cesare speaking no word, but lifting his cap with a low bow. Alexander almost made a motion as if he was wringing his hands; but recovered himself with an effort, and kissed his son on the cheek.

"So do the devils kiss." Lucrezia spoke these words under her breath, and I turned sharply round and looked at her. Her eyes fell beneath my glance of inquiry, and to raise some conversation I addressed Giulia Bella.

"So that is the Duke of Valentinois?"

"Yes—and the man immediately behind him is Don Michelotto."

"The strangler."

"You use strong terms, sir," the eyes of the Farnese flashed fire, and Lucrezia added hurriedly—

"Yes, yes—you are right—the strangler."

"Hush, fool!" and Giulia Bella laid her hand on her friend's shoulder. "See, they come this way—be cool!"

In fact, Cesare had turned from his father without either of them exchanging a word, and was coming directly towards us. On the way he passed a group consisting of D'Amboise, Bayard, and the Cardinal of Strigonia. Valentinois stopped, and in his speechless way, held out his hand to Bayard, who merely bowed stiffly. Cesare's dark face whitened with rage, and dropping his hand to his side he walked straight on, and I could see that D'Amboise was expostulating with Bayard, and Strigonia openly laughing. This insult, however, had not added to Cesare's good temper; in fact, he came up to us as angry as a man could be, and after greeting his sister coldly, turned to St. Armande and looked at him in silence.

"It is usual, signore," said Don Michelotto to the chevalier, "to stand in the presence of a prince."

"I was not aware that you were a prince, sir," replied St. Armande, entirely ignoring the Borgia.

"You can give this young gentleman a lesson in manners at your leisure," said Cesare. "By your leave, sir," and giving his hand to his sister, who took it passively, he led her to another apartment, followed by Giulia Bella, who tapped a good-bye on St. Armande's arm with her closed fan.

Our group now consisted of Michelotto and myself standing, and St. Armande still sitting comfortably in the lounge, evidently examining the contour of his small and shapely foot. As for me, although I knew St. Armande to be grossly in the wrong, I was delighted with the sudden spirit he had shown. The youngster had heart, after all, and there was the making of a man in him.

Michelotto behaved with great composure.

"I trust, signore—I do not know your name—that you will give me the chance of carrying out the duke's commands."

"My name is St. Armande," replied the chevalier; "and I am ready now, if you wish it."

"This is scarcely the place, signore; but the Vatican gardens are a few feet away. If you will meet me near the summer-house, in, say, half an hour from now, it would be a convenience. If we left together perhaps it would excite remark," and the Spaniard played with the inlaid hilt of his dagger.

"Very well."

Michelotto gave St. Armande a bow, made a slight inclination towards me, and strolled off. To all intents and purposes we might have been engaged in the most friendly of conversations.

"Well, cavaliere," said St. Armande looking up at me, "are you satisfied now?"

"I am satisfied, chevalier, that you are still too young to be trusted alone. If you wanted to pick a quarrel there were a hundred courses open to you: there are fifty other men with whom you might have crossed swords with no danger except to yourself, and you must needs insult Cesare, and get embroiled with a cut-throat and risk our plans. Where is your prudence? But the wine is poured out now. You must drink."

His colour kept coming and going. "I mean to fight it out. I shall step out in ten minutes, and await him. See! they are all gathering round the tables. What with the wine and the dice, no one will take heed who goes or who comes—good-bye!" and he held out his hand to me.

"Nonsense, man—you are not going alone. You will want a second."

"But not you," he replied, "any one but you. You have work to do—not you, Savelli." His voice had almost a choke in it as he spoke.

"Come," I said, "put an end to this, or you will be run through the ribs. I am going with you."

He gave in with a feminine gesture of agreement.

"The business will not take long——"

"It will take long enough, signore, if you go as you are going," and Corte stood beside us. "Signore," he added, "I have overheard every word of the scene. Do not go as you value your lives. If you do go, go with a strong party."

"Diavolo!" I exclaimed, "an affair of the dagger then!"

St. Armande looked from one to another of us in surprise. "This is a friend, chevalier," I said, "who has done us good service," and turning to Corte, "but we must meet the man—how on earth are we to do so in any force?"

"Look round you," he made answer, "like master, like man—stroll out. You have some swords at your back. Take them with you; but better not go at all. Ah! I see my new master, the Camulengo, looking towards me—be wise and do not go," and Corte moved off to where the Cardinal Ascanio Sforze was seated, surrounded by a little group of courtiers and priests.

"Who is that man?" asked St. Armande.

"I met him under circumstances too long to tell you here," I said, "some other day you may hear all about him. We will however take his advice, and meet Don Michelotto with an extra sword or so at our backs." So saying I took his arm, and we strolled through the apartments, where every one appeared to be giving full rein to his fancy. In fact the beginning of an orgie had set in. Alexander, apparently recovered from the shock of meeting with his son, was at the gaming table, playing heavily, with Giulia Bella at his side. Bayard and Gonsalvo de Cordova were engaged in earnest converse with each other, and Strigonia and D'Amboise were cracking a flask of wine. I heard D'Este say as we passed him—"It is adieu to your eminence after to-night. I am a sheep fat enough for the shambles, and must look to my throat and my fleece."

"You would be wise Strigonia," D'Amboise made answer, "if the shield of France did not cover me, I would not be here another hour. But it is an ill thing to lose a comrade such as you."

"To better times," and the prelate who could only eat, drained his glass to the prelate who could both eat and think.

We now began to hurry a little, and found that Corte was right, for the soldiers who had lined the passage inside the Bronze Gates had taken themselves off, and a considerable numbers of servants and followers were enjoying here the results of piratical raids on the supper tables.

Outside, however, everything was in order, for De Leyva was a thorough soldier. I found both the Spaniard and De Briconnet cursing their luck at being on the guards, and attacking a capon which they were washing down with copious draughts of Falernian. Their duties kept them outside, and it was a poor supper they were making, by the light of torches, seated together on the steps of the Vatican.

"What! out already, cavlaliere?" asked De Briconnet. "Is the cardinal going?"

"No, but there is a little business," I answered as I called Jacopo.

"*Nom du diable!* Can I not come?"

"It would be a relaxation," said De Leyva.

"I am afraid not, gentlemen, although we thank you. Here, Jacopo! Get three of our fellows and follow me. Tell the others to hold their horses."

It was done in a twinkling, and in a few steps, having harked back, we were in the Papal gardens. The casino or summer-house of the Pope was in full light, and we directed our steps there without difficulty. I made two of our men walk in front, Jacopo and the third behind us, and we remained in the middle. Strict orders were given to have swords ready, and to use them at once.

Except for the moonlight, the gardens themselves were not illuminated, and as we tramped along the paths, I thought to myself how easy it would have been for Michelotto to have got rid of both St. Armande and myself, if we had been fools enough to go without escort.

Nothing happened. We reached the casino and waited there a full hour; but there was no sign of Michelotto.

At last I lost patience.

"He never meant to cross a sword with you, chevalier. I can bear witness you were here, and kept tryst. We have escaped a felon's blow however. Come back—it is getting late—even for his eminence." We turned, and made our way back, but it was a good two hours before D'Amboise retired. Bayard had gone on long before, declining all offers of escort. When we reached the palace we found he had arrived safely.

I wished St. Armande a good night, with more respect for him in my heart than I ever felt before, and turned to seek my apartments. Late as it was, however, there was to be no sleep for me, as De Briconnet, whose brain the Falernian had merely made more lively, insisted on accompanying me, and we split another flask, and talked of falconry till the verge of the morning.

CHAPTER XVIII.

THE OPAL RING.

"His eminence will await the Signor' Donati at supper this evening."

Defaure delivered his message, received his answer, and tripped away, his little page's cap set jauntily on the side of his head, and the haft of his dagger clinking against the silver chain which held it to his belt. As for me, my heart leaped at the words, for I felt sure my business was come, and summoning Jacopo, I gave him the necessary orders to have our men in readiness for an immediate start. I then sought St. Armande, and told him what I expected.

"I am ready," he said simply.

"Very well, then sup lightly, and await me in my apartments."

I turned back, and on reaching my rooms, was surprised to find I had a visitor awaiting me. It was Corte. As I have said, he had cast aside his fantastic dress, and was robed as a doctor. He still kept his heavy book under his arm, and the features of his curious seamed face, and thin bloodless lips, were as pale as if he had arisen from the dead. His eyes alone blazed with an unnatural brilliancy, but he was outwardly calm.

"I came but to see if you were safe, signore, after last night," he said as he took my hand.

"Thanks," I replied, offering him a seat, "we are all

quite safe. Nothing happened. The Don was not there, either he had changed his mind, or we were in too strong force."

"A little of both, I should think," he said with a thin smile, as he placed his book on the table. "Signore," he went on, "are you not a little surprised and curious to see me as I am?"

"Well, Messer Corte, I will own to it. But I am honestly glad that Fortune has given the wheel a right turn for you."

"It is not Fortune," he said, "it is something greater. It is Fate. No chance turn of the wheel of a sleeping goddess. When I fled from you, signore, on that day," his voice choked a little, "I came to Rome. Never mind how. Here a great man found me. Great men pick up little things for their purposes sometimes. And Matthew Corte, who is but a little man, knows things the great man does not know. Ho! ho!" and he laughed mirthlessly.

"And that has put crowns in your purse?"

"Yes, crowns in my purse, crowns in my purse," he repeated, and then the old madness came upon him, and he rose and paced the room. "I could have done it last night, made the hilt of my dagger ring against his heart —the devil—the devil. But he is not to die this way— not thus—not thus. He will die as no other man has died, and it will come soon, very soon—Matthew Corte swears this."

He stopped suddenly, and turned to me with the question:

"Have you ever seen a mad dog die?"

"No," I answered, wondering what would come next.

"Well, my dog is dead."

"I am sorry," I began, but he interrupted.

"Dead, I say. Life went from it in writhings and

twistings, in screams of agony—the little beast, poor little beast! I would have ended its misery, but I wanted to see. I wanted to find some death so horrible, that it would pass the invention of man. And I have found it, signore. See this toy of a knife! This fairy's dagger!" and he held up a tiny lancet, "only a touch of it, and a man would die as that dog did, in writhings, in twistings, in screams——"

I rose and put my hand on his arm, keeping my eyes steadily on his face.

"Corte," I said, "this is not like you. You are not well. Here is some wine," and I poured him out a goblet of Orvieto. He drained it at a gulp, and sat with his head buried in his hands.

As he sat there the scene in the lonely hut, when I went forth an outcast from Arezzo came back to me, and there rose before me the dim light of the torch, the mad figure of my host, I could almost hear the pattering of the rain and the dying hisses of the log fire without. Then I saw other things as well, and a pity came on me for the man before me. A sudden thought struck me, and acting on the impulse of the moment, I spoke.

"See here, Corte! You are ill, you want rest, quiet. Throw off these dark thoughts, and do what I say. Two miles from Colza, in the Bergamasque, lies a small farm. It is mine. Mine still, though mortgaged. Go there. Ask for the Casino Savelli, and say you have come from me—from Ugo di Savelli. You know my name now, and they will want nothing more from you. Live there until you are better, or as long as you like. The air is pure, in the hills there is the bouqueton for you to hunt, the life is good. Will you do this?"

He lifted his head, and looked at me. Then rising, he placed one hand on each of my shoulders, thin hands they were, with long bony fingers that held like claws.

"Signore," he said with emotion, "Donati or Savelli—whoever you are—you are a good man. I thank you, but it cannot be. Good-bye!" and lifting up his book, he turned and strode out of the room, leaving me a little chilled. I was glad indeed to hear De Briconnet's gay voice a moment later, as he bustled in.

"*Sacré nom du Chien!*" he exclaimed. "But who is that old madman, cavaliere, who has just left your apartments? I met him on the stairs, muttering curses that would make a dead man's hair stand on end."

"You have hit it, De Briconnet. He is a madman. I have some acquaintance with him, and his story is a sad one. I believe he has found a protector in the Cardinal Sforza."

"A queer sort of pet for his eminence to keep—thanks," and he helped himself to the Orvieto. "*Ciel!* my head still hums after last night. So your little affair was but a flash in the pan—eh?"

"Yes, there was no blood letting, as I told you last night."

"Oh, I remember—no, I forget, last night is too far back to recall anything with certainty. I want a little exercise. Take pity on me. Come to my rooms, and have a turn with the foils. I have a new pair by Castagni, the Milanese, and want to try them."

"At your service—what! Not another glass! Then come on."

It was something to do, and passed away a full hour. After that I came back to my rooms, and, with an impatient heart, waited for my meeting with D'Amboise. I saw to the packing of a valise, went down and looked at the horses, closely inspected the arms and mounts of my men, who looked capable of anything, and, in one way and another, managed to get through the time, until about the sixth hour, when his eminence supped. I presented myself punctually, and was ushered into an inner apartment which I had not hitherto seen, and where the supper was evidently to be held, for the table was set out there. I was alone at first, and seating myself on a lounge, looked about me. The room was small, but beautifully fitted up, and had all the appearance of being the cardinal's private study. By my side was a table on which was spread a map, with various crosses marked on it in red chalk, the chalk itself lying on the map, where it had been carelessly flung. In front of me was an altar, surmounted by a silver crucifix, bearing an exquisitely carved Christ. Near it, in a corner, leaned a long straight sword, from whose cross handle hung a pair of fine steel gauntlets. Resting on a cushion, placed on a stand, was the cardinal's hat, and behind the stand I could see the brown outline of a pair of riding-boots, and the glitter of burnished spurs. In a corner of the room was a large table, set out with writing materials and covered with papers. Running my eyes over these idly, I finally let them rest on the supper-table which was arranged with lavish profusion. The curtains of the windows were drawn, and the light from eight tall candles, in jewelled holders, fell on the rose and amber of the wine in the quaint flasks, on the cheerful brown crusts of the pasties, on the gay enamelling of the comfitures, and on the red gold of the plate. I noticed, too, that the table was set for three only. It was evidently a private supper, where things were to be discussed, and I became glad, for I felt already a step onwards towards winning back my name, and—I seemed to see in the mirror on the wall to my left, a vision of a woman with dark hair, and dark eyes——

"Your eminence!" I fairly started up. I had not observed the entrance of D'Amboise, until he stood beside me, and touched me lightly on the shoulder.

"Dreaming, cavaliere! I did not think you were so given. I am afraid that, late as I am, I must still keep you from your supper, for I expect another guest. Ha! there he is!"

Indeed, as he spoke the door swung open noiselessly, and Machiavelli entered. He was plainly and simply dressed, and wore no sword, merely a dagger at his side. I thought, however, I caught the gleam of a steel corselet under his vest, as he greeted the cardinal, and D'Amboise's own sapphire was not more brilliant, than the single opal which blazed on the secretary's hand.

"This is the Cavaliere Donati, your excellency," said the cardinal, " but I think you know each other."

Machiavelli extended his hand to me, with his inscrutable smile; but as I met his eyes, I saw that they were troubled and anxious. He, however, spoke with easy unconcern.

"Well met, Messer Donati. I can only say I am sorry we parted so soon. I would have given much to have had you in Florence for a few days more."

"Your excellency is most kind."

"St. Dennis!" said the cardinal, "but are you gentlemen going to exchange compliments, and starve instead of sitting to supper. Burin, are we not ready?" and he turned to his grey-haired major-domo, who had entered the room.

"Your eminence is served," replied the man, and we took our seats on each side of the table, D'Amboise between us.

"You need not wait, Burin, but remain in the passage." Burin stepped out silently, and the cardinal said with an air of apology, "You must not mind so informal a repast, gentlemen; but we have much to discuss—pleasure first, however—my maitre d'hotel has an artist's soul, and he will have a fit if we do not touch this pasty."

The cardinal ate and talked. I now and then put in a word, but the secretary was very silent, and hardly touched anything.

"St. Dennis!" said D'Amboise, "but your excellency is a poor trencherman. And I heard so much of you!"

"Your eminence will excuse me, when I say I have had bad news."

D'Amboise became grave at once. "Let me say how sorry I am. It is not a matter of state?" and he glanced meaningly at the secretary.

"Not in the least; but much worse—a domestic matter. I do not see why I should not tell you. That cursed brigand Baglioni has seized on my ward Angiola Castellani, and holds her a fast prisoner in Perugia."

I felt cold all over to my feet.

"The Lady Angiola?" I exclaimed.

"Precisely," said Machiavelli, drily; "I think you have met."

"But this can be easily remedied," burst in D'Amboise; "a demand from the Signory, a word from France."

"Will not bring the dead to life again," put in the secretary.

"My God!" I burst out, "she is not dead?"

"Worse than that," he said; "it was done by Cesare's orders."

"Then Cesare Borgia will pay with his life for this," I exclaimed.

At this moment there was a knock at the door, and Burin entered, bearing a silver flagon, the stopper of which was made of a quaintly-carved dragon.

"Your eminence ordered this with the second service," he said, placing it before D'Amboise, and retiring.

"I pledge you my word, your excellency, that I will not rest until full reparation has been made for this outrage on an ally of France," said D'Amboise. "I could almost find it in my heart to let loose open war for this."

"We are not ready, your eminence. Rest assured of my thanks, and I will gladly accept your aid; but at present we can do nothing. This, however, has not decreased my zeal for the measures we are planning; and with your permission we will now discuss these, and put aside my private trouble."

For me, I could hardly breathe. A hundred feelings were tossing together within me, all that I could think of was to throw aside everything, to gallop to Perugia, to save her at any cost. The cardinal's voice came to me as from a distance.

"I agree—one glass each of this all round, and then—cavaliere, would you mind handing me those glasses?"

Three peculiar shaped, straw-coloured Venetian glasses were close to me, these I passed onwards mechanically to D'Amboise, and he went on, filling the glasses to the brim with wine from the flagon, as he spoke.

"I admired the rare workmanship of this flagon last night, and his holiness sent it home with me, full to the brim with this Falernian, which Giulia Bella herself poured into it. The wine is of a priceless brand, and our lord was good enough to say, that if I liked it, he would send me all in his cellars if I only let him know."

"We will drink this then, with your eminence's permission, to the success of the undertaking," said the secretary, poising his glass in the air.

"Right," said D'Amboise. "Gentlemen, success to our venture!"

He raised the wine to his lips. I silently did the same.

"Hold!"

We stopped in amaze, and Machiavelli, who had spoken, quietly emptied his glass into a bowl beside him.

"What does this mean?" said the cardinal.

"This, your eminence," and Machiavelli held out his hand, on which an opal was flashing a moment before. The stone was still there, in the gold band on his finger; but it was no longer an opal, but something black as jet, devoid of all lustre.

Startled by the movement, D'Amboise bent over the extended fingers, and I followed his example. The red on the cardinal's cheek went out, and his lips paled as he looked at the ring.

"Poison! Heart of Jesus!" he muttered through pale lips.

"Yes," said Machiavelli, slowly, withdrawing his hand, "the ring tells no lies. *Diavolo!* Was ever so grim a jest? Asking you to tell him if your eminence liked the wine!"

It was too near a matter to be pleasant, and the hideous jest, and the treachery of Alexander, filled me with a hot anger. It had the effect however of pulling me together at once, the sudden presence of death, and the danger, recalling me to myself, for all my thoughts of Angiola. I breathed a prayer of thanks for our escape. It was a good omen. My luck was not yet run out.

D'Amboise sprang to his feet. "By God!" he said, bringing his clenched fist into the palm of his hand, "the Borgia will rue this day; here, give me those glasses." He seized them, and drawing back the curtains flung them out of the window, where they fell into the court outside, breaking to splinters with a little tinkling crash. Then he emptied out the contents of the flagon, and hurled it into the grate where it lay, its fine work crushed and dented, the two emerald eyes of the dragon on the stopper blinking at us wickedly. This outburst made D'Amboise calmer, and it was with more composure that he struck a small gong, and reseated himself at the table. As he did so Burin entered the room.

"We want a clear table," said the cardinal, "remove these things, and hand me that map."

By the time Burin had done this, his eminence showed no further trace of excitement, except that his lips were very firmly set, and there was a slight frown on his forehead as he smoothed out the roll of the map. One corner kept obstinately turning up, and as Machiavelli quietly put his hand on it to keep it in position, he said, "See! The ring is as it was before."

We looked at the opal, and sure enough the poison-tint was gone, and under the pale, semi-opaque blue of its surface, lights of red, of green, and of orange, flitted to and fro.

"It is wonderful," I said, and D'Amboise smiled grimly to himself. The cardinal placed his finger on the map, where the port of Sinigaglia was marked.

"Is it here he lands?"

"Yes," replied Machiavelli, "and then straight to Rome."

"You have sure information?"

"Yes."

"Then will your excellency instruct M. Donati? As arranged, I pledge an immediate movement on the part of Tremouille, at the first sign of success."

"You have agreed, cavaliere, to undertake the task?" and the secretary turned to me.

"I have, your excellency."

Machiavelli then went on, speaking incisively, wasting no words. "In ten days or thereabouts from now, Monsignore Bozardo, the Papal envoy to the Grand Turk, will land at Sinigaglia and start for Rome. He brings with him a letter and a sum of money, forty thousand ducats. These are for his holiness. Bozardo and the letter may reach, if you like; the ducats must not."

"Where are they to go?"

"To the Duke de la Tremouille."

"I follow."

"Understand that you take this venture at your own risk."

I saw what he meant, if I failed I was to be sacrificed, and my mind was made up. I would accept, with a condition.

"I quite understand—there is one thing."

"What?"

"Ten days is a wide margin. I will stop Bozardo or die; but I propose effecting the release of the Lady Angiola as well."

A glad look came into Machiavelli's eyes; but the cardinal flashed out—

"*Nom du diable!* What grasshopper have you got in your head? Leave the demoiselle to us. You cannot do two things at once."

"Then with respect to your eminence I decline the affair of the ducats."

D'Amboise looked at me in sheer amazement.

"You decline—you dare;" but Machiavelli interposed.

"A moment, your eminence. Can we get another agent?"

"Not now; it is too late now."

"And we have no money for active measures?"

"Not a livre."

"It seems to me that the cavaliere has us in his hands, and we had better agree. After all he only risks his head twice, instead of once."

D'Amboise bit his lip, and with a frown began to drum on the table with his fingers. I sat silent but resolved, and Machiavelli, rising, went to the writing table, pulling out from his vest a parchment. In this he rapidly wrote something, and dusting it over with drying powder held it to the flame of a candle. Then he turned back leisurely, and, as he resumed his seat, handed me the paper.

"I have just filled in your name on this blank safe-conduct through the Papal States. I took the precaution of obtaining this from Sforza to-day. When can you start?"

"Now, your excellency," and I put the safe-conduct securely by.

"I suppose I must agree," said the cardinal suddenly. "If it fails, all is lost; if it succeeds——"

"There will probably be a new Conclave, your eminence," said Machiavelli.

D'Amboise's forehead flushed dark at the hidden meaning in the Florentine's words. But we all knew that the chair of St. Peter was ever before his eyes; and for this he schemed and saved, although profuse in his habits. George of Amboise never gained his desire; but when he died he left a fortune of eleven millions. This however was yet to be.

I had already arisen to take my leave as Machiavelli spoke, and the cardinal, taking no notice of his last remark, turned to me, with something of his old good temper. Perhaps the hint of Florentine support at the next papal election was not without its softening effect.

"Did I understand you to say you were ready to start at once, cavaliere?"

"Yes, your eminence."

"Then let me wish you good fortune—adieu!"

"Your eminence has my grateful thanks."

I bowed to D'Amboise and the secretary, and withdrew; but as the door swung behind me, I heard Machiavelli's voice.

"The air of Rome does not suit me, your eminence. No, thanks. No more Falernian."

CHAPTER XIX.

EXIT THE ANCIENT BRICO.

I HAD gained my point without waste of words or time, but it was to be my way or not at all. My lady was in dire peril. Against this could I for a moment weigh any thought of myself? What cared I whether France, Spain, or the Borgia ruled in Italy? What mattered it to me whether one crafty statesman held the reins of power, or another outdid him in craft and filched away his bone? My lady was in danger, and my honour might rot, and the Most Christian, the Most Catholic, and Most Holy wolves might tear each other's throats out before I would move a finger, take one step, until she was free. If I had to pull down Baglioni's hold with my hands, I would free her. If a hair of her head was injured I should take such vengeance as man never heard of, and then—my foot caught in the carpeting of the passage, I tripped up and fell heavily, the shock sending stars before my eyes.

"Too much haste, cavaliere," and a hand helped me to rise. As I gained my feet I saw Machiavelli beside me.

"I followed you at once," he said, "but you went so fast, I had missed you but for that lucky trip. A word more—if you free her, take her to the convent of St. Jerome, two miles north-west of Magione—the abbess will do the rest. I will see to that."

"Very well. God grant I succeed!"

"Amen to that," and Machiavelli took my hand. "Adieu, cavaliere, once again, I must go back to his eminence, we have a point or two to discuss yet, but no more Falernian. *Corpo di Bacco!* I grow cold when I think of our escape."

"Good-bye, your excellency," and we parted.

I went on with a little more care, and being a trifle cooled by my fall, was able to think better. By the time I reached my apartments I had decided on my route. I should leave by the Porta del Popolo, keep on the right bank of the river as far as Borghetto, there cross the Tiber, and on to Perugia in a straight line by Narni and Todi. It was close on three and thirty leagues; but I did not mean to spare horseflesh. As I reached the entrance which led to my rooms, I found Jacopo and my men ready, and Castor whinnied a glad welcome, pawing at the air with his forefoot in his impatience. St. Armande and the abbé, already mounted and attended by a couple of men, were a little to the right.

"I will not keep you a moment, chevalier," I called out as I passed him, and running up the stairs to my room, began to dress rapidly. Jacopo attended me, and as he handed me my sword, pointed to the open window.

"A fair night for a long ride, excellency!"

"Yes, the moon stands well—my cloak—quick," and we descended the stairs.

"All ready, Jacopo?"

"Your excellency."

"Steady, Castor," and I swung into the saddle.

There was the jingle of bit chains, the clank of steel scabbards, the ring of iron-shod hoofs on the pavement, and with St. Armande by my side and my troop behind me, I left the Palazzo Corneto.

To avoid risk of stoppage I did not go down by the

Alessandrina to the Ponte di San Angelo, but determined to cross at the Ripetta. Therefore, crossing the Borgi di San Angelo, we went northwards by the V. d. Tre Papazzi, up the Via Cancellieri, and then turning to the right, rode up the Via Crescenzio. To our right, as we rode, the moon hung over San Angelo and the dark outlines of the gloomy stronghold loomed like a vast shadow of evil above us. In front of us lay the Tiber, and the long line of fires of the charcoal-burners. The latter overhung by a blue cloud of smoke, into which the forked flames leaped and danced. At the bridge we were stopped by the guard, but the safe-conduct set us free, and we crossed at a slow pace. Above the hollow beat of the horses' hoofs, I heard the waters churning around the piers, and looking over the side, saw the grey river as it hummed past below me, flecked with white foam-tipped waves, chasing each other in lines of light across its surface, or, as they broke, catching the moon rays, and dying in a hundred colours with an angry hiss.

Over the bridge at last! And here Jacopo with a sudden " *Cospitto!* " put spurs to his horse, and galloped off down the Via Toma. So unexpected was the movement, that it almost brought us to a halt, and St. Armande called out—

" He is gone! "

" Not he, chevalier," I answered, " come on," and turning to the left we trotted up the Ripetta. I knew Jacopo too well not to feel sure he would catch us up again, and that he had some definite object, which was not desertion, in going off as he did. Yet I could not help being put out by his action, and resolved to give him the rough side of my tongue when he came back. We were almost up to the Porta del Popolo when he returned, coming with a loose rein, and as he drew in with the troop, I turned round.

"How now, sirrah! What does this prank mean?"

"Pardon, excellency, it was no bee that stung me. I suddenly remembered that we should have little luck on our journey if I did not pay her dues to our Lady of the Fountain."

"Our Lady of the Fountain?"

"Excellency, the fountain of Trevi. Does not your worship know that no one should leave Rome without dropping a piece of silver in her basin?"

"Indeed! I was not aware of it, but remember—no more sudden thoughts like this."

"Excellency!"

I said no more, and passing through the ruined Porta del Popolo where the breaches made by Charles' cannon were still unrepaired, we took the Flaminian Way, and galloped down the road almost in darkness owing to the shadows thrown by the high walls on each side of us. We recrossed the Tiber at the Ponte Molle, and, still keeping the Via Flaminia, turned our horses' heads in the direction of Castel Nuovo.

It was a wonderful night. There was no breeze, except that which we made ourselves as we galloped along. Not a cloud obscured the sky, arching deep blue over the yellow moon, now in her full strength. To the left the beacon fire from the top of the Tor di Vergara blazed like a red star low down in the horizon, and before us was the white road stretching in a ghostly line, its ups and downs accentuated by the moonlight. The Tiber lay to our right, but owing to the undulation of the ground we could not see it, although an occasional flash showed us where the waters reflected the rays of the moon.

Not the best horse in the world could keep up the pace we were going for long, and I was old enough soldier to know that our speed must be regulated by the slowest beast if we wanted to reach in full strength, so I slackened rein to a walk and gave the animals a rest.

Excepting once, when Jacopo rode off to make his duty to the Fountain of Trevi, I had not exchanged a word with St. Armande, indeed I was in no mind to talk; but he broke the silence with a question.

"Do we ride all night, cavaliere?"

"We have many leagues to go, St. Armande."

"*Ciel!*" he muttered under his breath, and I heard the abbé as he leaned forward whisper, "Courage! would you give way now? Courage!"

Clearly there was a mystery here to which I had no clue, and it troubled me. I glanced at St. Armande, and through the moonlight saw the white of his cheek, showing all the paler for the black patch he wore transversely across it; but looking at him did not explain matters.

"What the devil does this mean?" I said half aloud to myself.

"Did you speak?"

"Merely something to myself, chevalier. *Diavolo!* But this is a dull ride."

"Do you think so?" and his tone softened suddenly.

I made no reply, but stirred up Castor, and we jogged along. I left the mystery to take care of itself, and mapped out a line of action. I would take only two men with me into Perugia, and send the rest with St. Armande to the convent of St. Jerome to await the result of my attempt to free Angiola. It sounded like foolishness to give St. Armande the control of the stronger party, especially if he meant treachery; but this I was persuaded he did not. On the other hand a following of six troopers was a trifle too many to pay a peaceful visit to Baglioni, and might arouse suspicion, while they were too few to attempt open force. In short, if I could not do what I wanted with two men, I would not be able to effect it with six or a dozen, and made up my mind to split our party, either after crossing the Paglia, or beyond at San Fortunato.

In this manner, sometimes galloping, sometimes trotting, and at other times walking our horses to give them a rest, we reached Castel Nuovo but did not enter the town, skirting it by our right, although one of the troopers suggested our going westwards by Campagnano, a useless detour as it seemed to me. We passed the little town exactly at midnight, and the chime of bells striking the hour fell pleasantly on our ears. A short way beyond we found the road so cut into ruts and fissures that it was not possible to go at any other than a snail's pace, so that within the next two hours we barely covered as many leagues. The moon was now on the wane, the road became worse, and one or two of the horses showed signs of fatigue. Jacopo rode up beside me.

"By your leave, excellency! We have the road by Soratte to cross soon, and in the coming darkness may possibly lose our way. I would suggest, therefore, that we halt here until dawn. It will rest the horses, and with the light we could press on."

"Very well. Hark! Is not that the sound of water?"

"Yes, your worship."

"Then we will stop there."

A few yards beyond we came to a ruined temple, near which a fountain was bubbling. Here I gave the order to halt, and in less time than I take to write this, the troopers had sprung to earth, the saddle-girths were loosened, and all the preparations for a two hours' halt begun.

I shared a little wine with St. Armande and the abbé, and the former, rolling himself up in his cloak, leaned his back against a fallen pillar, and seemed to drop off at once into sleep.

The abbé followed his example; but my mind was too impatient for rest, and I walked up and down, watching the ending of the moon, until it finally sank out of sight, and darkness fell upon us.

Dark as it was around me, my mind was in a still greater darkness, for I was unable to think of any plan by which I could gain access to Angiola, after reaching Perugia. Time, too, was short; but that did not matter, for I was prepared to let the affair of the ducats slide, rather than lose any chance of rescuing her.

A straw yet remained. Luck might be on my side; and with luck and a strong heart one might do anything. There was nothing for it but to content myself for the present with this. Until I reached Perugia I could develop no plan. So I paced up and down with an unsettled mind, and finally, seating myself on a stone, awaited the morning, alternately nodding and awakening with a start.

At last! The east began to whiten, and getting up stiffly, I touched Jacopo with the end of my sword. He jumped up with an exclamation, and recognising me, began to apologise. This I cut short, and bade him arouse the men.

"This instant, your worship. *Cospetto!* To think I should have overslept myself! Ho, sluggards! Buffaloes! Awake! Think you that you are going to snore here all night?" and he began to stir the men up. They rose willingly enough, with tremendous yawnings, and stretching of arms, and we were soon on the march again, through the increasing daylight.

The coming day seemed to warm the hearts of the men, and one of them broke into song, the chorus being taken up by the others as we jogged along. When this had lasted some little time, I gave Castor's reins a shake, and off we went at a smart gallop.

Shortly after passing San Oreste the road led along the side of Soratte, and, the morning being young, besides very bright and clear, we had a glorious view. To the left lay Civita Castellana, the walls of the new citadel standing high above the town, which lay in the middle of a network of deep ravines; to the right and behind us the Sabine Hills extended in long, airy lines, and the wooded heights of Pellachio and San Gennaro, where, close to Palembara, was an old castle of our house, rose to the south-east. Above us was the monastery of St. Silvestre, and Soratte itself reached towards where Borghetto stood, on a bend of the Tiber, in a series of descending peaks. Cool puffs of air caught us, and freshened the horses as well as our hearts, and it was a cheery party that finally reached the Ponte Felice, and entered the town. Here our safe-conduct again stood us in good stead. Indeed, we had difficulty in getting away, for the Captain Lippi, who held Borghetto for the Borghia, wished to press his hospitality on us for a few days; but on my eventually taking him aside, and whispering to him that I was bound on a confidential mission, he gave in, but with some little reluctance. He, however, invited us to share his table at dinner. I accepted, but St. Armande, who was looking very wearied, declined, and dined quietly with the abbé at the "Silver Eel," where I quartered my men.

Lippi was an old soldier risen from the ranks, with a head more full of drill than suspicion; but in order to remove any such weed that might be growing there, I affected to be so delighted with his conversation at dinner, that I begged the favour of his accompanying me for a league or so on my way, after we had dined. To this he agreed with alacrity, and I was subsequently sorry for my pains, for the old bore did not quit me until we had all but reached the Nera, and saw the campanile of St. Juvenalis rising above Narni. We did this portion of the journey at a rapid pace, as I wanted, if possible, to shake off the captain, but, mounted on an Apulian, he stuck to me like a burr, dinning into my ears his opinion as to how the cross-bow was a weapon as superior to the arquebus as the mangonel was above even Novarro's new cannon. At length he wished us the day and departed, and the horses, scenting the end of their day's journey, put on fresh speed as we galloped through the oaks that studded the valley of the Nera. The river here was hemmed into a narrow ravine, and crossing by an ancient bridge of three spans, supposed to have been built by the Romans, we climbed up the steep ascent that led to Narni, and there found food and lodging for both man and beast, at an albergo, the name of which, somehow, I have forgotten. St. Armande was quite worn out, and I saw he was unfitted for any long strain. We supped together, and he retired almost at once. After supper I had a detailed examination of the horses, and found that one of them had a sore back. The trooper who owned him, vowed he would not part with him, so I had to dismiss the man, which I did. This reduced my fighting strength to six men, including Jacopo. I did not include St. Armande and his followers in estimating this, putting them down to so much encumbrance, of which I would soon take care to be rid. I was anxious, however, to hurry on, and so altered my original plans a little, and in the morning, after we had gone about a league, I turned to St. Armande, and said:

"Chevalier, it is necessary for me to press on with all speed. I want you, therefore, to do me a favour."

"Anything you like, cavaliere; but we do not part, do we?"

"It is this. I am going on at once; I want you to take four of my troopers, and with your own following make for the convent of St. Jerome. It lies a little beyond Magione. Your arrival will be expected. If not, say you are awaiting me. Await me for a week. If I do not come then, go back to Rome, and tell the cardinal what you have done."

"But I thought I was to go with you, and share your adventure."

"I give you my word of honour, St. Armande, that you will share in the adventure for which I agreed you should come—share up to the elbows—but you will spoil everything if you do not do what I say."

"There is no danger to you?"

"No more than there is to you; in one word, St. Armande, do you agree or not?"

"Very well."

"Then there is no time to lose. Jacopo!"

"Excellency."

"Pick out a man, and he, you, the lackey, and myself, will go on ahead. The rest can follow. I have given all other orders to the signor, St. Armande."

"There is Bande Nere, your worship."

"I am ready, cavaliere;" and a tall, thin, grey-moustached trooper saluted as he spoke.

He looked the man I wanted. My lackey was a stout horseman, and at a pinch might hold a sword as well as he held my valise. So, shaking hands with St. Armande, I put spurs to Castor, and we dashed off. Turning the corner of a belt of forest land, I looked back and waved my hand in further adieu to the chevalier. I caught the flutter of the white handkerchief the young dandy carried, as he loosed it to the air in reply to my salute, and the next moment the trees hid them from view.

We rode hard now, Castor going almost as freely as when we started. Indeed, I would have far outpaced the others, if I did not let him feel the bit once, and the noble beast, as if knowing his duty, required no further warning not to outstrip his companions.

Going as we were now Perugia was but a few hours away; but the pace was too great to last long, and from Todi to Perugia there were nine leagues and a trifle over of an ascending road. Castor might do it, the others I was sure would not. In order, therefore, to rest the horses, as well as to avoid question, I resolved that we should dine at Rosaro, and after an hour or so of rest press forwards, passing by Todi, and travelling all night, so as to reach Perugia in the morning. If we went faster, we would only reach at night, and so late as to find entrance into the town impossible.

We clattered past the villages of San Gemini and Castel Todino, and about noon drew up our now somewhat blown beasts at the gates of the "Man-at-Arms," the only inn in the village.

It was a poor place I saw at a glance, and as we pulled up, a crowd of yokels in holiday attire gathered around us. The inn seemed full, too, for the yard swarmed with people, and a half-score heads of contadini were at each window, staring at us open-eyed.

As I took this in, the landlord came running out, cap in hand and full of apologies.

"*Ohime!* But my house is full to the garrets, signore; and it is nothing I can do for you to-day. To-morrow is the feast of St. Mary of the Consolation, and all the country is going to Todi——"

"I do not want to stay. We merely halt here to bait our horses and to dine. Can you not manage that?"

"If that is all, excellency, yes, oh, yes. The beasts, they can rest anywhere, and there is a polenta and room for your excellency's followers; but for yourself, signore," and he shook his head mournfully.

"What is the difficulty?" And I dismounted, my men following suit.

"But this, signore. There is but one room in the house you could use, and that is occupied by two gentlemen of the army. Violent men, signore, who will not allow any one to share it. *Lasso me!* But not a paul have they paid me as yet!"

"Give them my compliments, and say that the Cavaliere Donati begs to be allowed a corner of their table for his dinner."

"Alas, signore! It is useless. They have been here two days——"

"Then it is time they made room for other travellers. Give my message, landlord, and say I am following."

Mine host trotted off with considerable misgivings expressed in his face, and followed by my lackey, bearing my valise, I went after him at a slower pace.

When I reached the room, which could hardly be missed, seeing it was the only one in the house that had any pretence of appearance, I found the door open, and heard a half-drunken voice shouting:

"Begone, dog! Blood of a king! But are two gentlemen to be disturbed because a signore with a long name wants to dine? Skull of St. Jerome! Did you ever hear the like of this? *Cospetto!* Tell him to go hang, or I'll spit him like a lark."

I heard enough to recognise the voice, and turning to the lackey said:

"Send Jacopo here at once with a stout cudgel—run."

The man went off on the double, and I remained without the door listening with amusement to the ancient Brico's bluster, for it was he, and he was having all the talk, his companion, whoever he was, now and then giving a grunt of assent.

"Mitre and cowl! Hell and sulphur! Will you begone, fool, or shall I slit your windpipe?" and I heard him beat the table with his fist. "Out, rascal," he roared, "and bring in another skin of chianti."

Out came the wretched inn-keeper, and seeing me at the door began to urge me to go; but at this moment Jacopo came running up with a stout stick in his hand, and pushing the landlord on one side I stepped into the room, followed by Jacopo.

Brico's friend, who was quite drunk as it seemed, had fallen asleep whilst he was talking, and lay with his head between his arms, half on the table, half on his chair. The ancient was seated with an empty skin before him, and rose in wrath as I entered.

"What the——," he began in a wine-blown voice, and then his face paled a little as he saw me.

I did not waste words. "Cudgel me this fellow out, Jacopo," I said, and Jacopo attended to the task as if he loved it. The ancient attempted to draw his sword, but it was useless, and a minute or two later he was flung out into the courtyard, beaten to a jelly and howling for mercy. He lay where he was flung, too bruised to move.

His friend slept through it all; but as my lackey lifted up his head in an attempt to eject him, I recognised Piero Luigi, and felt that some more stringent action than I had taken with Brico should be adopted here.

"This man is a thief," I said to the landlord, "and his friend little better."

"Then to the stocks they go; and now," almost screamed the host, "not a paul have they paid me, signore, I swear this, the bandits. Hi! Giuseppe! Giovanni!"

A couple of stout knaves came running in, and the inn-keeper, trembling with anger and fear combined, yelled out:

"Bind this brigand and his companion securely, keep them in the stables, and to-morrow we will hale them before the podesta."

I enjoyed my dinner comfortably, and on going out to see after the horses was met by Bande Nere, who took me aside to where, in a corner of the stables, two men were lying securely bound. One was Luigi, still happily drunk. The other was the ancient, whose bones must have ached sorely, for he had been beaten sober, and was feeling the full effect of the cudgel and the ropes. He was groaning terribly, and, being sorry for the wretch, I was about to intercede for him with the landlord, when Jacopo interposed with a whispered—

"Let the scotched snake lie, signore, he knows too much."

I let wisdom take its course, and left the ancient to his sorrows.

CHAPTER XX.

"A BROWN PAUL—A LITTLE COPPER."

SUCH as they were, the troubles of the ancient and his crony Luigi could not have ended soon, for although at first they were surrounded by a jeering crowd, fresh things caught the minds of the people after a little time, and they were left to themselves. As the following day was a holiday in Todi, the inn-keeper probably let them lie bound until he had more leisure on his hands, which were in truth full enough, as the albergo hummed with custom. I never heard or saw anything more of either of the villains again. We had time yet at our disposal; but after an early supper, the horses being rested, we started, and going slowly, with a halt on the right bank of the Paglia, we crossed the Tiber near San Fortunato, and Perugia lay before us, bright in the sunshine. In order to throw any pursuit off the scent, for if by chance inquiries were made about us, they would be at the southern gates, we made a turn east, then struck north, and getting over the numberless trenches lying between us and our point, eventually entered the city by the Porta del Carmine. Here Jacopo, under my secret instructions, let the guard handle his wine-skin, buzzing out as if in the confidence of the cup, that we had come from Fabriano in the Marches and then gave them the day. We rode on, leaving the ward at the gate to finish the skin, and found very comfortable house-room in the Rubicon, an hotel kept by Messer Passaro, which lay behind the house of the Piccinino family, "close to the Duomo, the citadel, and the gallows," as the landlord, who thought himself a merry wag, informed me whilst he received us at his door. I took the best room available for myself, and saw to the wants of my followers and the horses, who were as well as when they started. I left them in comfort, bidding Bande Nere make ready to accompany me out at noontide. Dinner I ordered at twelve, inviting the landlord to crack a flask of his best thereafter with me. He accepted with effusion; my object in doing this being to try and get as much information out of him as possible, as I saw he had a loose tongue and a gossiping heart, and I was resolved to leave no stone unturned in my search for Angiola. It wanted two hours or more for dinner, and having bathed and changed my attire, I sank me down in an arm-chair to enjoy an hour or so of repose.

After dinner mine host appeared, bearing with him a cob-webbed flask.

"It is a wine of France, excellency—Burgundy—and all my customers do not taste this, I can tell you."

"I am favoured, indeed, Messer Passaro; take a seat, and help yourself."

"The condescension of your excellency!" and with a bow he settled himself on the extreme edge of a chair.

We poured out our measures, and on testing the wine I found it most excellent; as for Passaro, he pushed himself back into his seat and let the liquid down his throat in drops, his eyes closed in an ecstacy. When he opened them, which he did after a time, he gasped out:

"Is not that glorious, signore? Have you ever lipped the brand?"

"I confess it is wine for the gods," I said. "Is there much in your cellar."

"Store of it, excellency; I was not butler to His Eminence of Strigonia for ten years for nothing."

"His eminence is a fine judge of wines."

"*Cospitto!* And your excellency's forgiveness for swearing. He is the finest judge in the world. There is no brand he could not name, nay, tell you the year of vintage, were he blindfold and a drop but touched his palate. *Corpo di Bacco!* But he is a true prince of the Church."

"Ah! you are a sly dog, Messer Passaro," and I filled him his glass; "I warrant me you could tell many a tale of the cardinal. But come now, has not the Baglioni as fine a taste in wines, and a better one for a neat ankle?"

"Hush!" he said, looking around him as he put down his empty glass, "in your ear, excellency—the Count Carlo has big teeth and bites hard. Let your tongue be still when his name comes up in Perugia."

"Thanks, friend, but Count Carlo owes me no grudge, or else I should not be here."

"Your worship has come to join him then?"

"As you see, Messer Passaro," and I filled his glass again, "I am a soldier and love to serve a soldier. Besides things will be on foot soon, for what with the French at Passignano, war cannot be delayed long."

"True, and a light has been put to the torch too."

"Hurrah! Another glass, man; we soldiers are sick of this truce. Our purses run dry in peace. But tell me."

"You must know, signore, that all the country east of Castiglione to the Tiber, and lying between the Nestore and Casale, is a fief of the Castellani, and the Count—ha! ha! It was glorious!" and he slapped his thigh—"ha! ha!"

Nothing irritates me so much as to hear a man laughing aimlessly, and it was in a sharp tone that I said, "go on."

"A moment, excellency," and he held up a fat hand, "ha! ha! I had it all from Messer Lambro, my cousin, and groom of the chambers to Count Carlo. Well, all the fief I spoke of is inherited by the Lady Angiola, the daughter of old Count Adriano. The family is Ghibelline, and have taken the French side, and seeing that Tremouille was between us and Casale, my lady must needs go down to visit her estates. The Count, who is looking for a wife, buckles on his armour, mounts his mare, and with two hundred lances at his back, gallops up the left bank of the Tiber, fords the stream, swoops down on the dovecote at Rossino, and brings back a bride to Perugia; ha! ha! It is superb."

"Ha! ha! Messer Passaro—diavolo! Are they married yet?"

"Not yet—ah! The wine is wine for the gods as your worship says—not married yet, for my lady is half beside herself they say, and the Count, receiving a sudden message from Cesare, has had to leave Perugia for a few days."

"*Cospitto!* How he must curse the Borgia for putting off his happiness! And she is handsome, eh?"

"For the matter of that, excellency, one does not squint at a sour face set in a golden coif. But they do say the lady is very beautiful."

"You have not seen her then?"

"*Corpo di Bacco!* She is under lock and key, and not for the likes of me to look upon."

"In the citadel I suppose—a gloomy cage for a fair bird."

"Maybe, but I have let my tongue wag too freely, signore, and must be going."

"Safe enough with me, Messer Passaro, for I am on the right side—adieu!"

I made no further attempt to detain him, and he waddled off with the best part of the now empty flask under his belt. I was sure he knew but little more, and what I had got out of him did not amount to much. At any rate I had discovered that Baglioni was out of Perugia, and that she was still here. This was better than nothing; but worse than nothing if I could not discover the place of her imprisonment. I threw myself back in my chair, and racked my brains to no purpose. There was nothing definite for me to get hold of, no clue of any kind. I thought of getting the landlord to invite the Count's valet to drink a bottle or so of his Burgundy with me, but the mere whisper of such a thing would excite suspicion of a further object, and the slightest suspicion would ruin the business. Bande Nere appearing at this time, in accordance with my orders, I resolved to hang about the Palazzo Publico, and see if I could pick up any information there. On second thoughts I resolved to go alone, and dismissing Bande Nere, sallied forth by myself. I went by way of the Piazza del Duomo, and here I stopped in an idle manner, and was for a moment struck by the entrance to the palace, which lies here. Over the gate was a splendid bronze of a lion and a griffin, set above a series of chains and bars of gates, trophies of an old victory gained over the Sienese. A crowd of beggars surrounded me, but I was in no mood for charity, and drove them off with a rough oath. One of the number, however, remained. He was lame in both feet, supported himself on crutches, and wore a huge patch over one of his eyes.

"That is right, excellency—drive them off—the scum, the goats—pestering every noble gentleman. It is only to the deserving your excellency will give—a paul, excellency—a brown copper for the poor cripple—a million thanks, excellency—may this copper be increased to you a thousandfold in gold."

"Begone, fool!" I said, and walked on; but he hobbled along at a great rate beside me.

"But a favour, excellency. If your worship would but come with me, I would show you a wonderful sight. A bird-cage, excellency; would your lordship be pleased to buy a bird—"

I turned round in my anger, and raised my hand to cuff the rascal's ears, cripple though he was, when he suddenly added: "Or *free* a bird, excellency—there is someone coming—a paul, quick—thanks, excellency—may your lordship die a prince."

As he spoke a couple of gentlemen and their servants pushed by us, and I gave them the road, the beggar hopping nimbly to my side. My heart was beating rapidly, and all my blood tingling. Was I on the edge of a discovery?

"No more riddles," I said, "who are you?"

"It is not safe to talk here, signore," he answered. "Follow me." He started off across the square, hobbling along on his crutches and wailing out, "A copper for the poor cripple—a brown paul—a little copper?"

"By God!" I exclaimed to myself as I followed behind, "what does this mean?" I had to find out for myself, however, and followed the man, who stumped along at a rare pace, notwithstanding the ups and downs of the side-streets by which we went. He never once looked behind him, but kept up his cry of "a copper for the poor cripple —a brown paul—a little copper," and once or twice, when I lost him in the crowd, the cry served as a signal to me telling me where he went. Finally he turned to the left, and on reaching the Via della Conca, made straight for the gate. Here a toll was collected, and paying his paul he went straight out of the town. I kept him in view now easily, and could have caught him up as I liked, for the speed at which he had hobbled along had no doubt breathed him. At last he left the road, and toiling somewhat painfully over the very uneven ground, vanished behind a spur of the hills on which Perugia is situated. I now put on my best walking pace, and in a minute or two turned the elbow of the spur myself, and found the mendicant seated on a stone mopping his brow, his crutches lying beside him. He stood up with the greatest ease as I approached.

"Well, fellow," I said, "what does all this mean? Beware, if you have attempted to trick me."

"Does not your excellency know me?"

"Never saw you before."

"I am Gian, excellency."

"Gian! Gian! That throws no light on the subject."

"The cavaliere remembers the garden of St. Michael in Florence?"

I was not likely to forget the place where I had received Angiola from Luigi, but I could not connect the man before me with the circumstance. "I remember perfectly, but I do not know you. Drop this foolery and speak plainly."

"I am speaking plainly, signore. I was not sure if it was you myself until now. I am Gian, the Lady Angiola's servant, and his excellency the secretary has sent me to you."

"But how did you hear I was in Perugia: his excellency did not himself know I was coming here until a half-hour before I started, and I have ridden hard?"

"The pigeon, your worship: it flew to Florence with a letter to the Lady Marietta. She sent another one on to the convent of St. Jerome, and the result is I am here. I was to seek out your worship, and inform you where my lady is confined."

"Basta! It was well conceived by his excellency. But where is she—in the citadel?"

"No, excellency; but in the Casino Baglioni, behind Santa Agnese."

"How did you find out?"

"I was brought here prisoner, excellency, and was allowed to be in attendance on her ladyship, together with Madonna Laura, her maid. I escaped back to Florence with a letter from the Lady Angiola a day or so after. It was by her orders I went."

"Then she may not be there now."

"I have made sure of that, excellency—but Madonna Laura——" he stopped.

"The maid—what of her—no doubt with her mistress?"

"Alas, no, excellency! She was killed by Pluto."

"Pluto!"

"Yes, your worship. A black bear that the cavaliere Paolo, who holds the house, has as a pet," and he commenced to weep.

I felt for the faithful fellow's grief, but said nothing, and after a little he composed himself.

"Come, Gian," I said, laying my hand on his shoulder, "be a man, and we will have an eye for an eye."

He ground his teeth but made no reply, I and went on—

"How far is the house from here?"

"Close," he said. "We can reach it by the Porto San Angelo."

"Come, then."

"There is no need for the crutches now," he remarked, as he tucked them under his arm. "I will use them when we come to the gate. Will your excellency follow?"

As we walked northward over the hills, I continued my questions:

"Who is the Cavaliere Paolo?"

"A cousin of Count Carlo Baglioni, your worship. A man in middle life—my age—and a perfect devil."

"I doubt not, the breed is a bad one. Has he many men with him?"

"About six, excellency, and then, of course, there is the guard at the Porta San Angelo always at hand."

"Now listen to me, for we may not have time to talk further of this. When you have shown me the house we must separate. Go to the Albergo of the Rubicon—you know it?"

"Alas! no, excellency."

"It is behind the Palazzo Piccinino; you cannot miss it. Go there, and await me a few steps from the doors—you follow?"

"Yes, your worship."

We had now crossed the Vici dell' Elce, but passing the gate of that name, went onwards, and after a stiff climb reached the Porta San Angelo. Here my companion, betaking himself once more to his crutches and keeping ahead of me, turned southwards along the road which lined the walls towards Santa Agnese. Shortly before reaching the church, we came to a small but solid-looking building, half fortress, half dwelling-house, and Gian, stopping dead in front of it, turned round and began his whine:

"A copper for the poor cripple—a brown copper. The house, signore," speaking the last words under his breath as I came up.

"Do you know the room?" I asked pretending to fumble for a coin.

"In the tower behind," he answered rapidly, "may the saints bless your lordship," and he limped away.

In order to gain time to look about, I put back my purse leisurely, and then, with the same object, proceeded to rearrange and retie the bows on my doublet. The face of the house was a little way back from the wall which it overlooked. The massive doorway was shut, and the windows on each side of it, as well as those set above, heavily grated. I was too near the house to see the tower behind, and it looked so deserted that it was hardly possible for six men to be on guard there.

"An odd sort of bower to place one's lady-love in," I said, half aloud, to myself; but then Baglioni's wooing was a rough one. There was obviously nothing to be got by staring at the front of the house, and I turned to my left, pausing between two dead walls, until I obtained a view of the tower behind. The windows of the topmost room were all closed and strongly barred, and it seemed deserted. I glanced lower down, and to my joy saw that the room below was evidently occupied, and once I caught a glimpse of a figure moving within. It was a brief glimpse; but the eyes of love are sharp, and I knew it was Angiola. I made up my mind at once, and stepping back quickly to the front of the house, hammered loudly at the door with the knocker. After a moment's silence, I heard the firm tread of a soldier. A small barrier was let down, a bearded face looked up, and a rough voice asked—

"Who knocks?"

"Diavolo!" I exclaimed. "You are polite. Is the Cavaliere Paolo within?"

"He is not," replied the man shortly.

"Expected soon?"

"Cannot say."

"If you do not answer more civilly it will be bad for you. Tell him when he comes that the Cavaliere di Savelli"—I gave my proper name—"has arrived from Rome on an urgent affair, and will call on him to-morrow; forget, and it will be the worse for you."

The man seemed a little surprised, and altered his tone at once.

"I will give your message, signore."

"Beware how you fail—harkee—is there a road to the Via Appia behind this house?"

"Yes, signore, straight on, after taking the passage."

I did not even thank him, but turned on my heel, and walked off whistling a catch. I went down the passage between the two walls, and after some considerable stumblings up and down the vile roads, reached the Via Appia and turned southwards to my hostel. I had formed the somewhat daring plan of trying to force the house in broad daylight, choosing my time an hour or so after dinner, and if done boldly this would probably be successful, as my own force was nearly equal to that of the garrison including Pluto.

As I was approaching the Rubicon, I heard a voice at my side.

"A copper, signore—a brown paul."

"Gian."

"Excellency."

"Drop the beggar, and attend—can you ride?"

"Yes, excellency."

"Very well!"

I said no more and went on in silence, but a little distance from the hostel I bade Gian stop, and entering the yard, sought out Jacopo.

"Has the landlord any horses for sale?"

"Two, your excellency."

"Good ones?"

"Fairly so, excellency—about twenty crowns a piece with saddle included."

"Then buy one—and here—a few steps to the right of the entrance you will find a cripple, he is one of my men, do not speak, but attend—go out quietly—get him decently clothed, and bring him back here, the horse will be for him. You can get clothes to fit him anywhere, for the shops do not shut until late; get him a sword too, there are some good and cheap weapons in Perugia."

"It shall be done, excellency."

"Then be off at once."

I went on, and had a look at the horses. Bande Nero was with them, seated on a rough wooden bench cleaning his corselet, which already shone like silver. He rose to the salute as I came up.

"How are the horses, Bande Nero?"

"As well as possible, signore, they are all in high mettle."

With a parting pat to Castor, I sought my chamber, reaching it a little after the supper hour. I kept up an outward composure, but my mind within me was aflame with excitement. I ordered another flask of the Burgundy and forced myself to eat and drink a little. Then I betook myself to the arm-chair, and my thoughts. So impatient was I, that the idea came on me to make the attempt there and then, and it was with difficulty I persuaded myself to abandon such a plan, which could have only ended in disaster. Finally, I was about to retire for want of something better to do, when Jacopo came in, followed by Gian.

The latter was entirely transformed, except for the patch which he still wore over his eye, and I was able to recall him now as the old servant who had come somewhat fiercely up to me in the garden of St. Michael. He had the art which I found so difficult, of completely disguising himself when he chose. Jacopo had performed his task well, and bidding them keep their tongues closed, I dismissed them with a good night.

CHAPTER XXI.

THE RESCUE OF ANGIOLA.

THE next day as the big gun from the citadel boomed out the twelfth hour, and all the bells of the town clanged forth the time, five horsemen rode through the gate of St. Angelo, whose doors were spread wide open. The single sentry on duty paced sleepily up and down, he was longing for his noontide siesta, and the guard of a half-score of Baglioni's lances, lay with their armour off, basking in the mellow sun. A subaltern officer, who had evidently dined to some purpose, reclined on his back, half in half out of the shade of a few olive trees that grew to the left of the gate, and the ruby on his cheeks showed up all the brighter against the green of the grass on which he was stretched. The horsemen were myself and my four followers. We had taken the route I went the day before with Gian, and the plan I had formed was this. On my gaining admittance to the house, Jacopo and Bande Nere were to put themselves at the door, and engage the guard there in conversation. Gian and the lackey were to hold the horses. As soon as I ascertained the position of Angiola's room, I would blow shrilly on a whistle I had purchased for the purpose. My men at the door, who were armed with arquebuses as well as their swords, would hold the passage, and I should try and account for the Cavaliere Paolo and bear off the prize. If we succeeded, we could easily make the gate, and then, the road to St. Jerome lay open before us. The fact that the attempt was to be made in broad daylight too would be a safeguard, as no one would deem that such a deed, usually done under cover of night, was to be adventured at this hour. I had partly paved the way for my entrance by my call of yesterday, and was provided with a sufficiently plausible story to keep the cavaliere engaged, whilst I took stock of his surroundings. Jacopo too had been carefully drilled as to how he was to announce me, and the question resolved itself into hard hitting, and a little luck. I had dressed myself with particular care, wearing my buff-coat under a gay jerkin, and a short velvet cloak hung from my shoulders. This almost gala attire was to act as a further blind, and give all the appearance of a mere visit of ceremony. There was of course the possibility of my being refused admittance, and of the Cavaliere Paolo declining to see me; but this was not probable, and if it did happen, I was ready for a bold stroke, and for this Bande Nere carried with him a grenade with which to blow open the door. As it turned out, however, we had no difficulty on this score. On reaching the house I glanced up, and saw a face peering at us through the caging of one of the windows above; but it was almost immediately withdrawn. Jacopo dismounted and knocked firmly. The same performance, I have described, of opening a grating was gone through, but on my name being mentioned the porter shut his peep-hole, there was the sound of the removal of a bar, the clank of chains, and the door swung open with a sullen groan, disclosing a hall, in which stood two men, completely armed, their arquebuses at the ready in their hands, whilst the door-keeper himself, a sturdy knave, stood full in the entrance, swinging a bunch of keys.

"Is the Cavaliere Paolo Baglioni within?" I asked as I dismounted, taking it for granted I was to be received, from the preparation I saw was made.

"He is, signore—be pleased to follow."

With a warning glance to Jacopo I stepped in, finding myself in a hall of middle size, the walls discoloured with age, and chipped and cracked in many places—clearly the Casino Baglioni needed repairs. At the end of the hall was a spiral staircase, whose stone steps, worn to a hollow in the middle, by the passing and repassing of feet, marked its great age. Up this narrow stairway I followed the man, until we reached a corridor, hung on each side with rusty suits of armour, and old and tattered banners. The place was very damp, and there was a musty smell about it, as if no pure air ever came that way. It was evident that the cavaliere was on the alert, for a man was on guard here, armed like those below, with sword and arquebus. To him my guide addressed himself.

"He has come," he said, jerking his thumb backwards at me.

"Well, announce him," said the sentinel.

"That is for you," answered the janitor, "I had enough of Pluto this morning." With this he turned on his heel and ran back downstairs, jingling his keys.

The sentry stood still, however, and after waiting for half a minute, I spoke, my blood rising a little within me.

"Will you be good enough to announce the Cavaliere di Savelli—on an urgent affair?"

The man turned round to a closed door behind him, rapping at it with his mailed hand. From inside I heard a shuffling noise, a heavy body lurched against the door, and there was a scratching at the wood. No answer, however, came to the knock.

"Knock again," I said, a little impatiently, and this time a deep voice called out—

"Enter."

I placed my hand on the door to open it when the sentry spoke with unexpected civility.

"Take care of the beast, signore!"

"The beast—what beast?" I asked, pretending not to know anything of Pluto's existence.

"His excellency's bear—do not fear it—else it might injure you—*cospetto!* But it is a perfect fiend if you run from it. It killed a poor woman the other day."

"Thanks, friend, I will beware," I answered, and pushed open the door, springing back a yard as I did so, for with a short roar that echoed through the house, a huge bear rose on his hind legs, and struck out at my face with his claws.

"*Diavolo!* go back," shouted the sentry to the brute, and I whipped out my sword; but the animal merely stood in the open doorway, making no further advance, his great jaws open, and puffing like a blacksmith's bellows.

"*Cospetto!* excellency, call off the bear," shouted the sentry again, indeed he seemed positively to hate the animal, and from inside came a low deep-toned but mocking laugh. "Come back, Pluto—down, you brute—down!" then there was a heavy "thud," the tinkling of shivered glass, and the bear dropping on its fore feet, shambled back into the room. I was considerably startled, and not a little angry; but concealing these feelings, stepped boldly into the room, keeping my drawn sword still in my hand.

"The Cavaliere di Baglioni?" I enquired.

"At the Cavaliere di Savelli's service," and a tall figure rose from a lounge chair and surveyed me. I confess that my heart began to beat a little fast when I saw the man against whom I was to pit myself. He was far above the middle height, and proportionately broad. His grizzled hair, parted in the middle, hung down straightly to his neck, and a thick grey beard and moustache hid his mouth and chin. A cruel hooked nose, almost Hebraic in shape, was set between a pair of small and piercing eyes. His complexion was deathly pale, and by the light which fell from the barred window, I saw beneath the skin the little red lines of swollen veins which marked an intemperate life. At a small table beside the chair was a pack of cards, and a glass half filled with red wine, the bottle from which the wine was taken was lying in fragments at the door, where it had fallen and broken to bits, after being flung at Pluto. The bear was now beside his master, facing me, his huge head held down and swaying from side to side. We remained for a half minute staring at each other, and then Baglioni spoke again, with his deep sneering accent, " Is it usual for the Cavaliere di Savelli to pay visits with a drawn sword in his hand ? "

" Is it usual," I replied, " for gentlemen to be received by having a savage beast set at them ? "

" Oh, Pluto ! " and he touched the bear, " Pluto was not set at you, man—you would not be here if he was."

" Probably—if however you will call the beast to one side, I would like to discuss my business with you, cavaliere."

" Shut the door, and sit down there," he replied, " Pluto will not disturb us—you can put back your sword. It would avail you little," he grinned.

It cost me an effort, but I did as I was bidden, and Baglioni sank back into his lounge, the bear still standing, and keeping its fierce eyes on me. Its master however kept running his hand up and down its shaggy coat, whilst he asked in his measured voice—

" Well, and to what do I owe the honour of this visit ? "

" You would prefer no beating about the bush ? "

" It is my way."

" Well, then, cavaliere, I have come from Rome with a special object, and that is to ask you to change sides, and to use your influence with your cousin, Count Carlo, to do likewise."

"I follow the head of my house."

"Exactly. You are aware that His Holiness is now over seventy years of age."

"The lambkin of God, Alexander—yes."

"Well, he cannot go on for ever, and if he were to die, it is an end to the Borgia."

"Ho! ho!" he laughed, "it is an end to the Borgia—Cavaliere, your employers are mad. It will take not a little to break Cesare—Cesare Borgia, Duke of Romagna, Imola and Faenza, Marquis of Rimini, Count of Forli, Lord of Pesaro and Fano, Gonfaloniere of the Church—good for a low-born bastard—eh? Ho! ho! break Cesare! Not you."

"Stronger trees have fallen, signore—remember we have France, and the Florentines on our side, and twenty thousand men, under Tremouille and Trevulzio, are not twenty miles from you."

I was playing a risky game. If I did succeed in inducing this man to listen to my proposals, and he actually persuaded his cousin to do likewise, it would be a terrible blow to the Borgia. On the other hand I ran the immediate risk of being arrested, and kept a prisoner, or killed outright. But it was the only way to gain time, and look about me; and whilst Baglioni reflectively stroked his strange pet, making no reply to my last speech, I glanced cautiously but carefully around the room. Like the passage outside, the walls were hung with old armour and old flags. Time had defaced the pictures on the ceiling, and such furniture as there was, was old, and the coverings of the chairs and tables moth-eaten and wine stained. The stale odour of wine mingled with the must of a long untouched room, and everywhere, on the tables, on the chairs, and strewn here and there on the floor, were cards. Evidently the cavaliere had a weakness in this direction, and like lightning it flashed upon me, that if he were a gambler the game was probably in my hands, and I would drop policy and turn to the cards. My thoughts were interrupted by Baglioni, who broke the silence. "What evidence have you, to show you are the person you represent yourself to be?"

"I can offer you none. In matters like this one does not carry evidence about—but if you like to send a trusted messenger to Rome, to the Cardinal d'Amboise—see the reception he will get—or nearer still to Tremouille?"

"And why come to me?"

"Because of your influence with your cousin, and because you are a man who will play for a big stake," and I risked the shot. His eyes flashed, and his hand stopped in its movement through the fur of the bear.

"My influence with my cousin is—that," he snapped his fingers, "but a big stake—yes—I like playing for big stakes."

I stooped and picked up a card, holding it idly up between my finger and thumb.

"This, what I propose, is a bigger stake than you could ever get on the king, cavaliere," and with a twist of my wrist I sent the card from me, it hit the wall opposite with a smart tap, and then floated slowly and noiselessly down to the floor of the room.

The man's eyes followed the card, and he muttered as if to himself—

"A big stake—yes—Carlo gives me nothing—I am his jailor—I, who in a single night have lost two lordships to Riario, have now not a ducat to fling in the air, except what the niggard allows me."

I did not like the part I was playing; but I knew enough of the state of affairs to be certain that D'Amboise would richly reward the person who could detach Baglioni from the Borgia. I said no more than the truth therefore when I added quietly—

"You would have another lordship, or two maybe, to stake, if my proposal were carried out."

"*Cospetto!*" he said, "it is useless."

"Then I am sorry," I replied, rising as if to depart, "but must wish you good day."

"*Diavolo!* Cavaliere, you are not going without some refreshment. Ho! without there," and his deep voice pealed out like a great bell.

The bear, which had stretched itself on the floor, rose with a grunt, but Baglioni pressed its head down, and it sank back, and began to hum to itself between its paws, like an enormous bee, or rather with the sound a thousand bees might make.

After a little delay there was a knock at the door, but apparently, as usual, the person outside, whoever he was, did not feel disposed to come in. My host rose in anger, and stepped across the room, followed by his beast, the latter passing unpleasantly close to me.

There was an altercation at the door, my host went out with his pet, and for a minute or two I was left alone. I moved my seat nearer to the small table beside Baglioni's lounge, and taking up the pack of cards began to shuffle and cut them.

The cavaliere came back very soon, a flask in one hand and a glass in the other.

"Blood of St. John!" he exclaimed as he set them down with a clink on the table, "those rascals—I will have their ears cut off—they fear this poor lamb," and he fondled the great bear, which rose on its hind feet and began muzzling its master.

"I am not surprised. *Corpo di Bacco!* The king again!" and I flung down the pack in apparent disgust.

"Down, Pluto!" and Baglioni turned to me, "The king again. What was that you said?"

"Cutting left hand against the right. I lost three times."

"I lost ten thousand one night over cutting—but help yourself," and he pushed the flask towards me, and then filled his own, which he drained at a gulp.

"Come, cavaliere—you are in no hurry—cut me through the pack."

"With pleasure; but my purse-bearer is downstairs—will you permit me to see him?"

"By all means—the heavier the purse the better for me."

"A favour—I cannot play with that beast near me—could you not send him away?"

"Send him away—my familiar," he said with an awful smile, "No, no, Di Savelli—he is my luck; but I shall keep him at a distance if you like."

I rose and went down to Jacopo, and found him and Bande Nero already on friendly terms with the guard. I took my purse from him, and found time to whisper a warning to strike the moment he heard my whistle. When I came back, I was relieved to find the bear fastened by a chain to a ring in the wall. The chain itself was weak, and could have been snapped with ease, but the animal made no effort to strain at it, and lay down as contentedly as a dog. Baglioni had pulled a table into the centre of the room, and was seated at it, impatiently ruffling the cards.

"Back at last," he said, and his voice had lost its measured cadence, "heavens, I have not spread the cards for a whole year—what stakes?"

"Simply cutting the cards?"

"Yes. It is the quickest game I know."

"Say a crown each turn to begin with."

We cut through four times, and I paid over two crowns.

Baglioni laughed as he put them on one side, "peddling stakes these, cavaliere—make them ten crowns a cut."

"Agreed—three cuts and a shuffle."

He nodded, and I paid ten crowns, feeling at this rate that my purse would soon be empty; but I saw that the fever was taking hold of him, and offered to double the stakes and won. From that moment luck favoured me, and at the end of half an hour's play the cavaliere had lost all his ready money, about sixty crowns, and owed me five hundred besides. He did not take his losses well, all the restrained self-command which he first exhibited, gave place to a wild excitement, and his hands shook as he shuffled the cards, his white face paling whiter than ever.

"Curse the cards!" he said, "I have no luck."

The moment had come for which I had been watching. Time after time I felt inclined to strike a sudden blow; but held myself in.

"No more to-day, cavaliere," I said, filling my glass, "I have business and must away."

A red flush came to his forehead, "I cannot pay you at once," he said in a low tone.

"Tush!" I replied, "the word of Baglioni is enough—but if you want a last try for your revenge, I will cut you——"

"Double or quits?" he burst in.

"No, cavaliere," and I dropped the words out slowly, "the five hundred against a five minutes' interview with the Lady Angiola."

He leaned back in his chair in amaze, and I went on, "Listen to me, I only want five minutes' speech with her —in your presence if you will—come, shall I cut or will you?"

"*Diavolo!*" he muttered, "if Carlo hears of this—well, yes—I will cut first—the ten—a bad card to beat."

I cut carelessly, and faced my card. It was a king.

"Hell and Furies!" he burst out. "You have won. Come, sir," and rising he advanced towards the bear.

"A moment, cavaliere. I said in *your* presence. I did not include Messer Pluto there in the interview."

He gave me an unpleasant look; but stopped short.

"Very well," he said, and taking a large key from his girdle, went on before me.

It cost me a great effort to keep cool, up to now my luck had been so great that every moment there was a temptation to put all to the hazard of one stroke. I smiled, under my beard, as I thought of the imposing fool Count Carlo had placed in charge of his prize, and when I saw the huge shaking hand clutching the key, I could not help thinking that nerves like that would never hold a sword straight, and that for all his size and courage, the cavaliere was not a very formidable foe.

In a few steps we reached the door he wanted, and Baglioni, after knocking once, simply turned the key and pushed open the door.

Looking over his shoulder I saw a small but well-furnished room, and standing in the middle of it, in startled surprise at this sudden intrusion, the figure of Angiola. Quick as thought I made a warning gesture, and almost at the moment Baglioni turned round with—

"A visitor for you, madam."

She did not seem to recognise me, but at the warning gesture I made, a faint flush came into her cheek. She stood looking at us half frightened, half indignant, and at last spoke.

"I do not recognise——"

"Ugo di Savelli, madam," and I bowed.

Her lips curled a little as she answered—

"Well, Messer Ugo di Savelli—Cavaliere Ugo di Savelli I should say—is it not so? May I ask your business? If it is any message from your master, I decline to hear it," and she turned away with a motion of supreme disdain, thinking no doubt that I was a follower of Count Carlo.

"Ho! ho!" laughed Baglioni, at my look of discomfiture, "the future countess can speak her mind. I pity Carlo. You had best cut short your five minutes, cavaliere, and come back to the cards."

At this moment I heard the bear whining below, impatient for his master, and I knew his bonds were all too slender to hold him. There was nothing for it, but to save Angiola in spite of herself. All this happened in a flash, and with my full strength I hit Baglioni below the left ear, just where the neck and head united. So sudden, so unexpected was the blow, that the huge man rolled over like an ox, and a short shrill scream broke from Angiola. My sword was out in a moment, and I stood over Baglioni.

"A cry, a movement, and I kill you like a dog," I gasped out, my breath coming thick and fast; "throw the key to the lady—pick it up, girl—quick—now run to the door and stand there—I am here to save you." It was done at once, for Baglioni saw he must obey or die, and springing back, I closed the door quickly and turned the key. Almost as I did so, I heard footsteps hurrying below, and blew loudly on my whistle. The sound of the whistle was followed by an angry shouting that was drowned by a terrible roar, and I saw Pluto before me, rushing up the stair, with the end of his broken chain still hanging to him. Baglioni was battering at the door behind me. He was safe enough, but my companion had dropped in a faint, and I wanted all my hands and all my nerve to meet the beast, who was now on the stairway, not ten feet away from me. Close to me was a heavy stool, I seized this, and flung it at the animal with all my strength, and getting between his forefeet, it caused him to stumble and slip back a half-dozen steps; but with another roar Pluto gathered himself together, and rushed up again, his jaws agape, and white with foam. I gave him the point deep into his neck. It might have been a pin-prick, and he dented the steel with his teeth. Rising to his feet, he struck at me, tearing my short cloak clean off my shoulders, and then, my sword was up to the hilt in his side, and we grappled. My left cheek was once touched by his claws, and seemed to be hanging in ribbons; but although almost blinded with blood, and choked by his fœtid breath, I held my head well down, and drove my dagger again and again into the beast. Angiola had recovered from her faint, and above the grunting of the bear, the battering at the door, and the clash of steel below, I heard her laughing in shrill hysterics. My strength was failing. I was about to give up all for lost, when there was a loud report, and with a howl the bear fell backwards. My hand somehow fastened itself to the hilt of my sword, sticking in the animal's side, and the weight of him, as he fell back, and as I shook myself clear, freed the blade. I stood half dazed, watching the huge black body sliding limply down the stairs, until it lay in a shapeless heap on the landing. Jacopo's voice brought me to myself.

"For the love of God—quick, excellency—quick!"

God, I suppose, gives men strength sometimes, for his own purposes. And so it must have been with me, for I picked my dear up in my arms, and half giddy, and staggering, made my way to the entrance door. I need not say I had no time to look about me; but Jacopo helped me with my burden. Lifting her to the pommel of the saddle, I sprang up behind, and drawing my darling close to me, with a shout of triumph, I set free my plunging horse and let him go with a loose rein.

CHAPTER XXII.

THE RIDE TO ST. JEROME.

We galloped at a break-neck pace to the gate, but the guard was already alarmed, and half-a-dozen men came hastening towards us. They were on foot, however, and had no mind to stand the shock of meeting horses coming at full speed down an incline, so skipped nimbly aside. The officer alone held his ground, paying for his courage with his life, for Bande Nere sliced his head in two like a ripe water-melon—poor wretch. Had they only closed the gates we were lost, but we reached them just in time, and passing through like a flash were free of the town. A bullet or two whizzed past us, but did no damage. It was done, and another half hour of the pace we were going would place us beyond pursuit. It was no easy matter, however, to sit the horse and hold Angiola as I was doing, and I very soon began to feel that the strain on my arm was getting beyond me, and that she was slipping from my grasp. She lay still and passive, her eyes closed, her head resting on my shoulder, and seemed in a faint. Perhaps I spoke roughly, but it was no time to mince words.

"Come, madam," I said, "you must rouse yourself—take another day to swoon—hold me as closely as you can—quick."

My words—and the tone they were spoken in—had the effect I wanted. She looked a little indignant, but held on, leaving my left arm, which was getting numbed, more free to guide the horse, and my sword arm greater liberty should occasion arise.

The country, rugged although it was, descended in a slope towards the basin of Trasimene, but I turned sharp aside from the road, fearing there might be a picquet thereon, and galloped across the open, far out-pacing my followers, who I saw were coming after me in a bunch, and at their utmost speed—the honest knaves. The glance over my shoulder that I took to observe this also showed me a strong body of horse spurring from the gate, and I chuckled to myself as I thought we had gained a mile's start and that they had to deal with Castor. Five leagues to go—it was nothing to the brave horse; and in answer to my call he stretched himself out as he had never done before. As for me, such thoughts as I had when I felt the arms of the woman I loved clasped about me are to be recalled for one's self alone, and concern none else beside. Once or twice I glanced down, meeting her eyes, and as she dropped her lids over them they seemed to me to be alive with a soft light. After a little I felt her arms beginning to relax.

"Hold tight," I said.

"I cannot; my strength is going."

"Courage, take heart; see, to our left is the Tower of Magione—a few minutes and we are safe."

I drew her closer towards me. With an effort she rallied, her arms again tightened in their clasp, and we sped down the long slope which led to Trasimene, Castor stretching himself like a greyhound. I looked again over my shoulder. Far behind my men were riding for their lives, and farther still was the dark line of our pursuers, coming on with dogged persistence, the sun lighting up their armour and flashing from their spears. Once beyond Magione we were comparatively safe, but a false step, a stumble, and all was lost. Magione itself was held by the Baglioni, and from the old watch-tower, built by the Sforza, which stood high above the country, we might have already been spied, and a party sent out to intercept us. The thought seemed to grow into a reality, and a despair began to come over me. "On, on, Castor!" I spoke to the good horse, and he laid his ears back at the sound of my voice, and even as he did so I saw a cloud of dust coming towards our left, and knew that the danger I feared was at hand. Going as we were I was riding right into the party from Magione, and therefore with a touch on the rein, I swung Castor round to the north, and we raced on, leaving the tower over my shoulder. The double burden and the tremendous pace, however, began to tell on the horse, and within the next five minutes he slackened perceptibly in his stride. To my horror I saw that the ground began to be furrowed and cut up by ravines and that we were approaching the bed of a river. I had therefore to slacken the pace, and at the same time our new pursuers sighting us, came on with all the speed of their fresh horses. Castor scrambled in and out of the ravines like a cat, but we were going slowly now, and the enemy had all the advantage of the level ground to come up, which they did at a dreadful rate. With the failing strength of my companion I dared not risk jumps, weighted as I was, but the brave horse did his utmost, as if knowing our danger.

"For God's sake hold on!" I cried out as we topped a deep ravine with a plunge that almost caused Angiola to slip from my grasp, and as I said this I heard a shot and a ball from an arquebus whistled over my head. The enemy were in the rough ground now themselves, but they were within gun-range, and I dreaded that some of them might dismount and pick me off. This however did not occur to them, and on we went, with every now and again a bullet, fired from horseback with an unsteady aim singing past us. My charge had twisted her arms into my shoulder belt and held on bravely, but I saw by her white face and the blue coming into her lips that this could not last, and if she fainted there was an end of all.

At the outside it was a matter of a few minutes now, one way or the other; but as I came to the crest of another ravine I saw before me a steep bank leading down to a small stream that was swishing along in a white flood, and on the opposite shore a sight that made my heart leap, for drawn up in array, evidently roused by the sound of the shots, was a strong body of men-at-arms, and over them fluttered the pennon of Hawkwood, a red hand on a white field. I knew in a moment we were within the king's outposts.

"Saved!" I shouted in my joy. "Saved!"—and risking all I made the horse fly the last ravine, and the next instant we had slid down the bank, and the white water was churning round Castor as he dashed into the stream.

A puff of smoke above us, a flash as of lightning, a deafening roar, and one of Novarro's nine pounders belched out a storm of grape, that hissed over our heads in the direction of our pursuers, and stopped them, beaten and baffled. One effort more, we were out of the stream, up the bank, and panting, breathless and still bleeding, with my companion in a dead faint in my arms, I reined in Castor. In a moment we were surrounded, but the faces were kindly, and dismounting slowly, I placed my lifeless burden on a heap of cloaks that were flung to the earth for her, and then turning round, saw Hawkwood before me. It was the first time we had met since the affair at Arezzo, when I was cast forth a dishonoured man. I did not know how to greet him, and there was a constraint in his face, for I saw he knew me, and was like myself at a loss for speech. I had, however, to take the matter in my hand.

18

"Signore," I said, "accept my thanks. This lady is the Countess Angiola Castellani, a ward of the Florentine secretary, whom I have brought off from Perugia, and have to take to the convent of St. Jerome."

He tugged at his tawny moustache.

"I have merely carried out orders—you have nothing to thank me for, signore. My instructions were to prevent any of Baglioni's men crossing the Sanguinetta, and to protect all fugitives from the territories of the Borgia."

I bowed and added, with a pain in my tone I could not conceal, for this man was once my friend—

"All the same I thank you, signore; I have, however, four followers."

"I can do nothing for them if they are on the other bank," he interrupted, and went on, "St. Jerome is not a half-league from here. My men will make up a litter, and help to bear the lady there. It will be easier for her. I wish you a good day." He turned on his heel and gave some orders to his men in English, a language I do not know, leaving me standing by the body of Angiola. All the misery of the past came back to me in a flash. Would the stain never be wiped out? All the kindness I had received from Bayard and the cardinal, all the efforts made by those who believed in me, seemed to be swept away as dust in the wind. Almost did I feel that I would accept the ban cast on me, and turn wolf in earnest. It cost me much to restrain myself from drawing on Hawkwood, but a glance at the still pale face before me recalled me to my duty. A man very kindly brought me a little wine, I knelt down and forced some of it between her blue lips. In a short time she revived, some colour came into her cheeks, and she attempted to rise, with a look of fear on her face at the number of armed men she saw around her.

"There is nothing to fear, madam," I said to reassure

her, " you are safe, and in an hour will be at St. Jerome—a litter is being made ready for you."

Without a word she held out her hand, and thanked me with this and the look in her eyes.

The litter was now ready, half-a-dozen men volunteered their services, and placing her therein, we started for the convent. Ere we had gone half a mile we heard shouts behind us, and I was more than glad to see Jacopo and my men riding up.

"How did you get off?" I asked as they came up.

"In the rear of the troop from Magione, excellency," was Jacopo's reply, "they did not observe us, having eyes only for you; and seeing you were safe, we forded the stream lower down and crossed—but, excellency, your face—are you hurt?"

"Somewhat, but at St. Jerome I will have it attended to."

In truth the left side of my face appeared to be laid open, and although I felt that the wound was not so dangerous as it seemed, yet I had bled freely, and now that the excitement was over, began to suffer much pain. Indeed at times I felt as if I could hardly hold myself straight in the saddle, succeeding in doing so only by an effort of will. I did not approach the litter. I was afraid that the sight of my face would alarm Angiola, for now she was probably able to look about her, and see that which she had not been able to observe before. Once, however, in a bend of the road, that fortunately went to the left and hid my wounded side, our eyes met, and I caught so bright a smile of thanks, that it paid me for my hurt. I reined in, for I knew my face showed too much, and henceforth kept well behind. I sent Gian on to the convent with the good news of Angiola's rescue, and on nearing the gates was met by St. Armande and the rest of my followers, whom I was glad indeed to see.

He came up with a merry greeting. " Welcome," he cried, " so, gallant knight, you have saved the damsel in distress;" then catching sight of my wounded face his tone changed. " Good God ! you are hurt."

" A little."

" You should have it seen to at once—come—we are not allowed to enter the convent; but the abbess has done all she can for us, and we camp or lodge, whichever way you put it, in that house there," he pointed to a small villa, set in what seemed a wilderness of holm-oak that hid all but its roof from view.

" Not so fast, chevalier. I must leave my charge at the convent first."

He had to rest satisfied with this, but I was surprised that he made no inquiry as to the condition of Angiola, an ordinary civility that might have been expected.

At the gates of the convent, within which we were not allowed to enter, we were met by the lady abbess and her train. I dismounted, intending to assist Angiola out of the litter, but as it was set down, she sprang out of it of her own accord, and the next minute she was in the arms of the abbess, and there was much kissing and many congratulations, mingled with tears of joy.

I did not stay to receive the thanks I saw would shortly be showered on me, and thrusting a handful of crowns into the hands of the leader of the good fellows who bore the litter, as some reward for himself and his men, I looped Castor's reins into my arm, and set forward to walk to the villa. The chevalier came with me, and by the time I reached it I was quite giddy, being weak with the pain and the loss of blood. The saturnine old abbé was there, with more concern in his face than I had seen for a long time, and seeing me stagger, he put an arm round me and, aided by St. Armande, assisted me to a couch. The chevalier himself dressed my wound, with a gentle and skilful hand, making as much of me as if I had been run through the vitals. As he finished dressing the wound, the abbé remarked that I would have to rest for a few days to enable it to heal, and I had replied with some difficulty, my jaw being bandaged up, that this was impossible, when Gian came in with a note. It was from Angiola, chiding me gently for not waiting to receive her thanks and those of the abbess, and begging me to come the following day, with a postscript to the effect that the lady abbess would so far relax the rules of the order, as to admit me within the courtyard. I dismissed Gian with thanks, and a message that I would be at the convent, charging him to say nothing of my wound, and then my thoughts went a wool-gathering, and I lay back with the missive in my hands. St. Armande was leaning against the window, his back to the light. He had taken up this position after whispering a word or two to the abbé, who left the room. I did not, however, observe him or anything else, my mind was full of mad thoughts, and for the moment I let them have full play, making no effort to resist. Folding the letter up carefully, I placed it under my pillow, and was about to close my eyes, when the abbé returned, bearing a bowl in his hands. This St. Armande took from him, and approaching me said—

"Come, cavaliere—you must drink this at once."

His tone was sharp and incisive, and looking up in some surprise, I saw he was pale to the lips, and wondered what bee had stung him. I rose to a sitting posture to take the cup; but he would not have it so, and passing his arm round my neck, made me drink like a child. The draught was cool and refreshing, and as I sank back on my pillows, my heart for a moment being gay at the thought of the letter, I said jestingly—

"Chevalier, you would make a most excellent nurse.

Shave off that little moustache of yours, put on a black hood and gown, and *diavolo!* But you would break as many hearts as you cured wounds." The words were barely out of my mouth, when he brought his foot down with an angry stamp on the carpet, and with a face as scarlet now as it had been pale before, turned on his heel and walked out of the room.

I looked to the abbé, who was sitting watching me, stroking his chin with his hand.

"St. John! But is he often taken this way?"

The cleric rose, and not answering my question, spoke.

"You had better try and sleep now, cavaliere, or else the potion may lose its effect." He then followed St. Armande.

I would have risen to apologise, but I felt a pleasant numbness stealing over me, and in a minute or so my thoughts began to grow confused, and I seemed to sink into a sleep. Not so profound a slumber, however, as to be unconscious of what was going on around me. I was sure I once heard Bande Nere and Jacopo in my room, and that I was being carried apparently to a more comfortable bed. Then I felt soft hands bathing my wound, and heard a gentle voice whispering words of deep love in my ear. It was a dream, of course, but all through the night that soon came, Doris d'Entrangues hung over me, and tended me with words I cannot repeat.

CHAPTER XXIII.

THE PAVILION OF TREMOUILLE.

WHEN I awoke the next morning, my head was still dazed, but I was otherwise strong. At least, I felt so, as I lay still in my bed, all sense of fatigue gone, and trying to collect my thoughts. After a little, I glanced round the chamber, which was not the room where I had taken the potion, but another and a larger apartment. It was no fancy then, the voices of Jacopo and Bande Nere I heard and the sensation of being lifted and moved, which I experienced in the night. My removal was doubtless effected whilst I was under the influence of the drug; but the voice of madame? The almost certainty that she was by me through the hours of the night? I could not account for this, and seeing any such effort was useless, ceased to rack my brain on the subject, putting it down to a mad dream. For some while I lay mustering up courage to rise, fanned by the mild breeze, which played in from the open window on my right. Outside I could see the branches of the trees, as they swayed to and fro in the wind, and the joyous song of a mavis trilled out sweetly through the morning, from the thorn bushes whence he piped. In about a half hour my head began to grow clearer, I remembered Angiola's letter, and thrust my hand under the pillow to find it. Of course it was not there, as I had been moved, and a short exclamation of annoyance broke from me.

"Excellency!"

It was Jacopo's voice, and the good fellow, who had evidently been watching me, came forward from behind the head of the bed.

"Ah, Jacopo! Is it you? Here, help me to rise."

"Signore—but is your worship able—the chevalier——"

"Never mind the chevalier. I am as well as ever, and there was no need of that to-do yesterday—*diavolo!*" and a twinge in my face brought me up sharply, and recalled Pluto's claws. I put my hand up to my face, and found I was still bandaged.

"It was lucky he only touched your worship."

"Luckier still your being there with your arquebus, else St. Peter and I had surely shaken hands—there—thanks—I will sit here for a few minutes," and I sank into an easy chair, being really weaker than I thought I was, the effects more of the narcotic than anything else.

"Will your worship breakfast here?"

"No—but before doing anything, go to the room where I was last evening, and bring me the letter you will find under the cushions of the couch there."

"Excellency!" and Jacopo left the room.

I now for the first time observed a bouquet of red and white roses, whose fragrance filled the chamber. I had been conscious of their perfume before, but thought the scent was borne in by the breeze from the garden outside. Whilst I was admiring the flowers, Jacopo returned.

"The letter."

"Is not there, signore, I have searched carefully."

It was a disappointment, but I said nothing, having determined to see for myself. As Jacopo assisted me to dress, I enquired to whom I was indebted for the flowers.

"I cannot say, excellency; they were here when I came

this morning. Possibly the Signor de St. Armande, who was with your worship all night."

"All night!"

"Signore."

I could not help being touched by this proof of devotion, and when I had dressed went down, with the intention of finding my letter, and thanking the chevalier for his kindness. I was, I saw, still a little weak, but a few hours' rest would make me fit for action, and I could not help thinking I had been made much over, on too small an occasion. St. Armande was in the room where I had left the letter, and at the first glance I saw he was haggard and worn, with dark circles under his eyes, eyes which many a beauty would have been proud to own. He seemed so slim, so small and delicate, as he came to meet me, that my heart began to misgive me again, as to his powers to endure the labour involved in the difficult adventure we had before us. He was much concerned at my having risen, made many enquiries about my condition, and put aside my thanks.

"*Per Bacco!* chevalier," I said, "you look more of an invalid than I. I fear me, I shall have to be nurse in my turn."

"It is but a touch of the megrims, I have; but you must not think of doing anything for a week."

"Or a month, or a year," I gibed, as I turned over the cushions of the couch, and in answer to St. Armande's enquiring look, went on, "The letter I received yesterday—I am certain I left it here."

He came forward to help me, but with no avail.

"It must have been blown away," he said.

"But I put it under the cushions!"

"True—but you forget you were moved, and the things were shifted. Come to breakfast now, and I will have a thorough search made afterwards."

"Not yet; I will but step over to the convent, and enquire after the Lady Angiola——"

"What! With a bandaged face?"

"It is a wound," I answered coldly, and turning, went out of the villa. My lackey ran forward to enquire if a horse should be made ready; but thinking the walk would do me good, I declined. I was right in this, the fresh air acted as a tonic, and when I reached the gates of the convent, all the giddiness had passed. There, to my dismay, I heard that Angiola was unable to leave her room, a thing I might have expected, and sending a civil message I retraced my steps, entering the villa by a side gate, and walking towards it through a deserted portion of the garden. I went leisurely, stopping every now and again to admire the flowers and the trees. In one of these rests, whilst I idly gazed about me, my eye was arrested by a number of fragments of paper, that lay on the green turf at my feet. Yielding to an impulse I could not control, I stopped and picked up one of the pieces, and saw in a moment it was a piece of Angiola's letter to me. I lost no time in collecting the remaining bits of the paper, and carefully placed them in my vest pocket. Then I retraced my steps to the villa.

As we sat down to breakfast, the chevalier explained that he had made a further search for the letter, but in vain.

"I ought to have told you," I said, "I have found it."

"Where?"

"In the garden—in shreds and tatters."

He became suddenly very silent, and so we finished our meal. All that day I rested, more for the horses' sake than my own, and be sure I did not fail to make frequent enquiry of Angiola's condition, hearing each time she was better, and would certainly see me on the morrow. Whilst

I lay resting, my mind was active. I cast up the time I had left at my disposal. I still had four clear days to carry out my mission, and to make my plans to intercept Bozardo. But after my adventure in Perugia I had need for extra care, and could not afford to throw away an hour of the four days that were left to me. There were many points to think of. Bozardo would no doubt be strongly escorted, and if the forty thousand ducats he had with him were in gold, they would be difficult to carry away, and would be a great temptation to my men. I could answer for Jacopo and Bande Nere; of course St. Armande was beyond suspicion, my doubts of him were at rest; but for the others? They might or might not yield to temptation. If they did yield, affairs would be serious indeed. I deliberated long and carefully, making up my mind to adopt the following course. Tremouille was but a few miles from me. I would see him, tell him of the enterprise which D'Amboise had entrusted to me, and ask him to send a troop, or some trusted men, to whom I could hand over the money in case I succeeded. If he could send these men on to Sassoferrato, I meant to ambuscade on the banks of the Misa, make my dash at Bozardo there, and if all went well, they could receive the money in a few hours, and relieve me of that anxiety. Of course Tremouille might refuse to see me; he might even do worse; but I would give him the chance and accept the risk.

When I came to think of it, it was hardly possible that he was unacquainted with the cardinal's design, and I could form no better plan than the one I had resolved upon. I would have to deny myself the pleasure of seeing Angiola on the morrow, but the four days gave me no margin. The day's repose did me much good, and, after supper, which we took about six o'clock, I ordered Castor to be saddled. St. Armande looked surprised, but I wasted no words, telling him briefly that I was bound on business, and that on my return we should have to make an immediate start. I refused all offer of companionship, and shortly after Castor and I were galloping through the glow of a late sunset to the camp of Tremouille.

I skirted the shores of Trasimene, the road being easier there, and as I went on, could not help wondering to myself what manner of reception I would have from the duke. Good or bad, I was determined to see him, and I soon caught sight of the line of tents, cresting the hills that overhung the defile where Hannibal caught the Romans. The tents were soon lost to view in the grey of the coming night. One by one the camp fires began to light the hills; the mist that rises here after sundown enveloped me, and slackening speed, I let Castor pick his way up an ascending road, covered with loose stones, and cut into ruts and fissures. In a while I came to an outpost, and at once challenged by the sentry, and surrounded by the piquet. I explained that I was from Rome to see the duke, and could not possibly give the pass word. The officer of the watch replied that this was my affair, not his, and that I would have to remain here until the morning, or until a field officer inspected the posts, in which case he would take his orders. There was no help for it, and I resigned myself to circumstances, with an impatient heart. So an hour or two passed, which I beguiled by discourse with the subaltern, telling him of Rome; he was a cadet of the house of Albani, and hearing petty items of news in return, the chief of which was that the Seigneur de Bayard had returned to the camp. Even as he said this, we heard the deep bay of a hound, and I recognised Bran's throat.

"*Per Bacco!* It is Bayard himself going the grand rounds," exclaimed the subaltern springing to his feet, and giving the order for the men to stand at attention. In a few minutes we heard the sound of horse's hoofs, the sharp clink of steel scabbards, and a half-dozen horsemen rode up. As they approached, Castor neighed in recognition of his twin brother, and an answering call showed that Pollux knew the greeting, and gave it back. The hound too came up, and rising on his hind feet, fawned a welcome on me. I made myself known to Bayard at once.

"*Ciel!*" he said, "you are the last man I expected to meet, and you want to see the duke, come with me then."

On the way I told him of the success of my attempt to free Angiola.

"We have just heard of it," he said, "and it has gone far in your favour. In fact Madame de la Tremouille, who is back again, could speak of nothing else at supper this evening. It was a brave deed, and I envied your luck, cavalier."

I told him of my plan, enquiring if he thought Tremouille would give me the assistance I wanted, pointing out that the movement of any troops, where I wanted the detachment to go, could not possibly be taken as a breach of the truce.

"As for the truce," he made answer, "it is in the air. The king has really left Maçon at last. It is said that the advance guard under the Seneschal of Beaucaire has already crossed the Ombrone. Tremouille cannot possibly refuse, and here we are."

We pulled up at the entrance to a large pavilion, out of whose open door a broad band of light streamed into the night.

"Follow me," said Bayard, and I did so, the guards saluting respectfully as we entered.

I had not time to look about me, but saw that Tremouille, who was in his armour, was pacing up and down the tent, with his limping gait, and dictating a despatch to his secretary. He stopped short in his walk, and greeting Bayard cheerfully, looked at me with a grave surprise.

"This is M. di Savelli," said Bayard, "he has business of such importance with your excellency, that I have taken it upon myself to bring him here."

The duke glanced at me keenly, the thin lines of his lips closing together.

"Are you aware of the risk you run by coming to my camp?" he asked.

"I am perfectly aware, your excellency, but——"

"You must either be a fool, or a very brave man," he interrupted.

"I lay claim to neither honour, my lord, and I take the risk: will you hear me?"

He nodded, and I laid my proposal before him. When I had finished his face expressed approval.

"Very well," he said, "I will detach Hawkwood. If you succeed, hand the money over to him."

"I understand, my lord," and bowing I retired. As I reached the door of the pavilion, I heard the duke's voice again:

"M. di Savelli."

"My lord," and I faced him.

"Succeed in this, and count me as a friend. I give you the word of Tremouille."

"I thank your excellency," and turning again I went forth. Bayard followed me out.

"I have half a mind to ask you to let me share your adventure," he said, "I am afraid, however, they will not allow me to go. At any rate I will ride back to the outposts with you — down, Bran," and he swung into the saddle.

When I shook hands with Bayard on parting from him, his last speech was—"Be careful, cavaliere, for Tremouille is a man of his word—if you fail, however, remember the game is not yet lost—good-bye, and good luck."

I turned Castor's head towards the convent, and leaving the camp fires behind me, went on through the darkness. It was midnight when I reached the villa. Those tough old soldiers Jacopo and Bande Nere were on the watch. Everything was ready; and after sharing a skin of wine all round, we rode out—shadowy figures through the mist, now faintly lit up by a young moon, whose thin crescent lay quietly in the sky. I looked back at the walls of the convent; from a window of an upper chamber a light was shining. Perhaps it was hers! And I bent down my head in a silent prayer, for God's help in my fight back to honour.

CHAPTER XXIV.

TOO DEARLY BOUGHT.

ABOUT a mile from Arcevia, the road from Sinigaglia to Rome, begins to ascend the oak-shrouded hills whence the Misa has its source, passes Sassoferrato, and then, turning due south, goes on for some nine miles over the mountains. At the point where this road, up to now following the banks of the Misa, and advancing in a gentle slope, begins the somewhat abrupt ascent of the outer chain of the Pennine Alps, on a high overhanging rock, covered with twisted and gnarled oaks, stood a ruined and deserted castle. It was of the eleventh century, and originally belonged to the Malatesta, whose battered and defaced scutcheon frowned over the half-falling arch of the gate. Now it was ownerless, but there were tenants there, for the falcon had made her eyrie in its rocks, in the crannies of the falling towers were numberless nests of swallows, on the ruined *débris* of the walls the little red lizard basked in the sunlight, and, when the night came, the melancholy hoot of the owl was heard, and tawny fox, and grey wild cat, stole forth on plundering quests, from their secure retreats amidst the thorn, the wild serpythum, and the fragments of the overthrown outer wall, which afforded these bandits of nature so safe a hiding place.

For once, however, for many years, the castle was again occupied by man. There were a dozen good horses under the lee of the north wall which still stood intact, and in the great hall, part of whose roof lay open to the sky, a fire of oak-logs was burning, whilst around it were gathered Jacopo and my men, cracking jokes, and finding the bottom of a wine skin. In a smaller chamber, a little to the right, I sat with St. Armande and the abbé. We, that is the chevalier and myself, had been dicing a little together to kill time, the abbé improving the occasion by reading from his Breviary. We had now been here for three days, on the watch for Bozardo's party, but there was no sign of them. They had certainly not gone on, for we had carefully enquired, and were doubtless detained by some reason, of which we knew not the details. In order not to be taken by surprise, I had sent Bande Nere on to scout, with instructions to come back with a free rein, the instant he had news of the party. Two days had passed since he went, there was no sign of him, and I was beginning to feel a little anxious.

"*Diavolo!*" I exclaimed, "I am getting sick of sitting like a vulture on a rock here. I wish Monsignore Bozardo would hasten his steps."

The abbé looked up in a mild surprise, and St. Armande put in gently—"The compulsory rest has done your wound good at any rate."

"I fancy, chevalier, I owe more thanks to your skilful doctoring than to the rest. *Per Bacco!* But I think I shall carry those claw marks to my grave."

"What one carries to the grave does not matter," said the abbé, "it is what one carries beyond the grave that the signor' cavaliere should think of."

"True, reverend sir, I trust I may ever remember that," and rising, I put my hand on St. Armande's shoulder, "come, chevalier, I go to take a turn outside, will you join me?"

He rose with pleasure on his face. On our way out we

passed through the great hall, and listened for a moment to Jacopo, who in a tuneful voice was singing a Tuscan love song. So absorbed was he and his audience, that they did not observe us, nor did our footfalls attract any attention as we passed out into the open air.

The moon was still young enough for all the stars to be visible, and leaning over the ruined battlements we looked out into the night. Far below us we heard the river, murmuring onwards towards the sea, behind us the castle stood grim and silent, a red light showing from the windows of the hall, through which we could catch the lilting chorus to Jacopo's song.

For a time neither of us spoke, and then to make some conversation I turned to my companion.

"Who is that abbé, chevalier, who accompanies you everywhere? Not a tutor surely?"

"In a way—yes," he answered, "he was born and brought up on our estates, and is a faithful servant of our house—you must know," he went on, "that in Picardy, the name of St. Armande is honoured as that of the king. I would trust Carillon with more than my life; my honour, if need be; for he and his fathers have served us more faithfully I fear than we have served France."

"Not more faithfully than you mean to though—eh, St. Armande?"

"If I live," was the reply, as he made a slight gesture, a movement of the head that brought back to me the shadowy memory I was always trying to grasp.

"Live—why of course you will live," I answered.

"I shall not see the sun set to-morrow."

I looked at him blankly for a moment. Moon and stars were sufficient to light his face, so that I could see the sad, far-away eyes, eyes more fit for a saint than a soldier.

"*Animo!* Do not talk like that. It is nonsense," but

I felt a foreboding myself that I could not account for, and it chilled me.

"It is not nonsense," he said in his dreamy voice, and then, as if rousing suddenly, "Cavaliere—di Savelli—I want you to promise me one thing. Do not hesitate; but promise. It is about myself I ask—will you?" and he held me by the arm with his slight fingers that I felt were shaking. To soothe him I answered gravely, "I promise."

"I know that I will not live beyond to-morrow. When I die, bury me as I am—here—here in this ruin—and—and you will not forget me, will you?"

As he said this his voice took a cadence, his face took an expression that suddenly brought back a hundred old memories, no longer vague and misty, but clear and distinct. In a moment the scales fell from my eyes, and I saw. I seemed to be once more hawking on the banks of the Chiana with madame, I was once more in the aisles of the church at Arezzo, treading down temptation, and bidding farewell to a woman who was trying to be strong.

"God in heaven!" I gasped to myself as I leaned back against the parapet, and drew my hand across my forehead, as if to wake myself from a dream. St. Armande did not notice my exclamation, he did not even observe my movement. His own excitement carried him away.

"Promise," he said, and shook my arm in his earnest entreaty.

"As there is a God above me I promise."

"I believe you," he said simply, "and now I am going in."

I made no offer to bear him company, and his slight figure drifted into the moonlight. I saw it clearly again, making a dark bar against the red glare in the open door of the hall, and then vanished from view. I was utterly thunderstruck by the discovery I had made. A hundred actions, a hundred tricks of gesture, of speech, of manner, should have disclosed St. Armande's identity to me. Now I knew it, it was all so simple and clear, that I wondered at my denseness in not having guessed through the disguise before. Now that I had discovered it however, now that my blindness was cured, what was I to do? I resolved on keeping the secret I had probed, and never once letting St. Armande know he was other than what he pretended to be. A great pity came up in my heart, for there was a time when I almost thought I loved this woman, and it required little conceit to see, after what had happened, that madame was prepared to make almost any sacrifice for my sake. I was sorry, more sorry than I can tell, for I knew my own hands were not clean in this matter, and I paced up and down, flinging bitter reproaches at myself, and utterly at a loss to plan out some way of escaping from the difficulty in which I was placed. I made up my mind that St. Armande, as I will still speak of the disguised chevalier, should be placed in no danger, resolving that as soon as the affair on which we were engaged was over, that I would send him, or rather her, with a message to the cardinal, and the message was to be one that, I hoped and trusted, would have the effect of making madame cease her foolish prank—I had it at this moment almost in my heart to be angry with her; but I could not, for the small voice that kept whispering to me—

"Thou art not free from blame." I was not; but nothing would induce me to add another wrong to the one I had committed. That in itself was sufficient to haunt me to the grave, and I shivered as I thought of the abbé's words, "It is what one carries beyond the grave that the Signor Cavaliere should think of."

So alternately reproaching myself, and praying for aid, prayers that brought no relief, I passed the night, and in the small hours of the morning stole back into the castle. Round the fire in the great hall, the figures of my followers were stretched, all but one, who kept watch, but recognising me did not challenge. I passed by softly, and entered the other room. The abbé had dropped asleep over his breviary, the lamp burning low beside him.

Rolled in a cloak, and half reclining against a saddle, St. Armande was in a profound slumber. I took the lamp in my hand, and holding it aloft, surveyed the sleeping figure. A last hope had come to my mind that I was mistaken, that perhaps I was jumping too quickly to conclusions. But no, there was not a doubt of it. There could be no mistaking that fair face with its delicate features, the straight nose, the curved bow of the lips, half hidden under its disguise, the small shapely head with its natural curls of short golden hair—oh! I knew all these too well. It was Doris d'Entrangues without shadow of doubt, and no blind beggar, who groped his way through a life-long darkness, was blinder than I had been. I set down the lamp softly, and with a sick heart stepped back into the hall, where I found room for myself until the morning, which indeed it was already. With the sunrise, I was awakened from a fitful sleep by hearing Bande Nere's voice.

"What news?" I asked as I drew the old soldier aside.

"I have been as far as Sinigaglia, excellency, and all goes well. The party left Sinigaglia the morning I arrived, and I followed in their track, letting them keep well ahead of me to avoid suspicion. Last night, however, I passed them. They will be here about noon, maybe a little before."

"The numbers?"

"Ten lances, excellency, for escort. It is those we have to deal with. Then there are about a score of mounted servants, four laden mules, and Monsignore Bozardo."

"*Um!* That is rather strong, if the servants carry weapons."

"But they march as through a friendly country, signore, the servants going on ahead to prepare for Monsignore's arrival. He himself keeps close to the mules, with one or two men, and of course the escort."

"Do you know who commands the escort?"

"No, excellency—I did not wish to risk anything, and asked no questions."

"You are right, and have done well—here are ten crowns."

"Your excellency is generosity itself."

"It is not more than you deserve. Go and get something to eat now, and take as much rest as you can within the next hour."

"Excellency," and Bande Nere stepped back to join his fellows, who surrounded him with eager questions, and there was a bustling and a buckling-to of arms and armour.

When we met a little later my face showed no signs of my discovery to St. Armande, and whilst we breakfasted together I told him that the time was come for which we had been waiting.

"Remember your promise," he said with an affected gaiety, but his voice nearly broke down and I saw the abbé glance at him with a deep compassion.

"I will not forget," I answered, "but God grant there may be no need to keep it."

"I should say 'Amen' to that," he answered, "only I cannot."

My plans were already made, and as soon as we had breakfasted we set forth from the castle. The road, as I have already explained, ascended abruptly a short distance from the base of the rock on which the castle was perched.

Between the base of the rock and the road was a narrow but thick belt of forest, which afforded admirable concealment, and here we posted ourselves secure from all view. The abbé and St. Armande insisted on accompanying us, and in order to put the chevalier from harm I placed him a little way up the rock, with instructions to charge down as soon as he heard my whistle, which I never intended to blow. The abbé took his station beside him, saying where the chevalier was it was his duty to be. St. Armande held out a small hand to me as I was turning away, and I took it gently for a moment in mine. The quick impulsive movement reminded me much of that day when madame had held the flowers I gathered to her husband's face. Something almost choked me as I turned away hastily, having only strength to repeat my warning—

"Do not move till you hear my whistle."

I borrowed an arquebus from one of my men, and the arrangement was that we were to charge out after a volley, the first shot of which I was to fire. All being now ready, it was only necessary for us to wait. I would merely add that in order to prevent discovery by the neighing of the horses, we had muzzled ours as far as possible. There was now a dead silence, that was only broken by the rustle of the leaves overhead, an occasional crack amongst the dry boughs as a squirrel moved against them, or the uneasy movement of a horse, which caused a clink of a chain-bit, and a straining sound made by the leathers of the saddlery, that was not in reality so loud as it seemed; but caused Jacopo and Bande Nere to scowl fiercely at the unfortunate rider, a scowl which was only equalled by their own stolidly impassive faces, when their own beasts sinned. We had not long to wait; presently we heard voices shouting, the clatter of horses trotting, a rapid reining in at the ascent, and a number of followers and lackeys, some mounted on horses, others on mules, with led mules beside them, came past, and went on, heedless of the eager faces watching them through the trees. One or two of our horses became so uneasy that I was afraid of immediate discovery, but so occupied were the knaves in babbling together, all at once, that what with this, and the thwacking of their animals, and in some cases the efforts to remain on, we remained unnoticed. Then there was a short interval, and the suspense was strained to breaking point. In a while we heard the firm beat of a war-horse's hoof, and our quarry came in view. First came Monsignore Bozardo, a tall thin man, wrapped in a purple cloak, with a fur cap on his head. He rode a strong ambling mule, and by his side was the commander of the escort. Immediately behind were four troopers, then the mules with the ducats, behind these again six other lances, whilst the rear was brought up by half-a-dozen lackeys, without a sword amongst them. But what struck me almost dumb with surprise was that the leader of the escort was none other than D'Entrangues himself. There could be no mistake, his visor was up, and I saw the sallow face, the long red moustaches, and almost caught the cold glint of his cruel eye. At last! I raised my arquebus and covered him. At last! But a touch of my finger and the man was dead. I could not miss, my heart was mad within me, but my wrist as firm as steel. In another moment he would be dead, dead, and my revenge accomplished. It was already in my hand. I looked aside for a second at the line of breathless faces watching me, then back again to the muzzle of my weapon. D'Entrangues was now not twenty yards away. I could scarcely breathe as I pointed the arquebus at his heart. I had already begun to press the trigger, when something seemed to come across my mind like lightning. I saw in a moment that lonely room in the Albizzi Palace, where I had kneeled to my God and sworn to put aside my vengeance. The weapon shook in my grasp.

"Fire, signore," whispered Jacopo hoarsely.

With an effort I jerked the muzzle in the air, and pulled the trigger. The report was followed by four others, and two of the troopers fell. The next moment we were on them with a shout, and there was the clash of steel, as fierce blows were struck and received, now and again a short angry oath, and sometimes a cry of pain. I did not want to take life, but a trooper came at me, so I had to run him through the heart, and the man fell forward under Castor's hoofs, with a yell I shall never forget. The next instant D'Entrangues and I crossed blades, and whether he recognised me or not I do not know, but he fought with a skill and fierceness I have never seen equalled. At last I lost my temper, and cut savagely at him. He parried on the forte of his blade, but so furious was the stroke that it broke the weapon in his hand, and almost unhorsed him. Reining back skilfully he avoided another cut I made at him, and drawing a wheel lock pistol from his holster, fired it straight at me. At the flash, someone dashed between us. I heard a scream which froze the blood in me, and a body lurched forwards and fell to my side, whilst a riderless horse plunged through the press, and galloped away. I saw the light of the golden head as it fell, and forgetting everything, forgetting D'Entrangues, forgetting all but the fact that a dreadful deed was done, I sprang down from Castor, and raised St. Armande in my arms. As I did this a hoarse yell from my men told me the day was won; but I had no ears for this, no eyes for anything, except the slight figure, which lay in my arms gasping out its life.

"Congratulations, signore, we have taken the lot," and Jacopo, bleeding and dusty, rode up beside me.

"At too great a price," I groaned; "help me to carry——," I could say no more.

"Here, two of you secure those mules—Bande Nere, see to the wounded—Queen of Heaven—the chevalier——" and Jacopo, giving his sharp orders, sprang down beside me, and together we bore our unconscious burden under the shadow of the oaks. A dark figure stepped to our side, and kneeling down supported the lifeless head on his arm, whilst hot tears fell from his eyes, as he prayed over her. It was the abbé.

"How did this happen?" I asked, "did I not say you were not to move?"

"It was done at once," he answered, "I could not prevent it—alas! How can I carry this tale back to St. Armande?"

"Water, excellency."

Jacopo had brought some clear water in his helmet. I thanked him with a look, and he stepped back, leaving us three together, two who were living, and one who was going away.

I bathed the forehead and drawn lips, from which flowed a thin stream of blood, and as I did so her eyes opened, but the film of death was on them.

"Di Savelli—Ugo—," and she was gone.

Gone like a flash, flung swiftly and fast into eternity, struck down, perhaps unwittingly, by the arm which should have been a shield to her. I have often wondered if D'Entrangues ever knew who fell to his pistol shot. If he did, God pity him! In the one glimpse I caught of his white face, as he swung round and rode off, I thought I saw a look of horror. But everything went so quickly, that then I had no time to think, and now I can recall but the end.

To her dead lips Carillon pressed his crucifix, into her

dead ears he mumbled prayers. I knelt tearless, and prayerless, beside him, thinking only of the great love that had laid down a life.

One by one my men stole up, and stood in a half circle, leaning on the cross-handles of their swords, over which the grim, bearded faces looked down on us in pity.

Suddenly Carillon raised his crucifix aloft.

"My Father," he cried, "receive her soul!"

And someone said softly,

"Amen!"

CHAPTER XXV.

THE VENGEANCE OF CORTE.

WE buried our dead; and madame slept beneath the ilex, in the courtyard of the castle, below the north wall. Over her nameless grave we raised a rude cross, and after it was done, Carillon bade me farewell. He was going, he said, to bear the story to St. Armande, and when he reached it, I wit there was sorrow in the Picard château, whence madame took her name. It was with a heart of lead that I rode into Sassoferrato, and there, as arranged, made over my prize to Hawkwood. The tale of the ducats was complete, and the Englishman, giving me my quittance, held out his hand, saying bluntly—

"I wronged you, Di Savelli; but I know now. We all know, for Bayard has told us."

I hesitated. Many memories came to me, and there was bitter resentment in my soul. They had all been too ready to believe. They had flung me forth as a thing too vile to touch, and now—it was an easy matter to hold out a hand, to say, "I am sorry," to think that a civil word would heal a hideous wound. The kind world was going to forgive me, because it had wronged me. Such as it was, however, it was the world, and things had made me a little humble. After all, if the positions were reversed; if I stood in Hawkwood's place, and he in mine, how should I have acted? I would not like to say.

"Come," said Hawkwood, "let the past be covered. Come back—we want you."

"As you will," and I took his grasp; "I will come back in a little time. Till then adieu!"

"Good-bye!" and we parted.

Five minutes later, I was spurring to Rome, my following at my heels. It was, in a manner, putting my neck on the block, for Bozardo was probably making his way thither with all speed, and doubtless D'Entrangues as well. Recognition was almost certain; but risk or no risk, I was bound to see the cardinal, and tell him my task was done. Little did I think, however, as Castor bore me, with his long, easy gallop, across the oak forests of the Nera, that the face of affairs in Rome had been changed in an hour, and that, had I so wished, I might have, in safety, proclaimed what I had done from the very house-tops. As we came nearer the city, it was evident that there was some great commotion within, for, from every quarter pillars of dim smoke rose up in spiral columns, and then spreading out like a fan hung sullenly in the yellow of the sunset. It was clear that houses were burning, and swords were out. We soon began to meet parties of fugitives, hurrying from the city, and making across country in all directions. They avoided us like the plague, and the mere glint of our arms was sufficient to make them scatter to right and left, leaving such property as they could not bear with them, to the tender mercies of the road-side. Some of my men were eager to ride after the runaways, and question them; but I forbade this, knowing we should hear soon enough, and that if there were danger, it would be best to hold together.

"*Per Bacco!*" and Jacopo, riding up beside me, pointed to a black cloud, which slowly rose, and settled above the vineyards of the Pincian Hill, "we had best go with a leaden boot, excellency. There is a devil's carnival in Rome, or I am foresworn."

At this juncture, we turned an abrupt corner of the road, coming upon a crowd of fugitives, who seemed to be running forwards, caring little where they went, so that they put a distance between them and Rome. Amongst the throng was a figure I recognised; and in a mean habit, mounted on a mule, which was seized with an obstinate fit, and refused to budge, although soundly thwacked, I saw the Cardinal of Strigonia. Bidding Jacopo keep the men together, I rode up to him, and asked—

"Can I render your eminence any aid?"

His round eyes, starting out of his head like a runaway hare's, glanced at me in fear, and the stick he bore dropped from his hand, no doubt much to the satisfaction of the mule. At first he was unable to speak, for my words seemed to fill the man with terror, and I had to repeat the question, before he stammered out—

"You are mistaken, sir; I am no eminence, but a poor brother of Mount Carmel, on my way to Foligno, out of this hell behind me," and he glanced over his shoulder towards Rome.

"I see," I answered with a smile, "but if the poor brother of Mount Carmel will look more closely at me, he will see a friend. In short, your eminence, I am Di Savelli."

"*Corpo di Bacco!* I mean our Lady be thanked. And so it is you, cavaliere! Take my advice, and turn your horse's head to Foligno. On beast!" and he kicked at the mule, which moved not an inch.

"I am for Rome, your eminence; but what has happened?"

"Oh, that I had a horse!" he groaned. "What has happened? Everything has happened. Alexander is dead or dying. Cesare dead, they say, and burning in Hades by this. Orsini and Colonna at the old game of hammer and tongs——"

"And the Cardinal—D'Amboise?"

"Safe enough I believe, as the Orsini hold the Borgo, and have declared for France."

"Trust me, your reverence, you will be safer in Rome than out of it. The whole country will rise at the news, and the habit of Mount Carmel will not save the Cardinal of Strigonia. Turn back with me, and I will escort you to the Palazzo Corneto."

To make a short story, D'Este agreed after a little persuasion, and the mule was kind enough to amble back very willingly to Rome. We placed his eminence in the centre of our troops, and went onwards, entering the city by the Porta Pinciana, riding along leisurely in the direction of S. Trinita di Monti, and thence straight on towards the Ripetta. It was a work of no little danger to make this last passage, for everywhere bands of plunderers were engaged in gutting the houses, many of which were in flames, and we continually came across dead bodies, or passed houses from which we heard shrieks of agony. We could help no one. It was all we could do to keep our own heads on our shoulders; but by dint of shouting, "*A Colonna!*" with the Colonna, and "*Orsini! Orsini!*" with their rivals, and sometimes hitting a shrewd blow or two, we crossed the Ripetta, and in a few minutes were safe in the Palazzo Corneto.

Here we were received by Le Clerc, who comforted the trembling Strigonia, with the assurance that an excellent supper awaited him, informing me, almost in the same breath, that D'Amboise was in the Vatican. I lost no time in repairing thither, which I did on foot, accompanied by Jacopo alone, and made my way without let or hindrance to the Torre Borgia. Here everything was in the wildest confusion, and the Spanish soldiers of the Pope were plundering right and left. I stumbled across De Leyva, who, with a few men at his back, was trying to maintain order. He gladly accepted the offer of my sword, and we did what we could to prevent the wholesale robbery from going on. In a brief interval of rest, I asked,

"Do you know where D'Amboise is?"

"In the Sistine Chapel, with half-a-dozen others; De Briconnet guards the entrance."

"And Alexander?"

"Dead or dying—I do not even know where he is; Don Michele has seized as much as he can, and carrying Cesare on a litter, has escaped to Ostia."

"Then Cesare is not dead——"

"No. Cross of St. James! see that?" and he pointed to a reeling drunken crowd, full with wine and plunder, who passed by us with yells, into the great reception rooms.

Followed by the few men who remained steady, De Leyva dashed after them, and with Jacopo at my heels, I made for the Sistine Chapel. I reached the Scala Regia, and although I knew the Sistine Chapel was but a few feet distant, yet, owing to the darkness that prevailed, I missed the way, and Jacopo was of course unable to help me. Groping onwards we came to a small door, and pushing it, found it to open easily. It led into a narrow, vaulted passage, where the darkness was as if a velvet curtain of black hung before us. "I like not the look of this, excellency," said Jacopo, as we halted in front of the door.

"Keep a drawn sword," I answered, "and follow me."

We could only go in single file, and picked our way with the greatest care, our feet ringing on the stone floor. Except for this, the silence was intense, and we could hear no sound of the devilry outside. The passage continued, until we almost began to think it had no end, but at last the darkness gave way to a semi-gloom, and a faint bar of light gleamed ahead of us. At this we increased our pace, finding a sharp corner, a little beyond which rose a winding flight of stairs, ending before a half-open door, through which the dim light came. I put my foot on the first of the steps, and was about to ascend, when we were startled by hearing a moan of mortal agony, followed by a laugh, so wild and shrill, so exultant, and yet so full of malice, that it chilled us to the bone. It pealed through the door, and echoed down the passage behind us, until the horrid cadence became fainter and fainter, finally dying away into the black darkness.

"God save us!" exclaimed Jacopo, "it is a fiend laughing its way to hell."

He went on, with chattering teeth, to adjure me to go no further; but crossing myself, I bade him be silent, and stepped forwards. Since that moan of agony, and terrible laugh of triumph, there was no sound, and I could almost hear my heart beating, as I reached the door. Jacopo had nerved himself to follow me, and stood pale and trembling at my shoulder, his sword quivering in his shaking hand. I was myself not free from fear, for no man may combat with spirits, but after a moment's hesitation, I looked cautiously in. I saw before me a room of great size, dimly lighted by two tall candles, burning on each side of a massive bedstead, on which lay a man bound, and writhing in the throes of death. The light, though faint around the room, fell full on the face of the man, and horribly as the features were changed, distorted as they were, I saw they were those of Alexander, and that he was in his last agony, alone and friendless in his splendid palace. Yet not alone, there was another figure in the room. As I looked, it stepped out of the gloom of the rich curtains at the window, and standing over the bed, laughed again, that terrible laugh of devilish joy. At the sound, the dying man moaned through his black, foam-clothed lips, and Corte, for it was he, bent over the body and mocked him.

"Roderigo Borgia, Vicar of Christ, hell yawns for you; but a few moments, Borgia, but a few moments of life; think you, that you suffer now? There is more coming—things I even cannot dream of." In the face of Alexander came so awful a look of entreaty that I could bear it no longer. I stepped into the room, and putting my hand on Corte's shoulder, said,

"Come, let him die in peace."

He turned on me with a snarl, but recognising me, laughed again.

"Ha! ha! Let him die in peace. Why, man, you saw her die, and can say this? But he is going too. It is a week since his doctor, Matthew Corte, bled him for an ague, and touched him with a little knife, just a little pin-prick. He began to die then; but hell is not yet hot enough for him. He dies in too much peace. Why, my dog died in more agony! But he has felt something. See those torn curtains! See this disordered room! He tore those curtains in his madness. He bit at the wood of the chairs, he howled like a dog at the moon, and they tied him here, and left him. I alone watch. I will let him die in peace. Ha! ha! It is good. I do not want him to die yet. I give him food, and he lives. In a little while perhaps he will die. But in peace! ha! ha! I could almost die with laughter, when I hear that. It is too good! Ha! ha!"

I saw it was hopeless to do anything with Corte, and the Pope was beyond repair. I might have cut down the madman, but it would have served no purpose. For a moment I thought I would pass my sword through the Borgia, and free him from pain. It would have been a mercy, but I luckily had the sense to restrain myself. Again, Alexander deserved his fate, and a few minutes more or less would make no difference. So I left the wretch to die the death of a dog, that befitted his life, and turning on my heel, went back through the passage.

Jacopo heaved a sigh of relief as we came out, and I felt a different man as I ran down the steps of the Scala Regia. Here I met with De Leyva again, and told him what I had seen.

"The Camerlengo has just gone to him," he answered, referring to the Pope, "and you have missed D'Amboise. He has returned to the Palazzo Corneto. I can do nothing here, and am going myself. Do you walk or ride? I have no horse."

"Walk," I answered, and the Spaniard linked his arm in mine, as, followed by Jacopo, we took our way back to the cardinal's house.

On reaching I sought D'Amboise at once. He had heard of my arrival, and was awaiting me. After a brief greeting, I told him his business was done, and handed him the quittance I had received from Hawkwood. He was mightily pleased, as may be imagined. I felt it my duty to inform him of the death of St. Armande, telling him how it occurred, without in any way disclosing my knowledge of the secret. He was much affected.

"It is a sad business," he said, "but we have other things to think of now. *Mon Dieu! mon Dieu!*" And to this day I am unaware if he knew or not.

But the night was not yet over, and late as it was, there were yet things to be done. About midnight we heard that Alexander was dead, and a few minutes later Gentil' Orsini hurried to the cardinal. They held a hasty council, and De Briconnet and I were summoned. News had come that Cesare had not yet left Ostia, that he was too ill to travel, and D'Amboise and Orsini resolved on a bold stroke. It was nothing less than the capture of Borgia. Orsini offered to lend two hundred lances for the purpose, but a leader was wanted. He could not go himself, as his arch-enemy, Fabrizio Colonna, held all Rome on the left bank of the Tiber, and was in sufficient force to make a dash for the Borgo at any moment. The short of it was, that at the cardinal's recommendation, I received the command, and about two in the morning set out for Ostia. If the ships Cesare had hired had arrived the matter was ended, and we could do nothing; but if not, there was every chance of his surrendering without a blow, as although he had about five hundred men with him, they were not to be relied on, except the half-dozen cut-throats who formed his personal guard, and who might be trusted to fight to the last. The luck which had followed me so far favoured me again, and pressing on as fast as our horses could bear us, we came up with the fugitives in the early morning. Only one ship, too small to hold all, had come, and they were crowded on the banks of the Tiber, making every effort to embark. The river-shore was strewn with the enormous quantity of baggage they had with them, and a scene of the utmost confusion took place on our arrival. The ship was drawing up to the quay, and we could see the litter of the Borgia, surrounded by the few men who meant to fight. The affair was over in five minutes, and Cesare was my prisoner. Seeing how matters stood, the master of the ship anchored in midstream, heedless of the yells and execrations of the followers of the Borgia, who were not spared by my men. Indeed, I had great difficulty in keeping Cesare from harm. He was in truth very ill, but was able to gasp out as he yielded:—

"*Maldetto!* It is my fate. I had prepared for everything except being ill." He then lay back in his litter, and spoke no more.

One short and desperate attempt was made to rescue him. About a dozen horsemen charged right at us, and for a moment it appeared as if they would succeed. But we were too strong, and although they inflicted severe loss on us, killing Bande Nere amongst others, they were cut down, all but one, who led them. This man, seeing all was lost, and determined not to be taken himself, galloped to the quay, and striking his spurs home, leaped his horse far into the river, and made for the vessel. The stream was running fast and strong, but the good beast, despite his burden, struggled bravely against the flood. To relieve the horse, the cavalier, having torn off his morion, slipped from the saddle, and with his hand on the pommel, attempted manfully to swim beside the animal. The weight of his cuirass, however, bore him down. Twice his head sank below the water, twice he rose again and battled with the flood. Those on the ship made no effort to save him, and we on shore could do nothing. He had now, fighting every inch of his way, drifted astern of the vessel, and someone flung a rope at him. His hand reached out to clasp it, but missed, and then the under-current caught man and horse and dragged them down. He rose yet once again, his white despairing face turned towards us, and with a supreme effort of hate, shook his clenched hand at me, and was gone.

So died Crépin D'Entrangues, the death of a brave man, unyielding and fighting to the last. The yellow Tiber hissed in white foam over the spot where he sank. Perchance the mad currents dragged his body down to the slime of the river-bed, picked it up again in their swirl, tossed it in sport from one to another, and finally flung it to rot on some lonely bank, where the gulls screamed above it, and the foxes of the Maremma gnawed at the rusty armour, and snapped and snarled over the white bones in the moonlight.

CHAPTER XXVI.

CONCERNING MANY THINGS.

EVERYONE knows the history of the times, and it is not my intention to dilate on this, but merely to set down, without comment, those matters of state in which Fortune allowed me to play a part. When Cesare surrendered at Ostia the Borgia were broken for ever, and Valentinois allowed, after a short confinement, to escape to Spain, where he died like a soldier. Now that the game was in their hands, the allies began to quarrel amongst themselves, the French king to drivel away his opportunities in gaiety, and the Venetians to step in, in their Most Serene way, and claim a share of the spoils for the Lion of St. Mark. Events moved quickly, the genius of the Great Captain won victory after victory for Spain, the death of Francis Piccolomini paved the way for the accession of Rouvere to the Papacy as Julius II., and the Holy League was formed, by means of which the French were finally driven from Italy. Thus, in a few years, the work of D'Amboise was scattered to the winds, but long before that time I had sheathed my sword, and concerned myself no more with war.

But on the day that I surrendered my prisoner to D'Amboise and Orsini, the former already in thought sat in St. Peter's Chair, and the latter, at the very least, imagined himself the Lord of the Romagna. I sent forward couriers, with the news of my success, to the cardinal, and ere we reached

Malafede, met with a return messenger from D'Amboise, bearing a brief note of congratulation, and adding that Colonna had made terms to evacuate the portions of the city he held. The messenger informed me, that the Bailly of Caen had already entered Rome by the Porta Pia, and that, finding himself between two fires, old Fabrizi Colonna had made a virtue of necessity, and by yielding now, reserved himself for another day. This enabled me to go back by an easier route than we had come, and as we rode through the Ostian Gate, I could not help contrasting my present entry to the day when Jacopo and I had reined in our weary steeds to let the Borgia pass, and give his following the road. At the Ponte S. Angelo, I surrendered my prisoner to Orsini in person, and truly thought he would have but a few hours more to live, for Gentil' Virginio had a long score to settle with the Borgia, and a longer memory for a wrong. The blood, too, of Paolo, whom Cesare strangled at Sinigaglia, and that of the Cardinal Orsini, whom he brutally murdered in Rome, called aloud for vengeance. Cesare himself seemed to be aware of this, for whereas up to now he had remained in a sullen silence, he found tongue to implore me, in the most servile manner, not to deliver him to Orsini, and when I told him I had no option, he tried to creep out of his litter, and lay his cap at the feet of his enemy. Orsini spoke nothing, merely ordering him to be borne to S. Angelo; but as the Borgia shrank back into his litter, he said with a grim smile that he trusted the duke would find his entertainment to his liking. How it happened that Cesare came off with a whole skin I never knew, but he did, as I have mentioned above, and it surpasses belief. He turned cur at the last, and the low blood showed in him; but he was one of those men who knew how to be thoroughly bad. Orsini took back his lances, saying he had need of them, so that it was with my own few men that I reached the Palazzo Corneto. I must except Bande Nere from this number, and I was truly sorry for his death, for his was an honest sword. The cardinal received me in the little chamber where we had supped with Machiavelli. He had thrown aside his clerical habit and was in mail, but wore his barettina on his head. He was more than kind, congratulating me heartily on my success, going so far as to say that by capturing Cesare I had given a kingdom to France. I then left him with further assurances of his goodwill towards me, and saw him no more for the day.

Towards the small hours of the next morning I was aroused from a deep sleep by Jacopo. Starting up, I inquired what was astir, and was told that Defaure, the page, was waiting to see me. I gave orders for his instant admission, and, on coming in, he informed me that his eminence desired my immediate attendance. Telling Jacopo to have Castor saddled, for I smelt work afoot, I flung myself into my clothes, and hastened to D'Amboise.

He had evidently not slept all night, and was pacing the room in agitation.

"St. Dennis!" he burst out, as I entered, "do you know what they have done? The king holds a tourney at Arezzo instead of marching on at once. What is worse, he has granted an extension of the truce to Spain, and Tremouille and the rest of them are off to the junkets. They are making a May-day with those ducats you captured. By God! they would dance away a kingdom."

"Your eminence has no doubt sent news of the capture of Cesare?"

"That was only yesterday, man," he snapped, "and De Briconnet is riding for his life to the king. But it is about this I sent for you," he went on rapidly. "De Briconnet may come to harm. Here are other despatches. Take them and follow him; overtake him if you can. When can you start?"

"Now."

"Good—here are the papers. And this for Tremouille. Adieu!"—and he held out his hand—"*Monsieur le Compte.*"

I started a little at the last words which he uttered in French, but had no time to ask for explanation or make inquiry. I hurried to my apartments and found Castor ready. Bidding Jacopo follow me to Arezzo with my men as soon as possible, I gave Castor the rein and rode out of Rome. At Citta del Pieve I got my first news of De Briconnet. At Cartona he was but two hours ahead of me, and when on the afternoon of the second day I reined in the staggering Castor at the gates of the Villa Accolti, where the king was, I saw in the courtyard a dead horse, his sides still bleeding from the spur marks, and judged that De Briconnet had barely beaten me by a head for all his twelve hours' start. So once again had I entered the Villa Accolti! And as I sprang to the ground, loosed the girths over Castor's heaving flanks, and resigned the reins to a willing groom who led the poor beast to rest, all the past came back to me with a vivid force, and I looked around, almost expecting to meet again the glances of scorn and contempt, to hear once more the hisses, the mockery, and the foul reproach of that day.

The cardinal was right enough when he said that high junkets were to be held. And the day seemed to be one of merry-making. Flags were flying from all parts of the villa, and the wide grounds were full of the followers of the court, and the townspeople either watching, or engaged in sports of wrestling, archery, and other games.

For the great ones, however, the out-of-door amusement of the day came to an end with the dinner-hour, and they were now disporting themselves within. From the open windows strains of music floated out into the sunlight and gay figures passed and repassed, or moved in and out of the balcony overhanging the grand entrance which seemed, from the constant movement and the brilliant dresses of those who crowded thereon, to be like a bed of flowers stirring in the wind. As I came below the balcony, I did not dare to look up, but with my sword in the loop of my arm and my despatches clenched in my right hand, walked up the marble steps.

"Post from Rome! Post from the Lord Cardinal!"

The sonorous voice of the ushers pealed this out, and I found myself at the entrance to the gallery leading to the great hall where I had been tried.

"Not here, sir—to the left." My way was barred by an equerry in violet and gold.

"Not so, De Brienne, the king receives these despatches in person," and Bayard had linked his arm in mine.

"But, my lord!"

"I take the blame," and Bayard, blazing in full mail, led me through the gallery whose sides were lined with the archers of the Scottish Guard. Archers in name only now, and little as my time was, I could not forbear glancing at these fine troops, who, although few in number, bore an unequalled reputation for service in the field. The doors at the entrance to the hall, which were guarded by two gigantic men-at-arms, were opened only at fixed intervals to let people in and out, and by this means an attempt was made to avoid overcrowding. There were a considerable number before us, and having to go slowly, we had time to exchange a few words.

"I suppose De Briconnet has passed in?" I asked, "he could only have just arrived, for his horse lies dead at the gates."

"I doubt it. All posts are received by De Vesci, whose

wrath we are going to brave. If De Briconnet came in here direct, he was probably stopped and sent to the seneschal's apartments."

"If so, as he was the first-comer, he should present the despatches," I urged; "I bear but duplicates?"

"There is no time to think of that now," replied Bayard, and as he spoke the doors unfolded, and in a crash of music and the murmur of voices, above which now and again trilled a peal of clear feminine laughter, we entered the hall. At first we were unobserved, for the interest of every one was gathered to the centre of the room, where to the strains of music a game of chess was being played with living figures. The king himself took part in it, and I had good opportunity of observing him. Time had not changed Louis much, although his reckless life had enfeebled his constitution. He had the features of his house, the wide forehead, the oval face, the pointed chin, below which his short brown beard was neatly trimmed. His grey eyes were set somewhat wide apart, and his hair, which was naturally straight, he wore carefully curled, in a length that all but touched his shoulders. He was dressed in a tight-fitting surcoat of green, with green trunk-hose and stockings of the same colour. A short cloak, also of green, fell from his shoulder, and below his left knee was bound the ribbon of the English Order of the Garter, of which he was very proud. On his head was a velvet cap lapelled in front and on either side, and alive with the light of jewels, with which it was studded. He was playing king in the game, Madame de la Tremouille acting as queen, and the rival king was Tremouille himself, who had for his partner Isabel the Good, the wife of Gonsaga of Mantua, a princess distinguished alike for her beauty and her virtue. A little apart from the players, and watching the game with a grave interest, stood Etienne de Vesci, the Seneschal of Beaucaire, who was, after the cardinal, the most powerful man in France, and, indeed, was supposed by many to have more of the king's ear. Close by him were a number of ladies, and I ran my eye amongst them and around the hall, hoping in vain to catch sight of the one face I longed to see. Whilst so engaged De Vesci observed me, and seeing the papers in my hand, made an imperious gesture, beckoning me towards him. This I pretended not to observe, and the seneschal, biting his lip, edged his way towards me. It was easy to see from my travelled and stained appearance, the red on my spurs, and the packet in my hand, that I was the bearer of news.

"Is not monsieur aware," he said in a harsh voice, speaking in French, "that papers for the king should be brought to me?"

"These are for the king's hand," I answered.

"It is enough. Give them to me," and he held forth his hand.

"I have said, my lord, that they are for His Majesty's own hands."

Bayard, who was watching the game now drawing to a close, turned round at this, and grasping the matter, cut in.

"*Ciel!* My Lord, let the cavaliere deliver his packet. It will come to you soon enough. Take a holiday for once."

De Vesci frowned, and was about to make a hot answer, when there was a sudden shout and a clapping of hands, and Louis, who had won the game, came forward leading Madame de la Tremouille in triumph. The last move was made but a few feet from us, and as the king faced round with his partner he caught sight of our group and called out as he advanced—

"Victory! We have won. Why those black looks, De Vesci? Come and congratulate us."

With an effort the seneschal smoothed his face, "Victory always attends your majesty, and with so fair a partner defeat would be impossible," and he bowed with a courtly grace; but the wrinkles of his frown were still on his forehead. The duchess grew red with pleasure at the compliment, and Louis clapped his hands like a boy.

"Excellent! Trust a courtier's lip for a soft speech;" and then, observing me, "but what have we here?"

"From Rome, your majesty," and dropping to my knee, I presented my papers, which the king took irresolutely in his hand.

"*Diable!*" he exclaimed, with an impatient gesture, "from my lord cardinal no doubt?" And he glanced at me.

"Your majesty, and of the most vital import," and I rose.

"I must read them, I suppose. A plague on the cardinal! We were just going to the minuet——"

"I will deal with the matter, sire. The papers should have come to me," and De Vesci, saying this in his harsh, grating voice, reached forth his hand. Usually a perfect master of his temper, he had somehow, for once, let it get the better of him; and his closing words and manner were almost those of command. Louis, though a brave man, had a weak nature and a hasty temper. A temper that was often aroused to fits of obstinacy, little short of mulish. He caught the seneschal's tone, and perhaps also the suppressed smile that flickered on the faces of his courtiers. His forehead darkened, "You mistake, my lord, these papers come rightly to me," and turning his back on the seneschal, he tore open the packet.

De Vesci stepped back, white to the lips, and the court gathered round the king in silence. Seeing Tremouille at hand, I made bold to step up to him, and give him D'Amboise's note. He glanced at it, and turning to me said, "I gave my word, and it shall be kept. The honour of Tremouille is pledged."

I was at a loss to understand; but had no time to think, for Louis suddenly called out, "Tremouille—Bayard—gentlemen! The Borgia is taken! Rome is ours!"

At once there was a buzz, and a murmur of voices, in eager congratulation at the glad tidings. Standing alone and apart from all, I could barely see Louis, so closely did the court press around him; but it seemed that Tremouille was urging something on him, and the duchess too, for I caught the flash of the jewels on her fingers, as in her eagerness she laid them on the king's arm. Then Bayard's deep voice came to me clearly, "If done, 'twere well done quickly, sire."

I do not exactly know how it happened; but I found myself kneeling before the king, who stood above me, his drawn sword in his hand.

"M. di Savelli," he said, "one king of France owed you his life, another all but owes you a kingdom. Wear again your cross. It was nobly won. Take back your knighthood." He laid the blade gently on my shoulder, "for God, for your King, for your Lady. Arise, Sir Knight!" He stretched forth his hand to aid me to my feet, and I stood up again, with my honour white, in the very hall, almost on the very spot, whence I had been cast out in ignominy and shame.

I could not speak—I was choked—my eyes were wet with tears. Seeing my emotion, Louis placed his hand kindly on my shoulder.

"Remember, Di Savelli," he said, "France needs you yet. To the minuet, my lords and ladies—to the minuet!"

And he turned down the hall, not waiting for my thanks. But friends sprang up everywhere. The first to give me her good wishes was the Duchesse de la Tremouille, then came the duke, old Ives d'Alegres, and others I can scarcely name. It was whilst in their midst that I saw a face I knew well, and Machiavelli came up.

"Late, but not the less warm in my congratulations," he said; "so the good ship is safe in port at last! We owe you too much for speech, and can never thank you enough."

"Your excellency is most kind. Is the Lady Angiola well?"

He was silent for a moment, and laughed to himself, as if something stirred him. "As well as ever she was," he answered at length, and added, "You must sup with us this evening. We lodge in the Borgo di San Vito, and never mind your attire. My wife longs to see you, and thank you in person."

Other friends coming up, our converse was brought to an end, and I managed to effect my escape, and take refuge in the pavilion of Bayard, who insisted on my being his guest. I would have willingly foregone the supper at the Borgo di San Vito, as I was weary; but having promised, borrowed a horse from my host, and set out. I reached the secretary's lodging, punctually to the hour, and was received by Gian, who, after a respectful inquiry concerning my health, ushered me into an apartment, where, on entering, I found myself alone. I had to wait some little time, and wondering at the strangeness of my reception, I walked towards a window, overlooking the private gardens of the house. As I reached it, I heard the rustle of trailing garments, and turning round beheld Angiola before me. She came up with outstretched hands, and I took them in mine, and looked into her eyes. Then I found words; they come to every man at the right time, and I spoke. She made no answer as I pleaded my cause, and fearing the worst, I dropped her hands, with a bitter reproach against my age and my scarred face. When I had done she remained still, with her eyes down, and there was a silence. Then she looked up again.

"Di Savelli," and her voice was very low, " you say your face is scarred by wounds. Do you know, cavaliere, I would I were a man, that I too might bear wounds on my face, and looking in my mirror, see how they became me." And the rest concerns not anyone.

. . . .

We were married before the end of the truce, and on my wedding day, I received from His Majesty the King, the patents of the county of Fresnoy, in Guienne, a distinction that was extended to me in Italy, by His Holiness Pope Pius III., who, on my purchasing a portion of my ancestral estates back from Amilcar Chigi, confirmed to me the title in my native land. But the gift I valued most of all, was a tari of Amalfi, to which still clung a shred of the gold link, by which it had been attached to a bracelet. And this was from my wife!

CHAPTER XXVII.

MY LORD, THE COUNT.

Portion of a letter from the Countess di Savelli to her cousin Vittoria Ordelaffi of Forli.

. . . .

It is, as you know, gentle cousin, six years since my lord, having lost his sword-arm at the storming of Santa Croce, retired to his castle of Aquila in the Sabine Mountains, and ceased to help further in stirring the times. In truth, he has yielded to my wish in this matter, and although, in the war of the Holy League, he was offered a command, Di Savelli, at my entreaty, refused the honour.

The count, my lord, is well, but his wounds troubling him in the winter, he may no longer follow the wolf in our mountains, yet still hunts the stag in the Ciminian Forests of our kinsman, Amilcar Chigi, to whom we have been reconciled, and whom we visit yearly.

Last winter we spent in France, at the château of the Seigneur de Bayard, which lies on the Garonne, and met there, amongst others, Madame de la Tremouille, who is now a widow, the Duke having died of a tertian ague at Milan. There also was a very gay and noble gentleman, the Viscompte de Briconnet, who avers that my lord owes him a county for having forestalled him in bearing to the king the news of the surrender of Borgia. My Lord of Bayard, whom the Count thinks above all men, visits us in the autumn; and, gentle cousin, come you too, for we are to have a house full. The children are well, and Ugo grows a strong boy, but wilful. He has his father's features, but my eyes. They have just gone a riding, my lord on his great war horse Castor, and Ugo on his little white pony, bred on our farm in the Bergamasque. I see them as I write, going down the avenue.

Your namesake Vittoria, sends you a hundred kisses, and bids you come and be heartily welcome. I send this by a sure hand, that of my lord's esquire, Messer Jacopo Jacopi, a faithful servant and a good sword, though his tongue be ever wagging. Give him an answer, to say you are coming.

   .   .   .   .

THE END.

www.ingramcontent.com/pod-product-compliance
Lightning Source LLC
Chambersburg PA
CBHW022018240426
43667CB00042B/908